CHADD
EDUCATOR'S MANUAL

on Attention-Deficit/Hyperactivity Disorder (AD/HD)
AN IN-DEPTH LOOK FROM AN EDUCATIONAL PERSPECTIVE

A project of CHADD and CHADD's President Council

CHADD is a national nonprofit organization composed of parents,
health care professionals, and educators, with the mission of improving
the lives of people affected by AD/HD

EDITOR AND PROJECT COMMITTEE CHAIR
Chris A. Zeigler Dendy, M.S.

CONTRIBUTING EDITORS
Mary Durheim, B.S.
Anne Teeter Ellison, Ed.D.

CHADD®
CHILDREN AND ADULTS WITH
ATTENTION-DEFICIT/HYPERACTIVITY DISORDER

Copy Editor: Winnie Imperio
Cover Design: © LJ Design
Book Design: © LJ Design
Iceberg Illustration: Alex Zeigler
Photographers: Parents of children and teens featured in this book
                 Bobby Stroud Photography
                 Leonard Kong and Green Lake Crew

Printed in the United States of America by Progress Printing, Lynchburg, VA

CHADD
8181 Professional Place, Suite 150
Landover, MD 20785
http://www.chadd.org
http://www.help4adhd.org

ISBN 0-9634875-4-X

Library of Congress Control Number: 2006932825

"It would be nice if you would leave, Albert.
Your behavior at school, so distracted and
absentminded, and your poor interest in all
I teach set a bad example for the whole class."

A teacher's comment to young Albert Einstein,
from *Albert Einstein* by Ibi Lepscky

Children with learning differences including those with AD/HD often struggle
to meet teacher expectations. Our hope is that this manual will provide
teachers with the tools to help future Einsteins or expert computer programmers,
musicians, or car mechanics reach their full potential in life.

A Heartfelt Message for Our Partners in Education

Since school often represents the most difficult years of life for students with attention deficit disorders, the importance of having teachers who understand the impact of AD/HD on academic performance is obvious. CHADD parents recognize that the more knowledgeable teachers are about effective strategies for teaching these students, the more successful these children will be in school. CHADD hopes to help teachers with this task by providing the most up-to-date science-based information available on AD/HD and related educational issues. Thus we have spent the last two years developing our Educator's Manual on AD/HD.

In developing this document, we sought out three sets of experts: researchers, veteran classroom teachers, and parents. Information from researchers gave us the science-based facts as a foundation. Next, a number of veteran teachers identified key challenges, gave feedback on strengthening the Manual content, and shared their favorite teaching strategies. Parents also provided input regarding strategies that have worked well for their children. It is our hope that this guidebook will be a practical resource offering concrete strategies that teachers will use frequently.

As this Manual explains, AD/HD is a complex cognitive disorder affecting both boys and girls of all ages and ethnic groups. The severity and complexity of AD/HD varies with each student; consequently the challenges facing these students are not all the same. Hidden coexisting academic challenges related to AD/HD are often one of the greatest challenges students face because they remain undetected. Further compounding the student's problems, some of the primary characteristics of AD/HD, such as disorganization and forgetfulness, look like simple matters of laziness and a lack of willpower.

Understandably, teachers may not be particularly sympathetic with students who appear to be lazy and unmotivated. Fortunately, the schools of today offer numerous resources that greatly enhance the likelihood of school success for those students who are struggling. Teachers, school psychologists, and other student support personnel provide the all-important in-depth evaluation to identify any related learning challenges, including deficits in executive functions. School teams of veteran educators are also available both before and after the challenges are identified to develop a comprehensive educational plan for these students in conjunction with their parents. CHADD families are extremely grateful for the provision of these outstanding services.

CHADD parents recognize that teachers are a pivotal factor in the lives of our children; you are the cornerstone of the "educational treatment" plan. Experts provide this documentation for our statement: When adults with AD/HD were asked how they had managed to cope successfully with their AD/HD, they said, "Someone believed in me!" While parents were ranked first, teachers were ranked second as having the greatest impact on their lives. Teachers *do* have a profound impact on making or breaking our children. In fact, any adult with AD/HD can quote a teacher

Continues on next page

comment that is etched in their memory from their school years, whether it is positive or negative. So ask yourself this question: "What will my students with AD/HD say about my impact on their lives?"

From all of us at CHADD, we wish to express our appreciation to four key groups of people: first to members of the CHADD President's Council and other donors for making it possible to disseminate this Manual to every public school in the country. Second, a special thank you goes to all the authors who worked hard to construct teacher-friendly material. Third, to all the children and teenagers who struggle with AD/HD every day of their lives. And finally to educators, our partners, we thank you for caring about our children and working so hard to help them succeed in school!

Sincerely,

Chris A. Zeigler Dendy, M.S.
Editor and Project Committee Chair

Phyllis Anne Teeter Ellison, Ed.D.
CHADD President

Contents

Overview of the Diagnosis and Treatment of AD/HD

AD/HD research data, common coexisting conditions, developmental implications, executive function issues, multimodal treatment, diagnosis, a cultural perspective, and lifespan issues.

Overview of Key Academic Issues

Establishing a Strong Foundation During the Early Years

Developmental challenges, academic challenges, instructional strategies, social challenges, medication consideration and suggested resources.

Avoiding the "Brick Wall" in Middle and High School

Developmental challenges, academic challenges, instructional strategies, social challenges, unique challenges
for girls, medication consideration, and suggested resources.

Key Issues Impacting Students with AD/HD

Model Programs

Contributing Authors

Thomas E. Brown, Ph.D.

Dr. Brown is a clinical psychologist who maintains a private practice in Hamden, CT, specializing in the assessment and treatment of high-IQ children, adolescents, and adults with AD/HD and related problems. He is an Assistant Clinical Professor of Psychiatry at the Yale University School of Medicine and is Associate Director of the Yale Clinic for Attention and Related Disorders. He is author of the *Brown ADD Scales* and is editor of *Attention Deficit Disorders and Comorbidities in Children, Adolescents and Adults*. His most recent book is *Attention Deficit Disorder: The Unfocused Mind in Children and Adults*. He is the author of several other highly respected books on AD/HD and is a frequently sought-after speaker both nationally and internationally.

Chris A. Zeigler Dendy, M.S.

During her 40-year professional career, Dendy has been a teacher, school psychologist, mental health professional, and an author and publisher. Chris is also the mother of three grown children and three grandchildren with AD/HD. She is the author of two popular books on AD/HD (*Teenagers with ADD and ADHD* and *Teaching Teens with ADD and ADHD*) and co-author with her son, Alex, of a survival guide for teens (*A Bird's-Eye View of Life with ADD and ADHD*). As a member of CHADD's President's Council, Dendy has spearheaded efforts to create the Educator's Manual. She is a popular speaker nationally. Chris is also a former member of the CHADD National Board of Directors and Executive Committee and also served as Secretary, Treasurer, and Conference Program Chair.

Mary Durheim, B.S.

Durheim, an educational consultant, is a trained mediator, Section 504 hearing officer, and behavior strategist. She is the Immediate Past-President of CHADD and serves on the international board of directors for the development of an international alliance on AD/HD. She was selected by the governors of Texas (Bush and Perry) to serve on the Texas Council for Developmental Disabilities and has also previously served on the state Mental Health PAC. She is the mother of a grown son with AD/HD and a daughter with AD/HD inattentive type.

Anne Teeter Ellison, Ed.D.

Dr. Teeter Ellison, the current president of CHADD, is a Professor of Educational Psychology at the University of Wisconsin-Milwaukee and serves as the Training Director of the School Psychology Doctoral Program. She is the author or coauthor of several books, including *Child Neuropsychology: Assessment and Interventions for Neurodevelopmental Disorders; Interventions for ADHD: Treatment in Developmental Context;* and *Clinician's Guide to Adult ADHD: Assessment and Interventions*. Professor Ellison has served CHADD in numerous capacities since 2002: Secretary, President-Elect, and now President of the Board of Directors. She has also chaired the CHADD Professional Advisory Board and served as Conference Chair for two national meetings. Prior to service on the national level, Anne was a professional advisor to the Wisconsin ADHD Project and was a member of the State of Wisconsin ADD Council.

Joan Helbing, M.S.

Helbing, a veteran educator, is the regional ADD consultant with the Appleton Area School District in Wisconsin. She has been a classroom teacher, diagnostician, and support person for 32 years in the areas of learning, cognitive, and emotional/behavioral disabilities. Her former students range in age from three to adults. She is the coordinator for the Appleton Area CHADD support group and a former member of the CHADD National Board of Directors. She served as cochair of the Educator's Manual Committee. She is also the mother of two daughters with AD/HD.

Terry Illes, Ph.D.

Dr. Illes, a school psychologist, has been employed by the Jordan School District in Salt Lake City for over 20 years. He works with the Utah Collaboration for AD/HD, a task force that is working to improve the quality of AD/HD health care services in Utah, and has taught classes on the educational and home management of AD/HD. An adult with AD/HD, Dr. Illes was involved in the development of a treatment model for AD/HD for Intermountain Health Care, the largest health system in Utah. Currently, he is a member of the CHADD National Board of Directors.

Clare B. Jones, Ph.D.

Dr. Jones is a diagnostic specialist and educational consultant in private practice in Scottsdale, AZ. She is the former Director of Education for the Phoenix Children's Hospital and former Director of Special Education Services in Ohio and Minnesota. The recipient of the Master Teacher of the Year in Ohio and the CHADD Hall of Fame, Dr. Jones is the author of seven books, including *Practical Suggestions for ADHD* and *The Source for Brain-Based Learning*. A popular national speaker, she has written numerous articles and contributed chapters to five different books. Currently, she is a member of the CHADD National Professional Advisory Board.

Mark Katz, Ph.D.

Dr. Katz, a clinical and consulting psychologist, is the Director of Learning Development Services, an educational, psychological, and neuropsychological center in San Diego, CA. Dr. Katz is also the author of a book that addresses the importance of resilience (*On Playing a Poor Hand Well*). He writes an ongoing column for *Attention!* Magazine on innovative programs from around the country. Previously, he served as a member of the CHADD National Professional Advisory Board.

Sandra F. Rief, M.A.

Rief is an award-winning educator, consultant, speaker, teacher-trainer, and author of several best-selling books on AD/HD, including *How to Reach and Teach ADD/ADHD Children, 2nd edition* and *The ADHD Book of Lists*. Sandra specializes in strategies and interventions for meeting the needs of children with learning, attention, and behavioral challenges. She was on the faculty of the AD/HD projects of the National Initiative for Children's Healthcare Quality (NICHQ) and is a former member of the CHADD National Professional Advisory Board. Sandra is an educational expert for *ADHDbalance.net* and instructor for continuing education courses offered through Seattle Pacific University and California State University, East Bay.

Adele A. Sebben, M.A.

Sebben is a licensed professional counselor and nationally certified school psychologist from Fairfax, VA. Currently, she is in private practice at a private mental health facility where she specializes in helping those with AD/HD and helping children and parents deal with social skills deficits. As a school psychologist, she was involved in the collaborative efforts between public schools and her local CHADD chapter. She previously served on the National Board of Directors for CHADD.

Joan K. Teach, Ph.D.

Dr. Teach, a veteran educator with 46 years experience, was the Director of Lullwater School for over 17 years. Lullwater offered innovative programming for students with special needs, such as AD/HD and learning disabilities. She and her staff designed individualized alternative learning programs for their students. Dr. Teach started one of the first CHADD chapters in Georgia and now facilitates two monthly adult AD/HD support groups. She recently served on the CHADD National Board of Directors as Chair of the Membership and Chapter Services Committee. She is also President of the Learning Disability Association of Georgia. An adult with AD/HD, Joan is also the mother of three grown children with AD/HD.

Ann B. Welch, Ph.D.

Dr. Welch has over 25 years experience teaching students with AD/HD and learning disabilities. A former Council for Exceptional Children Teacher of the Year, she is now an Assistant Professor at Bridgewater College in Bridgewater, VA. She has published several articles on effective classroom strategies for students with AD/HD and other behavioral challenges. Her responsibilities include preparing prospective special education teachers.

Sharon K. Weiss, M.Ed.

Weiss is a behavioral consultant in private practice in Northern Virginia. She has worked as a teacher of special needs children and supervisor of behavioral intervention programs. She has been on the faculty for courses for the American Academy of Pediatrics. She has coauthored several books and is featured in a training video on AD/HD. A former member of the CHADD National Professional Advisory Board, she recently served as a member of the CHADD National Board of Directors and Executive Committee. She is also the coauthor of the popular book, *From Chaos to Calm: Effective Parenting of Challenging Children with ADHD and Other Behavioral Problems.*

Acknowledgements

CHADD wishes to express its deep appreciation to everyone who contributed to the development of our Educator's Manual: Committee members, CHADD members, reviewers, veteran teachers, school administrators, student support staff, and the children themselves who contributed photos for our Manual.

Editor and Committee Chair
Chris A. Zeigler Dendy, M.S.

Contributing Editors
Mary Durheim, B.S.
Anne Teeter Ellison, Ed.D.

Committee Members
Joan Helbing, M.S., Co-chair
Thomas E. Brown, Ph.D.
Clare B. Jones, Ph.D.
Sandra F. Rief, M.A.
Adele A. Sebben, M.A.
Mindy Street, B.A.
Joan K. Teach, Ph.D.
Ann B. Welch, Ph.D.

Project Manager
Russell Shipley, B.S.

CHADD Contributors & Reviewers
José J. Bauermeister, Ph.D.
Pamper Garner, B.S.
Soleil Gregg, M.A.
Terry Illes, Ph.D.
Brenda Webb Johnson, M.C.S.W.
Beth Kaplanek, R.N.
Mark Katz, Ph.D.

Jar Lampard, A.B.
Harvey Parker, Ph.D.
Arthur Robin, Ph.D.
Carl Smith, Ph.D.
Linda Smith, B.A.
Sharon K. Weiss, M.Ed.
Karen White, M.L.S.

Contributing Educators
Several veteran teachers participated in interviews regarding the most common AD/HD-related problems and their favorite intervention strategies. In addition, some read draft copies of the Manual and gave suggestions for making it better.

TEACHERS
Preschool
Jackie Castleberry, GA, 28 years
Jacquie Chappell, UT, 20 years

Elementary School (1-6)
Linda Armstrong, TX, 21 years
Margaret Bennett, AL, 30+ years
Laurie Lemery Burns, WI, 16 years
Deb Cox, WI, 28 years
Jennifer Dansby, AL, 25 years
Sandra Dendy, AL, 15 years
Sue Duven, WI, 34 years

Elementary School (1-6) (Cont.)

Robin Fischer, WI, 10 years

Cindy Garfield, UT, 18 years

Jean Housley, UT, 20 years

Glenda Liddle, GA, 33 years

Karen Pass, AL, 25 years

Debbie Patterson, AL, 29 years

Mary Sue Rabe, WI, 15 years

Maureen Syring, WI, 19 years

Dorothy Warren, WI, 40 years

Vickie Young, AL, 14 years

Diane Zwiers, WI, 18 years

Middle and High School

Cindy Evans, GA, 23 years

Sherri Guenther, AL, 18 years

Bari Levin, IL, 19 years

Deanine Lilley, VA, 10 years

Glen Orme, UT, 33 years

Linda Sorensen, UT, 11 years

Kathy Hubbard Weeks, M.S.W., WI, 22 years
(AD/HD consultant)

Reviewed all sections

Claudia Dickerson, Ph.D., GA, 30 years
(school psychologist)

Joan Helbing, M.S. (co-chair), WI, 32 years
(AD/HD consultant)

Joan K. Teach, Ph.D., GA, 46 years
(school principal)

Other Reviewers

David Kinsley, Pharm.D.

Christina Kloker Young, B.S.

CONTRIBUTING CHILDREN AND TEENAGERS:

These young people submitted photographs of themselves and their families for inclusion in the Educator's Manual.

Allie	Emily H.	Kyle	Robert
Alyssa	Hunter	Marina	Samantha
Andrew	Jay	Max	Spencer
Chris	Kara	Marlie	Stephanie
Dan	Kati	Nathan G.	Steven
Eric	Katie	Nathan K.	Tate
Erik	Khris	Nick	
Emily D.	Kristin	Perry	

Overview of the Diagnosis and Treatment of AD/HD

The first two chapters address AD/HD research, diagnosis, common coexisting conditions, developmental implications, executive function issues, cultural issues, multimodal treatment, and lifespan issues.

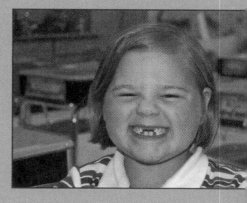

Chapter 1: New Understandings of AD/HD

✓ Several different types of AD/HD
✓ The science of AD/HD: Inherited problems in the brain's chemistry
✓ AD/HD and executive functions
✓ Problems show up early for some, later for others
✓ "Hitting the brick wall" in middle school
✓ Extra support needed for school success
✓ Improving academic success may also improve behavior
✓ Key characteristics of AD/HD and executive function impairment
✓ Cognitive self-management: Why is that important?
✓ Assessment of AD/HD
✓ The teacher's role in assessment
✓ Coexisting conditions are common
✓ Learning disorders
✓ Coexisting psychiatric disorders
✓ Helping families cope
✓ Helping reluctant parents
✓ Don't overlook strengths
✓ Treatment for AD/HD
✓ Medication
✓ Medication issues during adolescence
✓ The educator's role in monitoring medication
✓ Conclusion

Chapter 2: Diagnosis and Evaluation of AD/HD

✓ What do students with AD/HD look like?
✓ DSM diagnostic criteria
✓ Comprehensive assessment of AD/HD in the schools
✓ Underdiagnosis vs. overdiagnosis
✓ Students typically overlooked
  a. More about girls
  b. More about racial and ethnic minority populations
✓ Students sometimes overdiagnosed
✓ The teacher's role in evaluation and treatment
✓ Working as a team
✓ Summary

SIDEBARS
✓ Stages of a comprehensive assessment of AD/HD in the schools
✓ Common parent and teacher rating scales for AD/HD

CHAPTER 1

New Understandings of AD/HD

Thomas E. Brown, Ph.D.

According to a recent study by the U.S. Centers for Disease Control and Prevention, about 7.8 percent of children aged 4 to 17 years are currently diagnosed with Attention-Deficit/ Hyperactivity Disorder (AD/HD).[1] This means that most teachers are likely to have in every class they teach, on average, at least a couple of students with AD/HD. Clearly, it is extremely important for each teacher to have at least a basic grasp of what attention disorders are and what they are not.

Over the years, attention disorders have been known by several names. Currently, educators and medical professionals use different terms to describe this condition. Based upon federal law, educators use the terms ADD and ADHD to differentiate between students who are inattentive and those who are primarily hyperactive, respectively. Doctors diagnose students as having AD/HD that is either predominately hyperactive-impulsive, inattentive, or a combination of the two. Throughout this book, the term AD/HD will be used. Information specific only to the AD/HD inattentive type will be noted.

Understanding this disorder is not so easy. There are many widespread myths, and scientific understanding of AD/HD has changed a lot over recent years. It is now clear that attention disorders are a much more complicated set of problems than was previously understood.

Several Different Types of AD/HD

There are three types of AD/HD:

1. **AD/HD Combined Type:** Some students with AD/HD have significant and chronic problems with both *inattention* and *hyperactivity/impulsivity.*
2. **AD/HD Predominately Inattentive Type:** Others have a lot of difficulty with *inattention* and not much trouble with hyperactivity or impulsivity; some of them sit quietly staring into space and daydreaming.
3. **AD/HD Predominately Hyperactive-Impulsive Type:** Still others show little difficulty with inattention but have serious problems with *excessive hyperactivity and impulsivity.* Usually these students

* In most cases, AD/HD is used interchangeably throughout this Manual to describe both AD/HD predominately hyperactive-impulsive and AD/HD predominately inattentive. IDEA regulations refer to these two conditions as ADHD and ADD, respectively.

are very young children who are not expected to pay attention very well and who are likely to develop combined-type AD/HD.

Specific diagnostic criteria for each of the three types of attention disorder are provided in Chapter 2.

AD/HD is seen about three times more often in boys than in girls; it affects children of all ethnic backgrounds and all socioeconomic levels.

The Science of AD/HD: Inherited Problems in the Brain's Chemistry

Although some media coverage suggests otherwise, there is now very strong evidence that AD/HD is a neurobiological disorder, a problem with the brain and its neurotransmitters. After a review of the research on AD/HD, the American Medical Association concluded that "AD/HD is one of the best-researched disorders in medicine, and the overall data on its validity are far more compelling than for many medical conditions."[2]

Differences in brain functioning have been shown in multiple imaging studies of people with AD/HD compared to those without AD/HD. Typically those with AD/HD show less activation in critical areas of the brain when performing tasks that require concentration, decision-making, or self-control.[3,4] Some imaging studies have also found differences in the volume of specific brain regions in children with AD/HD.[5]

There is also strong evidence that the primary cause of AD/HD is genetic, due not to any single gene, but to combined effects of a number of genes.[6,7] Simply stated, AD/HD runs in families. If a parent has AD/HD, their child has more than 50 percent chance of having AD/HD; for siblings of a child with AD/HD, the risk is 32 percent. Environmental and perinatal factors can play a part, but twin studies have shown that more than 80 percent of problems with inattention, hyperactivity, and impulsivity are the result of genetic factors.[8]

Causes of AD/HD are linked to chronic problems in the release and reloading of two specific neurotransmitter chemicals, *dopamine* and *norepinephrine,* that are crucial for effective communication in the management system of the brain. The brain of someone with AD/HD apparently makes these chemicals, as does everyone else, but often it does not release and reload them effectively. This leads to significant inconsistency in the student's ability to focus and get things done, especially if the task is not a high-interest activity.[9]

AD/HD and Executive Functions

Many still think of AD/HD as essentially a behavior problem — students who are unwilling or unable to sit still, listen to the teacher, and follow classroom rules. But researchers now have recognized that AD/HD is not so much a behavior disorder as it is an inherited problem in the development of executive functions, the management system of the brain. [10,11,12]

One way of thinking about executive functions is to picture a symphony orchestra whose members are all very fine musicians. Even when the musicians are excellent, if there is no conductor, who can organize and integrate the efforts of the individual musicians in the same piece at the same time, the music will not be very good.

The problems with AD/HD are not with those parts of the brain that would correspond to the individual musicians. The problems originate one level up in the management system that starts, stops, controls, and manages these activities, integrating them moment by moment to allow us to perform the tasks at hand. This management system is what is referred to as *executive functions.*

It is important to recognize that executive functions are not the same as intelligence. Some students who are extremely bright have significant impairment in executive function. And among those with average or below average intelligence, as measured by IQ tests, are many with adequate or better than average executive function.[13,14]

The brain's executive functions are not fully developed at birth. They gradually develop as the prefrontal cortex develops through early childhood and adolescence and into young adulthood. As executive functions develop, parents, teachers and others in the child's life often expect the student to exercise an increasing measure of self-management, from the simple tasks of dressing and self-care to the more adult responsibilities of managing a high school courseload or driving a car.

One way of thinking about children with AD/HD is that they are delayed in the development of their executive functions, unable to manage themselves at the same level as their peers. Students with AD/HD often experience a roughly 30 percent developmental delay.[15] For example, an 18-year-old may have executive function skills that are comparable to those of a 12- or 13-year-old. Because this delay often has a profound impact on academic performance, parents and teachers must provide more supervision and support that is commensurate with the student's developmental age rather than the chronological age.

Problems Show Up Early for Some, Later for Others

For some children, problems with AD/HD are obvious very early in their development. As preschoolers, these children are extremely difficult to manage, primarily because they are unable to follow even the most basic directions and, if frustrated, are excessively quick to run off or lash out at other students. Such children are often unable to fit into preschool and day-care settings without specialized staffing and services.

Other children with AD/HD may have much less extreme behavior problems. Their difficulties appear more in their academic work and may not become noticeable until third or fourth grade when more sustained attention and self-management is expected. Although some may *speak out impulsively* without being called on, *socialize excessively,* and be more *restless* than their peers, others may quietly withdraw and daydream their way through class each day. However, the primary difficulties shared by both groups of students can be seen more in chronic problems with *disorganization* of books and papers, *the inability to complete work,* or frequent *failure to understand instructions* quickly grasped by their classmates.

Not surprisingly, academic underachievement is frequently a hallmark of students with AD/HD. These students are at-risk and most will experience major problems at some time in their school career. In one study of students progressing through the school system, 29 percent failed a grade, 35 percent dropped out of school, 46 percent were suspended, and 11 percent were expelled. Providing proper supports and accommodations should prevent many of these students from experiencing these failures.

"Hitting the Brick Wall" in Middle School

Some students have AD/HD impairments that are not very noticeable until they move into middle school or junior high, where they are no longer in one classroom with one teacher for most of the day. The significant increase in demands on executive functions and increased expectations for planning and self-management are two of the primary reasons for the increased academic struggles at this level. When faced daily with multiple teachers and frequent changes of classroom, these students tend to have much more difficulty than classmates in keeping track of homework assignments, due dates, and test schedules. They show up in class lacking necessary books and materials that have been left at home or in their locker. They forget to take home materials needed for homework or may complete homework assignments and then forget to bring their work to class or hand it in.

Extra Support Needed for School Success

Many students with AD/HD are successful in school because their parents are very good at providing a scaffolding of reminders and supports to help them manage day-to-day activities. Basically parents are providing the executive functions that their child lacks. The students' impairments may emerge only when their parents are not present to provide this intensified support, for example, when the student has to write essays in class or has long-term assignments with multiple due dates, of which the parents are not aware. When the parental scaffolding is removed or when the student moves away from home to attend college, these adolescents' level of achievement can suddenly decline or they can experience unprecedented failure.

Improving Academic Success May Also Improve Behavior

A common misconception held by most professionals and parents is that students must behave properly before academic learning is possible. Consequently, teachers often address behavior problems first in hopes of enhancing the student's academic performance. However, research on students with emotional and behavioral disorders is beginning to *paint a different story*. One study revealed that when academic tutoring was provided, the student's behavior and grades improved. However, the converse was not true; grades did not improve for students who received behavioral interventions alone. This is consistent with other research that suggest that some students may act out to avoid aversive academic tasks — tasks that do not match the student's level, either being too easy or too difficult. Tutoring to improve academic performance also had a positive effect on social skills that was comparable to psychosocial interventions, such as counseling or skills training. Clearly, interventions that focus primarily on improving learning are more likely to improve behavior than interventions that target behavior problems directly.

Key Characteristics of AD/HD and Executive Function Impairment

In a recent study, children, adolescents, and adults with AD/HD described their chronic problems at school, home, or work. When their reports were compared with those of people who did not have AD/HD, their impairments could be categorized into six clusters:[16]

✓ **Activation:** *Organizing tasks and materials, estimating time, prioritizing tasks, and trouble getting started on work.* Individuals with AD/HD describe difficulty with excessive procrastination. Often they put off getting started on a task, even a task they recognize as very important to them, until the very last minute. It is as though they cannot get themselves started until the point where they perceive the task as an acute emergency.

✓ **Focus:** *Focusing, sustaining focus, and shifting focus to tasks.* For some, sustaining focus is like trying to listen to the car radio when the signal is fading in and out. They say they are distracted easily not only by things that are going on around them, but also by thoughts in their own minds. In addition, reading comprehension and retention pose difficulties; words are generally understood as they are read but have to be read over and over again in order for concepts to be understood.

✓ **Effort:** *Regulating alertness, sustaining effort, and processing speed.* Many students with AD/HD report they can perform short-term projects well but have much more difficulty with sustained effort over longer periods of time. They also find it difficult to complete tasks on time, especially in writing, and experience difficulty regulating sleep and alertness. "I can't shut my head off and get to sleep when I want to. I have to wait until I am absolutely exhausted. Then I sleep like a dead person and have great difficulty in waking up. During the day, I am okay so long as I am up and moving around or talking a lot. But if I have to sit still for a long time, read, listen in a meeting or lecture, or paperwork, my eyelids often get so heavy that I can barely keep myself awake."

✓ **Emotion:** *Managing frustration and modulating emotions.* Although DSM-IV does not designate any symptoms related to the management of emotion, many with AD/HD describe chronic difficulties managing their frustration, anger, worry, disappointment, desire, and other emotions in order to complete the task at hand. They speak as though these emotions take over their thinking, making it impossible for them to pay attention to anything else. They find it very difficult to put the emotion into perspective, put it in the back of their mind, and get on with what they need to do. Because of their difficulty with self-control and impulsivity, relationships with peers are often problematic, especially for those who are hyperactive and impulsive.

✓ **Memory:** *Utilizing working memory and accessing recall.* Very often, students with AD/HD have adequate or exceptional memory for things that happened long ago but great difficulty in remembering where they just put something or what they were about to say. In addition, children with AD/HD often complain that they cannot pull information out of memory when they need it. In students with AD/HD, stored memories cannot be activated and integrated with current information to guide their thoughts and actions. This deficit in working memory impacts the student's ability to hold information in mind and manipulate it while writing an essay or report or completing complex math problems. Students with AD/HD also experience memory retrieval problems when they study for tests. While studying, they may appear to have mastery of the material and be able to give correct answers when quizzed by parents or classmates. Yet, when it is time to take the test, significant portions of what they knew earlier seem to have disappeared. Hours or days later, something may jog their memory and the missing information becomes available once again. The information is in there, but they cannot retrieve it when needed.

✓ **Action:** *Monitoring and regulating self-action.* Many students with AD/HD, even those without hyperactive behavior, report chronic problems in regulating their actions. They are often too impulsive in what they say or do and in the way they think, jumping too quickly to inaccurate conclusions. They are unable to hold off and think to themselves, "What is going to happen if I do this?" or "Is the way I am seeing this the only reasonable way to see it?" Such impulsivity can be quite problematic at any age. In addition, people with AD/HD often have problems in assessing the situations in which they are interacting. They often fail to notice when others are puzzled, hurt, or annoyed by what they have just said or done and, consequently, fail to modify their behavior in response to the circumstances. Behavioral issues do not necessarily always revolve around hyperactivity but can manifest in social situations, as well as the inability to modify behavior according to specific circumstances. They also report experiencing chronic difficulty in regulating the pace of their actions, controlling actions, slowing down, or speeding up as needed for specific tasks.

These six clusters of impairment are reported as chronic by many children, adolescents, and adults with AD/HD and tend to overlap and interact with one another. For example, sustaining attention requires the use of working memory to keep important information in mind. Likewise, sustaining attention requires activating and sustaining alertness. Executive function impairment is complex and multi-faceted, just as the neural networks of the brain are complex and multi-faceted.[17]

Cognitive Self-Management: Why is that Important?

This emerging view of AD/HD as impairments in the development of cognitive self-management skills is very different from the old view that assumed children with AD/HD simply outgrew their impairments as they reached puberty. The earlier view was based on observations of hyperactive children, many of whom do become less hyperactive as they approach adolescence. However, this view did not take into consideration the attentional problems that are the primary and most persistent impairments of AD/HD, whether the individual is hyperactive in childhood or not. We now know that 70 to 80 percent of children with AD/HD continue to have significant impairments from their symptoms well into adulthood.

Assessment of AD/HD

This newer understanding of AD/HD as a developmental impairment of the brain's executive function has important implications for the assessment of the disorder. When AD/HD was seen as just a disruptive behavior disorder in childhood, diagnosis was based simply on observing behavior. This is no longer an adequate approach. Since executive function impairments are largely cognitive and not easily observed, a different approach to assessment is needed. It is not always possible to notice a child with AD/HD simply by observing classroom behavior, because many with this disorder do not misbehave and can appear to be attending to instruction even when their minds are continually spacing in and out. More information on assessment of AD/HD in preschool, elementary school and secondary school, students is provided in Chapters 2, 6, 7, and 9, respectively.

Assessment of AD/HD should take into account two important characteristics of AD/HD symptoms; symptoms of this disorder are *dimensional* and they are *situation-specific*. In other words, virtually all individuals suffer some impairment in these functions sometimes. Anyone looking at the list of symptoms of AD/HD is likely to say, "I have trouble with that sometimes; doesn't everybody?" But occasional occurrence of AD/HD symptoms is not enough to warrant diagnosis. Only AD/HD symptoms that are persistent and pervasive in at least two domains of activity, for example, school, work or home, are considered sufficient for a diagnosis of AD/HD. The extent to which these symptoms impair life functions, for example, socially, academically, or occupationally, must be considered for a diagnosis.

Most people find it difficult to understand the situational variability of AD/HD. Students with AD/HD can often engage in activities of intense interest for them without any difficulty paying attention or utilizing executive functions, such as playing sports or video games, drawing, and building Lego creations. When asked how they can concentrate so well on one particular activity when they have so much difficulty sustaining attention for virtually everything else, students with AD/HD say they can pay attention when they are "doing something that's really interesting" to them or if they will "get in big trouble right away unless it's done now." "If it is not interesting to me, then I usually can't make myself pay attention, even when I know it's important and I really want to get it done." This makes it appear that

AD/HD is simply a problem of willpower, but clinical evidence suggests otherwise.

As explained in Chapter 2, treatment for AD/HD should be preceded by a comprehensive evaluation that uses clinical interviews with the child and family in addition to information from the school. It should assess the child's past and current functioning in home, school and social relationships, health history, and possible coexisting disorders, including substance abuse. If a learning disorder is suspected, a psychoeducational evaluation should also be done. Diagnostic assessment should be done by a physician or psychologist familiar not only with AD/HD, but also with the variety of related disorders.

The Teacher's Role in Assessment

When a child is with one teacher most of each day, that teacher is likely to notice patterns of inattention, failure to understand directions, disorganization, chronic problems in recall of reading assignments, and excessive difficulties with chronic forgetfulness and in sustaining effort for assigned tasks. Every student has occasional problems of this sort, but if a student seems to have chronic difficulties that significantly impair learning, referral for an evaluation by the school's "child study team" is warranted.

For students in middle school or high school, where each teacher sees a student in large classes for only one period, it is easy to overlook students with AD/HD unless they have disruptive behavior problems as well as chronic inattention. Research suggests that girls with AD/HD and very bright students with AD/HD who are not hyperactive are at special risk of having their inattention problems overlooked or of being seen simply as lacking motivation.

Coexisting Conditions Are Common

AD/HD is not only a multifaceted disorder in and of itself, it is also often complicated by additional psychiatric or learning disorders. In a National Institute of Mental Health (NIMH) study of 579 children, aged 7 to 9 years, who had a diagnosis of AD/HD combined type, 70 percent experienced at least one other *psychiatric disorder,* such as anxiety, depression, or behavior disorder, within the previous year.[18]

Learning Disorders

As many as half of all children with AD/HD also have a specific learning disability in reading, math, or written expression. *Speech and language disorders* also have been found to occur frequently with AD/HD.[19]

Often the overlap between AD/HD and *learning disorders* is difficult to disentangle. For example, many individuals with AD/HD report that they have chronic impairment in their ability to *recall* adequately what they have read, even just moments after the reading. These individuals have a problem with reading, but, in and of itself, this problem may not constitute a specific learning disability in reading.

The core problem in the reading disorder, dyslexia, is severe impairment in phoneme recognition, the ability to recognize the pronunciation of specific letter combinations that make up words. Those with a learning disability in reading have severe difficulty in making the connections between how a word sounds and how it appears on the page. Yet reading disorders also involve impairments in *fluency* and in *working memory,* problems often found in AD/HD.

Some students with AD/HD are *dyslexic,* but many with AD/HD have adequate phoneme recognition while still having chronic difficulty remembering what they have just read, recalling it from one word, sentence or paragraph, and then integrating it into another. This can severely impair their *reading fluency* and their *reading comprehension.* These impairments in reading can also be secondary to impairment of *working memory,* an essential aspect of the executive function deficits in AD/HD.

Coexisting Psychiatric Disorders

Other psychiatric disorders are also prevalent among children with AD/HD. Among children with AD/HD, 25 percent have significant anxiety disorders, compared to 5 percent of the general population of children.[20] When compared to others without AD/HD, these children are also three to five times more likely to experience oppositional defiant disorder, obsessive

compulsive disorder, substance abuse, and sleep disorders.[21,22] Sleep disorders, which occur in 56 percent of those with AD/HD, can also have a significant impact on related school issues.[23] Students can have difficulty falling asleep at night, waking up each morning, or getting restful sleep, causing the student to be late to school, arrive at school in an agitated state of mind, have difficulty staying awake in class, or have an impaired memory.

Returning to the example of the orchestra, if executive function impairment is best described as an orchestra without a conductor, coexisting disorders can be represented as impaired musicians, such as violinists playing with broken strings. An orchestra can have a poor or absent conductor, poor musicians, or both, just as children with AD/HD can have the disorder alone, another psychiatric or learning disorder, or both.

Helping Families Cope

Students who suffer from AD/HD can be helped in a variety of ways. Often getting an adequate *assessment of the student's strengths and problems* is in itself a big help. When a teacher notices a student having chronic difficulties in school that may be due to AD/HD, it can be useful to describe those specific difficulties to the student's parents and ask if this pattern is familiar. If the parents corroborate the persistent pattern of behavior, they should be encouraged to seek an evaluation either through the school or in the community. If AD/HD is diagnosed, making them aware of community resources like local CHADD parent support groups can also be very helpful.

Sometimes it is difficult for teachers or parents to determine whether a student's attentional problems are due to AD/HD or to other causes such as a difficult life situation. The student may show many symptoms of AD/HD but also be living with a lot of stress related to an unemployed father, parents who argue a lot, a mother's worsening depression, an older brother's drug problems, a grandparent's progressive decline due to cancer, or coping with a new sibling or bullies.

Sometimes a child without AD/HD episodically shows significant symptoms of inattention in reaction to such stressors. However, if the child has AD/HD and a stressful life situation, evaluation and interventions for AD/HD can help equip the student to cope more effectively with the other life stresses.

Although a diagnosis can be made only after a comprehensive evaluation by an experienced physician or psychologist, teachers play an important role in alerting parents to specific problems in the classroom and referring them to appropriate resources.

Helping Reluctant Parents

Sometimes parents are reluctant to seek an evaluation for their child, even when the student is having considerable difficulty. They may insist that the child is simply being lazy or oppositional, or they may blame the teacher or themselves. They may worry that the evaluator will recommend medications for the child, a treatment they fear as risky or dangerous. In such cases, it can be helpful for the teacher to emphasize that getting a good evaluation does not commit the parents to any specific intervention. The first step is to find out if the student has a real problem, and if so, to get a clear picture of the specific difficulties. Once that is done, the parents can consider with the evaluator the available options to help the student and then decide upon the best course of action for their child.

Don't Overlook Strengths

Students with attention deficits often have many wonderful qualities and special talents that can get lost in the rush to address their disorder. Teachers and parents have a responsibility to identify each child's strengths and build on his or her "islands of competence."[24] The high energy and zest for living exhibited by students with AD/HD, when properly channeled, can bring joy and enthusiasm to a classroom. These students often see the world in different and interesting ways in comparison to other children. Sometimes their unique analytical skills lead to creative solutions that others may not have considered.

Treatment for AD/HD

The good news about AD/HD is that this disorder can, in most cases, be successfully treated. The American Academy of Pediatrics (AAP)[25] and the American Academy of Child and Adolescent Psychiatry (AACAP)[26] have published science-based guidelines for treatment, which are based on careful study of the voluminous research done on AD/HD over the past 60 years. The AAP has also published a review of assessment and treatment of AD/HD in adolescents.[27]

The NIMH study discussed earlier assessed the effectiveness of four different treatments: carefully managed medication treatment only; intensive behavioral treatment at day camp, school, and home without any medication; combination of medication management and intensive behavioral treatment; and standard community care, with or without medication, by a pediatrician, neurologist, psychologist, or other local professional selected by the parents.[28] Each child with combined-type AD/HD was randomly assigned to receive one of the four different treatments for 14 months. The two groups that received the careful medication management experienced a greater reduction in core AD/HD symptoms than the group with intensive behavioral treatment and no medication and those who received standard community care.

What surprised many was that the group of children who received medication alone showed improvement in AD/HD symptoms comparable to those who received the combination of medication and the intensive behavioral treatment.[29] However, this combination of interventions, known as *multimodal treatment,* was better in reducing other non–AD/HD problems, including oppositional and aggressive tendencies, feelings of anxiety, teacher-rated social problems, parent-child relations, and reading. In general, parents and teachers favored the combined treatments. These results suggest that carefully managed medication treatment is the key ingredient for successful treatment of most children with AD/HD. However, since most children with AD/HD do not have the disorder alone, comprehensive multimodal treatment should be helpful in treating some of the coexisting conditions.

Medication

Medications approved by the Food and Drug Administration (FDA) for the treatment of AD/HD are the stimulant medications, methylphenidate and amphetamine, both of which are available in several different brands and formulations, and a non-stimulant medication, atomoxetine. Stimulant medications, like Ritalin,® have been used to treat AD/HD for more than 50 years and have been carefully researched in more than 200 controlled scientific studies.[30] Although atomoxetine, sold as Strattera,® is more recently developed, it has already been studied in more than 1,600 individuals. No medication is guaranteed to be totally risk-free, but the safety record of these medications is very good.[31,32]

AD/HD medications do not cure symptoms like an antibiotic may cure a strep throat. But for 70 to 90 percent of those treated, these medications significantly alleviate AD/HD symptoms throughout the portion of the day when the medication is active.[33] This is comparable to the correction of vision with eyeglasses. These devices do not cure poor eyesight, but they can significantly improve vision during the time they are worn. It is important to note that preschool children can have more variable responses and side effects from stimulant medications, compared to older school-aged children.

Some stimulant medications for AD/HD are effective for only a few hours while other formulations can be effective for 10 to 12 hours. Additionally, some reports suggest that the nonstimulant, atomoxetine, may be effective for up to 24 hours. In years past,

students taking medication for AD/HD usually needed three doses each day. Now many students with AD/HD are treated once-a-day with longer-acting formulations that eliminate the need for a midday dose at school. The most important factor in medication treatment for AD/HD is that the medication be carefully monitored and fine-tuned to the individual's body sensitivity and schedule. More detailed information about medications for AD/HD is available in the "What We Know" information sheets on the National Resource Center on AD/HD website, http://www.help4adhd.org.

Although medication is usually the most effective treatment for many children and adolescents with AD/HD, behavioral treatments are especially important when families choose not to use medication or medication is not fully effective.[34] Behavioral treatment strategies have been demonstrated effective for many of the behavioral and learning problems often associated with AD/HD. Information on adapting these strategies in the school setting and at home in collaboration with parents is available in several books, on the CHADD website, and in other sections of this Manual.[35,36,37,38] A recent study with teens found that stimulant medications in combination with behavioral interventions improved a range of academic outcomes, including note taking, homework completion, daily assignments, and quiz scores.[39]

Medication Issues During Adolescence

Unique medication issues often surface during adolescence. During the middle and high school years, it is not uncommon for a medication that worked well in elementary school to lose its effectiveness.[40] Teenagers grow and gain weight, and their hormones change. All of these factors can *reduce medication effectiveness.* In addition, some students build up a *tolerance* to medications, especially long-acting forms, and may periodically need to increase the dosage or change to a different medication. In some instances, *the dosage of medication is simply too low* for maximum effectiveness.

If the student is currently taking medication, but symptoms are still evident, most likely the dose is no

> "The typical classroom is a terrible place for an AD/HD child...after all, we are asking children who have profound problems attending, organizing and controlling their actions to spend hours per day attending, organizing, and controlling their actions"
>
> • Michael Gordon, Ph.D., psychologist

longer effective. If medication effectiveness declines, grades can drop and the student can become more irritable. Sometimes this change is so gradual that parents and teachers can miss the underlying reasons for this problem. They may assume the worst, the student is lazy and simply doesn't care about school. If parents are not aware of these potential medication problems, teachers can suggest that they discuss them with their doctor, especially if the student's academic performance has declined.

Another medication issue that can arise during adolescence is refusal to take medication. Teens may complain that they don't like the way medicine makes them feel; they may be more focused but feel less outgoing. Teens may be angry that they have to rely on medication to do well in school or they may feel self-conscious or embarrassed about taking medication, especially at school. Occasionally, there is pressure to share medication with peers who want to try it.

Sometimes, medication refusal is mistaken for *simple forgetfulness* that is so common among teenagers with attention deficits. Unfortunately, that means that medication can unnecessarily become a focal point for major power struggles between students and their parents. A pattern of medication refusal can evolve as a way for the teen to retaliate. If this is the case, teachers can encourage parents to avoid power struggles and talk with their doctor about this challenge.

The Educators' Role in Monitoring Medication

The teacher is often in the best position to provide feedback to both parents and the physician regarding the impact of medication on the student's academic performance and progress.[41] Physicians must rely on teacher and parent reports to ensure that a student's medication is working at peak effectiveness at school. Specifically, if medication is working effectively, teachers should see improvements such as better grades, increased attention in class, completed homework, and compliance with teacher requests. A few rating scales to give teachers a more objective assessment of academic improvement of students on medication are listed in Chapter 2. The teacher can convey this information to parents who in turn can notify the physician when there are problems and adjustments in medication may be needed. Having rating scales completed by all the teachers who interact with a student will help the doctor make better informed decisions about medication.

Conclusion

AD/HD is a complex cognitive disorder, affecting all age groups of both genders. AD/HD is increasingly recognized as a developmental impairment of executive functions of the brain, a disorder that is chronic and often persists well into adulthood. The disorder is dimensional; most students experience symptoms of AD/HD to varying degrees and extent, which can appear as a simple problem of insufficient willpower. AD/HD is not easily assessed by observation alone; comprehensive evaluations, including student, teacher, and family interviews, are essential to diagnosis. AD/HD is implicated in many psychiatric and learning disorders. About 80 percent of children who have AD/HD benefit substantially from careful evaluation and appropriate treatment.

CHAPTER 2

Diagnosis and Evaluation of AD/HD in the Schools

Chris A. Zeigler Dendy, M.S.
Anne Teeter Ellison, Ed.D.
Joan Helbing, M.S.
Brenda W. Johnson, L.C.S.W.
Jose J. Bauermeister, Ph.D.

Contrary to widely held beliefs, most students, even elementary school youngsters with AD/HD, do not exhibit classic "Dennis the Menace" hyperactivity. They are active but not extremely hyperactive. Teachers are more likely to notice a student's impulsivity — difficulty stopping and thinking before they act or speak inappropriately. Additionally, they don't learn easily from their mistakes and are likely to repeat misbehavior. Students with AD/HD inattentive, on the other hand, are easy to overlook since they are quietly daydreaming their way through class. (In federal education regulations, AD/HD inattentive is referred to as ADD.) By the teenage years, students with AD/HD typically are not particularly hyperactive but can be restless or fidgety. Let's begin by talking about the common behaviors that teachers may observe from these students in the classroom.

What Do Students with AD/HD Look Like?

Veteran educators who are currently teaching in the classroom identify the following behaviors of concern as common in students struggling with AD/HD:

PRESCHOOL TO KINDERGARTEN
✓ Talking excessively, blurting out, disrupting class
✓ Easily distracted, off task, drawn to more interesting subjects
✓ Difficulty paying attention
✓ Difficulty staying in their seats
✓ Occasionally, low frustration and aggressive tendencies

ELEMENTARY SCHOOL
✓ Failure to complete work and turn it in
✓ Difficulty paying attention and staying on task
✓ Disrupting class, talking excessively, blurting out, making noises
✓ Disorganization
✓ Poor handwriting
✓ Occasionally, low frustration and aggressive tendencies

MIDDLE AND HIGH SCHOOL
✓ Failure to complete work and turn it in
✓ Chronic disorganization
✓ Not following directions
  - Difficulty understanding what is expected

✓ Weak written expression skills
✓ Low productivity of written assignments
✓ Off-task, distracting behavior, talking impulsively
✓ Inconsistent academic performance

At the middle and high school levels, many academic problems are linked to deficits in executive function skills. For example, students are often extremely disorganized, have poor working memory, and have difficulty identifying relevant information and figuring out how information fits together. In addition, two other classic characteristics of AD/HD are forgetfulness and losing things, such as assignments, books, and homework. Although teachers may not be aware, daydreaming and slow processing speed are often symptomatic of students with AD/HD inattentive (ADD), many of whom are girls. Some of these students also lack an awareness of their own behavior and how it impacts others, especially those with AD/HD combined type (hyperactive, impulsive, and inattentive). These students may be socially "clueless" at times and have poor social skills and few friends.

DSM Diagnostic Criteria

The best description of AD/HD behaviors is in the official diagnostic criteria of the disorder, published in the American Psychiatric Association's *Diagnostic and Statistical Manual of Mental Disorders* (DSM). (The official DSM-IV criteria are contained in Table 2–1.) There are four diagnostic categories: 1) AD/HD, predominately hyperactive and impulsive; 2) AD/HD, predominately inattentive; 3) AD/HD, combined; and 4) AD/HD not otherwise specified (NOS). The DSM uses different terms than educators use when referring to attention deficits. Educational law utilizes two terms to indicate the two most commonly recognized types of attention disorders: ADD and ADHD.

Comprehensive Assessment of AD/HD in the Schools

Most teachers easily recognize the more outgoing, talkative, hyperactive students who have a diagnosis of AD/HD. However, students with AD/HD inattentive type, who are quiet daydreamers, are more difficult to identify. Since there is no single test for AD/HD, a comprehensive evaluation must be completed. Generally

---

Table 2–1. DSM-IV-TR Diagnostic Criteria for Attention Deficit Disorders*

Possible Diagnoses

Attention-Deficit/Hyperactivity Disorder, Predominately Inattentive Type: If criterion A(1) is met, but criterion A(2) is not met for the past six months.

Attention-Deficit/Hyperactivity Disorder, Predominately Hyperactive-Impulsive Type: If criterion A(2) is met, but criterion A(1) is not met for the past six months.

Attention-Deficit/Hyperactivity Disorder, Combined Type: If both criteria A(1) and A(2) are met for the past six months.

Attention-Deficit/Hyperactivity Disorder Not Otherwise Specified: This category is for disorders with prominent symptoms of inattention or hyperactivity-impulsivity that do not meet criteria for Attention-Deficit/Hyperactivity Disorder.

*Reprinted with permission from the Diagnostic and Statistical Manual of Mental Disorders, Fourth Edition, Text Revision. Washington, DC: American Psychiatric Association, 1994.

CONTINUED NEXT PAGE

Table 2–1. Continued

Official Criteria

A. Either (1) or (2).

(1) Six (or more) of the following symptoms of inattention have persisted for at least six months to a degree that is maladaptive and inconsistent with developmental level:

Inattention
(a) Often fails to give close attention to details or makes careless mistakes in schoolwork, work, or other activities
(b) Often has difficult sustaining attention in tasks or play activities
(c) Often does not seem to listen when spoken to directly
(d) Often does not follow through on instructions and fails to finish schoolwork, chores, or duties in the work place (not due to oppositional behavior or failure to understand directions)
(e) Often has difficulty organizing tasks and activities
(f) Often avoids, dislikes, or is reluctant to engage in tasks that require sustained mental effort (such as schoolwork or homework)
(g) Often loses things necessary for tasks or activities at school, home, or the work place, (e.g., toys, school assignments, pencils, books, or tools)
(h) Is often easily distracted by extraneous stimuli
(i) Is often forgetful in daily activities

(2) Six (or more) of the following symptoms of hyperactivity-impulsivity have persisted for at least six months to a degree that is maladaptive and inconsistent with developmental level:

Hyperactivity
(a) Often fidgets with hands or feet or squirms in seat
(b) Often leaves seat in classroom or in other situations in which remaining seated is expected
(c) Often runs about or climbs excessively in situations where it is inappropriate (in adolescents or adults, may be limited to subjective feelings of restlessness)
(d) Often has difficulty playing or engaging in leisure activities quietly
(e) Is often "on the go" or often acts as if "driven by motor"
(f) Often talks excessively

Impulsivity
(g) Often blurts out answers before questions have been completed
(h) Often has difficulty awaiting turn
(i) Often interrupts or intrudes on others (e.g., butts into conversations or games)

Most of the symptoms in A(2) above describe the behaviors of younger children. Parents can compare their teenager's behavior as a young child with these criteria to determine if AD/HD is present.

B. Some hyperactive-impulsive or inattentive symptoms that caused impairment were present before age 7 years.

C. Some impairment from the symptoms is present in two or more situations (e.g., at school [or work] and at home).

D. There must be clear evidence of clinically significant impairment in social, academic, or occupational functioning.

E. The symptoms do not occur exclusively during the course of a Pervasive Developmental Disorder, Schizophrenia, or other Psychotic Disorder and are not better accounted for by another mental disorder (e.g., Mood Disorder, Anxiety Disorder, Dissociative Disorder, or a Personality Disorder).

speaking, underachievement in school is a red flag signaling the need for an evaluation for AD/HD or other learning problems.

Most experts suggest that AD/HD assessment in the schools is best accomplished in multiple stages:[1]

✓ **Stage I: Screening for AD/HD symptoms.** The teacher completes a behavior rating scale that lists AD/HD behaviors.

✓ **Stage II: Comprehensive Multimethod Assessment.** The school psychologist conducts parent and teacher interviews to discuss academic, behavioral and medical history, strengths, and problems. Formal and informal academic assessment, such as group test results and a review of samples of the student's work and records of work productivity, are also conducted. Two other invaluable assessment measures are direct observation of the student and assessment of executive functions such as organization, managing homework, and planning ahead.

✓ **Stage III: Interpretation of Assessment Data.** Next, the school psychologist interprets the child's academic, behavioral, and functional performance based upon the comprehensive assessment. Functional performance refers to the child's overall ability to manage responsibilities necessary for functioning successfully in a classroom.

✓ **Stage IV: Intervention Planning.** The IEP (Individualized Education Plan), Section 504 plan, or educational plan is developed, based on the results of the assessment. Both the child's strengths and weaknesses are taken into consideration.

✓ **Stage V: Progress Monitoring.** The student's progress must be monitored to determine the effectiveness of the plan. If the student is not successful, changes must be made to the plan.

A more detailed description of this process and a list of common rating scales are available at the end of this chapter.

Subsequent chapters in this Manual provide a wealth of intervention options that can be selected based upon the individual and unique needs of each child with AD/HD. It is important to remember that when other coexisting problems accompany AD/HD, these problems must be targeted separately for the best results. For example, interventions that reduce AD/HD symptoms will not necessarily increase friendships, reduce stress or frustration, or increase reading accuracy. These problems must be addressed specifically in the student's educational plan.

Underdiagnosis vs. Overdiagnosis

Although educators may worry about overdiagnosis of this condition, researchers tell us that the greater problem is often underdiagnosis.[2] According to Peter Jensen, M.D., a leading researcher on AD/HD, only 50 percent of youth with AD/HD ever receive a diagnosis, and at any given time, only half of those are on medication. According to the U.S. Surgeon General, AD/HD is not the only disorder being underdiagnosed. A variety of other mental health disorders, like anxiety and depression, are also not being addressed.[3] Recent changes in educational laws in the United States have increased general awareness that AD/HD is a handicapping condition and that more children have this condition than originally thought. However, this increased awareness has led some educators to erroneously conclude that AD/HD is a new disorder that is overdiagnosed.

Students Typically Overlooked

Several groups of youngsters with AD/HD, however, never receive a diagnosis until middle or high school. Further compounding this problem, some middle and high school teachers assume incorrectly that students who truly have AD/HD would have received a diagnosis during elementary school. Thus, they may not consider attention disorders as possible contributing factors to problems that appear during middle and high school.

Common reasons for overlooking these students prior to high school include:

✓ Students are smart enough to compensate and complete the work.

✓ They work extra hard and spend long hours to compensate for their deficits.

More about AD/HD in Girls

According to a report from the National Institute on Mental Health (NIMH) Conference on Sex Differences in AD/HD, there are significant differences in the manifestation of AD/HD in girls versus boys. As a result, girls with AD/HD are being neglected. In an analysis of studies conducted on girls with AD/HD, Miranda Gaub and Caryn L. Carlson, Ph.D.,[a] found that girls with AD/HD have greater intellectual impairment but lower rates of hyperactivity and externalizing disorders, compared to boys with AD/HD. These differences may result in a referral bias; that is, girls are not referred for evaluation.

Other studies of clinic-referred girls indicate that girls with AD/HD combined type are indistinguishable from boys with AD/HD on measures of coexisting disorders, behavioral ratings of core symptoms, psychological functioning, and family history of psychopathology.[b] When differences did occur, girls had lower reading scores and higher parent-rated measures of inattention. Furthermore, referred girls were a more extreme sample than were the boys, with higher rates of AD/HD in other family members.

Researchers at Massachusetts General Hospital in Boston, one of the leading AD/HD research and clinical practice settings, found similar results in girls referred to pediatricians and psychiatrists. Girls referred for AD/HD were more likely to show conduct problems, mood and anxiety disorders, lower IQ, and greater impairment in social, family and school functioning than non-referred girls.[c] Conduct problems were fewer in girls than in boys with AD/HD, which may account for lower referral rates.

In summary, teachers should be aware that this data describes the most severe cases of AD/HD in girls. Since most girls with AD/HD are not behavior problems, they are often overlooked and suffer quietly while struggling with overwhelming academic tasks.

✓ Parents provide extra supervision and supports to ensure completion of homework and projects.

✓ Demands for strong executive function skills, often lacking in children with AD/HD, expand exponentially in middle and high school, often overwhelming these students.

Specific groups that may be overlooked include:

✓ **Children with AD/HD Inattentive Type (ADD).** Most students with *AD/HD inattentive* are not hyperactive nor are they aggressive. Because they often sit quietly in their seats, teachers are less likely to recognize their attention deficits until later, when they are unable to meet the demands of middle and high school.

✓ **Girls.** Typically, *girls with AD/HD* are less likely to come to a teacher's attention because they are less aggressive and cause fewer behavioral problems in class than boys with AD/HD. In general, girls are more concerned with being compliant and gaining teacher acceptance. In their eagerness to please, they may work long hours to finish schoolwork. Because most girls with AD/HD are not behavior problems, typically their AD/HD must be more severe than in boys if it is to be diagnosed. This means that most girls who are facing serious academic struggles with their AD/HD are overlooked. For more information, read *More about AD/HD in Girls.*

✓ **Gifted.** Many *bright, intellectually gifted students* are able to compensate so that their AD/HD goes unrecognized until middle or high school where academic and organizational demands increase significantly, often overwhelming them.

✓ **Ethnic and Racial Minorities.** AD/HD is less likely to be diagnosed and treated in *students of ethnic and racial minorities.* African American youth are two and a half times less likely than Caucasian children to receive a diagnosis of AD/HD, even though the incidence of the disorder is comparable in both

More about AD/HD in Racial and Ethnic Minority Populations

Anne Teeter Ellison, Ed.D.
Brenda W. Johnson, L.C.S.W.
Jose J. Bauermeister, Ph.D.

Although the rate of AD/HD in African American and Hispanic youth is comparable to the rate in Caucasian children, they are less likely to receive treatment than white children.[a,b,c] One study also found lower medication use in non-white youth: 5 percent in African Americans and 2 percent of Hispanics, compared with 8 percent of Caucasians.[d]

Regina Bussing, M.D., M.S.H.S., of the Department of Psychiatry at the University of Florida also found that service delivery to black children was deficient even though there was no evidence that the incidence of AD/HD was lower among black children than white children.[e] Dr. Bussing also reported that (1) only 50 percent of children with AD/HD were receiving treatment, (2) girls were underserved at a rate three times lower than males, and (3) white children were three times more likely than black children to be referred.

Furthermore, *Mental Health: Culture, Race, and Ethnicity, A Supplement to Mental Health: A Report of the Surgeon General* concludes that African American children are over-represented in arrests, detentions, incarcerations, classes for emotional disorders, and the child welfare system.

Barriers to treatment. According to the Office of the Surgeon General, all racial and ethnic minorities "in America face severe economic, cultural, linguistic and physical barriers for treatment of mental illness, difficulties that prevent thousands from being properly treated."

Gail Mattox, M.D., Professor and Chair of the Department of Psychiatry at Morehouse School of Medicine, agrees that African American children are not receiving optimal care.[f] She identified two factors that are possible barriers to treatment: 1) African American parents may be less informed about AD/HD and 2) they are more likely to believe that AD/HD symptoms are caused by other factors such as "sugar intake." In her longitudinal study, Dr. Bussing also found that African American families are less likely to view AD/HD as a medical condition and tend to believe there is a dietary influence.

A Harris Interactive poll of parents further identified several barriers to diagnosis and treatment of diverse ethnic groups:[g]

1) Concern that their child will be "labeled"
2) Belief that their child was identified because of race or ethnic background
3) Belief that AD/HD is a condition that occurs mainly in white children
4) Lack of adequate information on AD/HD
5) Not knowing where to go for treatment
6) Poor access to care
7) Language barriers

Dr. Bussing also identified similar barriers and found that the cost of services could also be a barrier to seeking and receiving treatment.

According to Jose J. Bauermeister, Ph.D., a researcher at the Behavioral Sciences Research Institute, University of Puerto Rico, Hispanic families have similar reasons for avoiding treatment.[h] Many fear that medication use leads to drug addiction and parents often disagree about the need for medication. He adds that some adolescents may refuse medication because they do not necessarily view improvements in self-control associated with this treatment as desirable changes in the school setting. These teenagers enjoy the Puerto Rican cultural script of horsing around and joking, standing up for themselves and gaining respect, and being loyal and defending friends at school.

CONTINUED NEXT PAGE

More about AD/HD in Racial and Ethnic Minority Populations, Cont.

The importance of being culturally competent. Teachers who are culturally sensitive are better able to serve all students with AD/HD regardless of their ethnic and racial backgrounds. Cultural sensitivity refers to viewing all students in a non-judgmental and unbiased fashion. Studies have shown that a lack of understanding of cultural differences leads to negative judgments and penalties for children of color. Some of those penalties negatively impact special education placement and the achievement of this group of children:

✓ The U.S. Department of Education's Office of Civil Rights investigates allegations of discrimination and has found that African American students receive disciplinary actions at disproportionate rates, experience higher drop-out rates, and are more likely to be steered into special education and away from accelerated programs.
✓ Dr. Bussing reported a "communication disconnect between African American parents and the school system" when it came to AD/HD and treatment options.

What can teachers do to be culturally sensitive to the needs of students? Teachers must recognize the need for cultural sensitivity across a diverse spectrum of backgrounds:

✓ *Race* — African Americans, Hispanics, Native Americans
✓ *Religion* — Catholics, Jews, Protestants
✓ *Socioeconomic level* — rich, poor
✓ *Gender* — boys, girls
✓ *Locale* — urban, rural
✓ *Family educational background* — college graduates, high school drop-outs
✓ *Disabilities* — mental, learning, neurobiological

Of course, we are all different. In fact, all students have unique "qualities inherited and learned from their environment, families and community."

Strategies for teachers. Teachers are challenged to recognize and build on each student's strengths and talents. Here are a few strategies that can help teachers be more culturally aware:

✓ Educate yourself on being sensitive to differences and disparities in the health and mental health of underserved populations. For example, stay current on new information and professional studies such as those cited in this article.
✓ Seek expert advice not only from medical professionals but also from nonprofit family organizations such as CHADD to stay abreast of the most current scientific and culturally specific material.
✓ Build relationships with the child and family. This can be done in the classroom and through correspondence, conferences, events, or a home visit.
✓ Accept and celebrate differences in ALL of your children.
✓ Don't underestimate the importance of natural support systems such as extended family members, the church, and local community leaders. These supports can be useful if you are seeking to positively influence the child.
✓ Don't underestimate the importance of helping minority families address more basic needs prior to seeking their attention and support with educational needs. Be prepared to refer them to the school social worker or the local social services agency.
✓ Sometimes adults demand respect and then talk down to children; however, mutual respect goes a long way in developing a spirit of cooperation between teachers and students. Today, children are sensitive to and react to adult attitudes and judgments.
✓ Be conscious of how you say things to ALL children, especially to those who are struggling academically or behaviorally.

groups.[4] The identification rate of Hispanic youth is even lower. Additionally, African American males are categorized as having emotional and behavior disorders (ED) at a higher rate than white males.[5] Undiagnosed and untreated AD/HD should not be overlooked as a possible contributor to the over-representation of African American males in programs for children with ED. For additional details, read *More about AD/HD in Racial and Ethnic Minority Populations.*

✓ **Special education.** Students in *special education* may be given only one diagnosis, such as a specific learning disability. Evaluators may not always look for coexisting problems despite research showing rates of overlapping learning disabilities and AD/HD ranging from 25 to 50 percent.

Students Sometimes Overdiagnosed

Researchers tell us that some students, especially boys in kindergarten and first grade, are immature, lacking the motor and language skills necessary to meet academic demands.[6] These students can appear distractible and restless but are simply overwhelmed by the demands of school and probably do not have AD/HD.

The Teacher's Role in Evaluation and Treatment

As explained earlier, *multimodal treatment,* a comprehensive approach to treatment, is considered one of the most effective ways to help children and teenagers succeed in school. Although teachers may not think of themselves as providing treatment, educators do play a critical role in multimodal treatment plans. Ideally, treatment should be defined broadly, and academic success should be a top therapeutic priority. In fact, *succeeding in school is often one of the most therapeutic things that can happen to children and teenager.*[7]

Typically, multimodal treatment includes parent training, AD/HD education, classroom accommodations, academic and social skills training, and medication management. In some cases, therapy or counseling may be appropriate for other associated problems, including anxiety, depression and social rejection. Ultimately, the long-term goal is to teach children and teens the necessary skills and knowledge about AD/HD so they can eventually manage this challenging condition independently.

A shift in the treatment approach and behavior intervention strategies is critical, especially during the teenage years. The increased involvement of the student in planning and problem solving is imperative as he or she gets older. Students must be treated with respect, educated about their condition, and taught compensatory skills. Any intervention strategy is much more likely to be successful if the students, especially middle and high schoolers, help develop and agrees with the plan.

Some students may even be capable of collecting data to evaluate the benefit of any interventions. For example, the student may ask to do schoolwork without taking any medication, but parents and teachers believe it will impact his grades negatively. Parents and teachers can help the student plan an experiment to determine if homework and test grades change when he doesn't take medication. Oftentimes, facts can be more persuasive for students than adult arguments.

Working as a Team

Ultimately, everyone who touches a student's life has a role to play in treatment. Ideally, everyone, including the student, parents, teachers, administrators, guidance counselor, school psychologist, therapist, and the physician, should sit down together and plan for the student, but, in reality, it seldom happens. Parents typically convey information back and forth between the school and the physician or therapist. However, during the middle and high school years, the number of adults involved with each student increases significantly. Regular communication is extremely difficult but essential. Consequently, identifying one educator as the primary contact person at the secondary school level is helpful.

Summary

A thorough evaluation and development of a comprehensive IEP, 504 plan, or educational plan are essential and greatly increase a student's chance for success in school. Ideally, the evaluation will identify key problem areas and help teachers develop teaching strategies and accommodations to address each learning problem.

2

Stages of a Comprehensive Assessment of AD/HD in the Schools

Anne Teeter Ellison, Ed.D.

Most experts suggest that AD/HD assessment in the schools is best accomplished in multiple stages.

Stage I: Screening for AD/HD Symptoms

During Stage I, teachers are asked to document the presence, intensity, and duration of AD/HD symptoms. Generally, teachers complete AD/HD screening measures (for example, an AD/HD Rating Scale) to determine the number of DSM symptoms present. If there are sufficient symptoms rated as "very much" or "most of the time" (generally 8 of 14), a comprehensive Stage II assessment is appropriate. When there are fewer symptoms present but the child has other problems (academic difficulties), further evaluation may still be warranted. Older children may also show fewer symptoms of AD/HD and may require additional evaluation to determine the nature of their difficulties.

Stage II: Comprehensive Multimethod Assessment

Since there is no single test for AD/HD, a comprehensive evaluation must be completed:

Parent and Teacher Interviews. Parents are interviewed to determine the child's medical and academic history, particularly developmental milestones, such as walking and talking, and academic history from preschool to the current grade placement. This helps document school-related, behavioral, and other social adjustment difficulties that accompany AD/HD. It is important to determine when the problems began and the degree to which the AD/HD symptoms interfere with school (work productivity, homework compliance)[a] and social functioning (relations with family members and peers in the community). The interview should also explore the presence of other emotional-behavioral problems that exist at home (for example, oppositional defiance, depression, and anxiety). As noted in Chapter 1, the child's strengths should also be identified and incorporated into strategies in the IEP (Individualized Education Program) or Section 504 Plan.

The teacher interview focuses on the nature of the academic and behavioral problems in the classroom, particularly where academic problems occur and situations or circumstances in which the problems are most severe. Teachers provide valuable details about the antecedents (what happened before) and the consequences of the behaviors (gained attention, avoided work). The student's strengths should also be discussed.

A review of school records also yields information about the child's academic history, including when the problems were first reported, the nature of the difficulties, and the interventions used to reduce the problems.

Parent and Teacher Rating Scales. Teachers and parents generally fill out a number of behavioral rating scales to measure AD/HD-related problems as well as other coexisting behavioral disorders (oppositional, conduct-related problems) and emotional problems (anxiety and depression). Common parent and teacher rating scales for AD/HD are listed at the end of this chapter.

CONTINUED NEXT PAGE

Stages of a Comprehensive Assessment of AD/HD in the Schools, Cont.

Behavioral rating scales are useful in screening for AD/HD symptoms, determining the presence and severity of AD/HD symptoms, identifying coexisting disorders, identifying associated problems, and measuring response to interventions (medication, behavioral, academic). A number of the rating scales include self-report forms (ASEBA, BASC-2, Brown ADD Scales, Conners) and should be included in Stage II assessment for older youths and teens.

Direct Observations. Direct observations should be included in Stage II assessment because they help document specific behavioral problems across various settings (classroom, playground) and at different times throughout the day (morning, afternoon). Direct observations typically target behaviors such as being off task, fidgeting, negative vocalizing (blurting out, swearing), being out of seat, and social interactions (positive, negative, aggressive). The child's antecedent behavior and the teachers' response can also be noted. Other information that can be useful when planning interventions (Stage IV) include the number of times teachers reward positive behaviors and provide prompts for prosocial behaviors, reprimands, and corrective feedback. Several of the measures listed at the end of the chapter include direct observation forms (ASEBA, BASC-2).

Academic Performance. Academic performance can be measured both formally and informally. Informal methods typically include behavioral observations of daily classroom performance, work completion and work accuracy, homework completion and accuracy, independent seatwork, and organizational skills. Checking for organization and messiness (desk, locker, backpack, file folders) can be helpful as well.

Formal methods of assessing academic performance, such as standardized group and individual achievement tests, are not always as sensitive in measuring the impact of AD/HD on schoolwork. However, standardized tests are helpful for ruling out or identifying learning disabilities. Performance on formal tests also gives us insight into the child's need for testing accommodations such as extra time, which is especially important for high-stakes testing that is employed in schools today.

Other Assessment Measures. While new conceptualizations of AD/HD emphasize deficits in executive functions (EF), the measurement of EF is not an exact science. Although deficits in goal-directed behaviors, planning, organization, decision-making, and self-regulation have been found in children and adolescents with AD/HD, tests of EF are not always sensitive to the complexity of these problems.[b] A number of promising EF measures have been developed. The Behavior Rating Inventory of Executive Functions (BRIEF) comprises parent and teacher forms and measures global executive functions, behavioral self-regulation (initiation, emotional control), metacognition (memory and organization), and other behaviors such as goal setting, monitoring of one's own behaviors, and getting started. The Brown ADD Scales also measure six clusters: organizing, focusing attention, regulating alertness and processing speed, managing emotions, using working memory, and self-regulation.

There are several laboratory tests of sustained attention that have been used for assessing AD/HD symptoms, including the Continuous Performance Test II (CPT-II), the Test of Visual Attention (TOVA), and the Gordon Diagnostic System. Care should be taken when incorporating these measures into the assessment of AD/HD because they lack sensitivity and specificity; that is, they do not always differentiate between AD/HD and non-AD/HD children because some children with AD/HD *do well* on these measures and some children without AD/HD *do not*. However, the Gordon Diagnostic System does provide a valid measure of vigilance (sustained attention) and can be used in a comprehensive battery but not as the sole measure of AD/HD. These measures can also have utility for measuring responsiveness to medication and treatment efficacy.

The extent to which measures of EF add to the specific diagnosis of AD/HD is unclear, but they can be useful in identifying problems that can be targeted for intervention. They can also be helpful in measuring outcomes in Stage V.

CONTINUED NEXT PAGE

Stages of a Comprehensive Assessment of AD/HD in the Schools, Cont.

Stage III: Interpretation of Assessment Data

In Stage III, assessment data are interpreted to determine the presence and severity of AD/HD symptoms, identify coexisting disorders (for example, oppositional defiance, conduct problems), or rule out competing diagnoses, such as reading or anxiety disorders. It is important to measure the extent to which AD/HD impacts academic performance and social functioning.

The data collected in Stage II is used to determine whether the child shows significant signs of inattention (6 of 9 symptoms), hyperactivity-impulsivity (6 of 9 symptoms), or combined type (symptoms of both inattention and hyperactivity), according to DSM criteria. The data gathered from the parent and teacher rating scales should also be used to determine the severity of symptoms. It is generally accepted that scores two standard deviations above the mean suggest significant AD/HD problems. Scores falling between 1 and 1.5 standard deviations suggest borderline or mild AD/HD. While these children with mild symptoms may not receive a diagnosis of AD/HD, they may still need interventions, particularly behavioral, psychosocial or academic, to cope with their difficulties. (George DuPaul, Ph.D., and Gary Stoner, Ph.D., provide an in-depth discussion of these distinctions in their book, *ADHD in the schools: Assessment and intervention strategies*.) DSM also requires that the child show symptoms before the age of 7 years and that symptoms manifest for at least one year. However, for some very bright children and for those with AD/HD inattentive type, problems may not show up until later in childhood or even early adolescence.

During this phase of the assessment, the extent to which AD/HD symptoms interfere with the child's functioning — functional impairment — can be measured. The observational data and academic record review can be valuable for making this determination. It is critical to document the impact of AD/HD symptoms on academic performance (low work productivity), as well as social competence and social adjustment (impaired social relations). These functional impairments can further result in emotional adjustment difficulties and can lead to other disorders of childhood and adolescence (anxiety, depression, conduct, oppositional defiance).

Stage IV: Intervention Planning

While rating scales are important in determining the level and severity of AD/HD symptoms, they also help identify problem behaviors that can be targeted for change. Intervention planning can be assisted with a complete picture of the child's strengths as well as weaknesses. While there are many behaviors that teachers would like to reduce, they must not forget to focus on the child's unique talents and strengths when planning interventions. Educators can lose children if they focus primarily on a student's problems and forget about the charming, lovable, and real assets that these students bring to the classroom. By building strengths and assets into the intervention plan, teachers are more likely to increase the child's motivation and willingness to engage in the process of change. It is also critical that educators identify realistic goals for children, goals that can be clearly understood and easily measured by the teacher, parent, or child.

Stage V: Progress Monitoring

During this final stage, progress toward meeting intervention goals is monitored by collecting various data. It is important to determine how well the intervention plan is working and whether intervention goals or strategies need to be revised. Observation of classroom behaviors, work completion, and work accuracy are frequently used to measure progress. It is important to make data-based decisions when determining the effectiveness of the intervention plan, so charting behavioral progress, academic productivity, and other behavioral changes (increased positive social interactions, decreased out bursts) are recommended. Several forms are sensitive to change and can be easily used to monitor treatment efficacy and response to medication, including ACTeRs, BASC-2 Monitor for AD/HD, and SNAP.

Table 2–2. Common Parent and Teacher Rating Scales for AD/HD

Numerous rating scales have shown to be valid measures of AD/HD symptoms and related problems.

Scales	Behaviors/Problems Measured
ADD-H Comprehensive Teacher's Rating Scale (ACTeRs)	AD/HD Specific
ADHD Rating Scale-IV	AD/HD Specific/Subtypes AD/HD Inattentive AD/HD Hyperactive-Impulsive AD/HD Combined
Attention Deficit Disorders Evaluation Scales-Third (ADDES-3)	AD/HD Specific/Subtypes
Achenbach System of Internalizing Disorders Empirically Based Assessment (ASEBA)	Externalizing Disorders Total Behavior Disorders Syndrome Scales Anxiety/Depression Withdrawal/Depression Social Problems Thought Problems Rule Breaking Attention Aggression
Behavior Assessment System for Children-2nd	Comorbid Disorders Aggression Anxiety Attention Atypicality Conduct problems Depression Hyperactivity Activities of Daily Living Functional Communication Adaptability Leadership Learning problems Social Skills Study Skills
Brown Attention Deficit Disorder Scale for Children & Adolescents	AD/HD Subtypes Executive Functions Screening Comorbid Learning & Psychiatric Disorders

CONTINUED NEXT PAGE

Table 2–2. Cont.

Scales	Behaviors/Problems Measured
Behavioral & Emotional Rating Scale (BERS)	Strengths & Weaknesses
Conners Rating Scales–Revised	ADHD + Other Problems ADHD Index Hyperactivity Oppositional Cognitive Problems/Inattention Anxious/Shy Perfectionism Social Problems
SNAP–IV	AD/HD Specific
SWAN	AD/HD Specific Strengths & Weaknesses
Vanderbilt ADHD Rating Scale	AD/HD + Other Problems AD/HD Subtypes Oppositional/Conduct Anxious/Depressed School Function Academic Performance Behavioral Performance

2

Overview of Key Academic Issues

To teach is to touch a life forever.

• *Joan Teach, Ph.D., principal*

The next three chapters provide an overview of key academic issues for all age groups.

Chapter 3: Impact of AD/HD on School Performance

✓ Developmental characteristics of students with AD/HD

✓ Common learning problems for students with AD/HD

- Distractibility and inattention
- Poor inhibition and self–control
- Difficulty regulating activity level, emotions, and responses
- Disorganization and poor time management
- Deficits in executive function, self–monitoring, and metacognitive skills
- Poor memory (active working memory, short–term memory)
- Slow processing speed
- Poor visual motor, fine motor, and spatial organizational skills
- Poor language processing and communication skills

Photo: Bobby Stroud Photography

Chapter 4: Basic Instructional Strategies and Accommodations

✓ Sustained attention, memory, and on–task behavior

✓ Writing, output, and processing speed

✓ Organization, time management, and study skills

✓ Learning strategies and metacognitive skills

✓ Inhibition and self–control

Chapter 5: Creating a Positive Learning Environment

✓ Proactive classroom management

✓ Environmental supports

✓ Strategies to address the antecedents of misbehavior and consequences

✓ Behavioral interventions/accommodations

✓ Positive behavioral supports: A continuum of interventions

CHAPTER 3

Impact of AD/HD on School Performance*

Sandra F. Rief, M.A.

Developmental Characteristics of Students with AD/HD

Children and teenagers with AD/HD generally experience the most difficulty and impairment in the school setting. Problem areas include poor academic performance, behavioral acting out, and sometimes poor social relationships with peers. Russell Barkley, Ph.D., reports that students with AD/HD are approximately 30 percent delayed in their ability to control and manage their own behavior.[1] This means that many age and grade level expectations for students, for example, working independently, following through on tasks with minimal supervision, organizing assignments and materials, demonstrating self-discipline, and "acting their age," are unrealistic for students with AD/HD. Typically, these students are functioning like a much younger child. In fact, Dr. Barkley explains that from a developmental perspective, a 10-year-old student behaves more like a 7-year-old.

Compared to other children and teens their age, students with AD/HD have developmental weaknesses in regulating activity level, impulse control, emotions, and attention, which interferes with their ability to make full use of their executive functions. Deficits in executive functions, in turn, can result in a host of learning problems. Executive function deficits can have a profound impact on the performance of students, especially middle and high school students. More information on executive function is also provided in Chapters 1 and 9.

As many as one-third to one-half of students with AD/HD have coexisting learning disabilities, which makes the acquisition of some academic skills, such as learning how to read and write and understanding the abstract language and concepts of mathematics, much more difficult. On the other hand, for students with AD/HD who do not have coexisting learning disabilities, the acquisition of information and skills — learning, per se — is not the problem. The main academic challenge is performance — the output and production of required tasks.

Variability of performance is a classic characteristic of AD/HD. At times, students with AD/HD are able to produce the schoolwork and demonstrate their knowledge/skills; at other times, they cannot. This inconsistency in performance and production is frustrating to teachers and parents alike and leads to the unfair and erroneous assumption that the child could perform as expected if he or she wanted to and just tried harder.

Common Learning Problems for Students with AD/HD

Every child or teen with AD/HD presents his or her own unique profile based upon learning style, strengths, and weaknesses. In addition, the symptoms

---

* In most cases, AD/HD is used interchangeably throughout this Manual to describe both AD/HD predominately hyperactive-impulsive and AD/HD predominately inattentive. IDEA regulations refer to these two conditions as ADHD and ADD, respectively.

of AD/HD will vary from student to student. Quite often, their academic difficulties are linked to their symptoms of AD/HD and executive function deficits. The following is a general overview of common learning and behavioral problems in students with AD/HD.[2,3,4] More detailed information and instructional strategies are provided in subsequent sections for preschool, elementary, and middle and high school students.

1. **DISTRACTIBILITY AND INATTENTION OFTEN RESULT IN:**
   ✓ **Off-task behavior:** lack of productivity and work production
   ✓ **Not getting started** on assigned tasks or getting very little work done without someone monitoring and focusing to the task
   ✓ **Poor listening and communication:** not following directions; pulled off topic in conversations; not focusing on the speaker
   ✓ **Lack of engagement** in lessons and activities
   ✓ **Making many careless errors** in math computation: inattention to mathematical processing signs; difficulty maintaining the level of attention required to complete problems with accuracy; not checking for errors and self-correcting
   ✓ **Lack of attention to detail** on written work: capitalization; punctuation; spelling; incomplete sentences; poor editing skills; difficulty maintaining focus and train of thought when writing
   ✓ **Reading difficulties:** particularly with silent reading (maintaining focus and processing what is being read); having to read the same material several times to "sink in," losing one's place when reading; missing important details, causing "spotty comprehension"
   ✓ **Not sustaining attention and effort for tasks** that are difficult or not of choice or interest, leading to many incomplete, late, or undone assignments
   ✓ **Missing important verbal and nonverbal cues,** which affects social skills

2. **POOR INHIBITION AND SELF-CONTROL OFTEN RESULT IN:**
   ✓ **Making many careless errors** due to not reading or waiting to listen for full directions before beginning tasks; rushing through assignments
   ✓ **Disruptive behaviors** interfering with work production and interpersonal relationships
   ✓ **Difficulty transitioning** between activities (stopping or disengaging from one task to do another)
   ✓ **Being easily pulled off task,** affecting work performance and class participation
   ✓ **A greater challenge to motivate and discipline** (not responding as well to typical rewards or punishments effective for most students)

3. **DIFFICULTY REGULATING ACTIVITY LEVEL, EMOTIONS, AND RESPONSES OFTEN RESULTS IN:**
   ✓ **Inability to sit still** long enough to perform required tasks
   ✓ **Becoming easily overstimulated and excitable;** having difficulty calming oneself or settling down
   ✓ **Poor coping skills and handling of negative emotions** (frustration, anger)
   ✓ **Over-reactivity;** easily provoked to fighting and inappropriate means of resolving conflicts
   ✓ **Above behaviors interfering** with academic productivity, peer and adult interactions, and the ability to work and play cooperatively with classmates

4. **DISORGANIZATION AND POOR TIME MANAGEMENT OFTEN RESULT IN:**
   ✓ **Being unprepared** with materials and textbooks needed for schoolwork and homework
   ✓ **Disorganized workspace, lockers, and notebooks;** losing or misplacing important materials or belongings
   ✓ **Poor planning** for assignments and projects
   ✓ **Lack of awareness or sense of time;** poor estimation of time required to pace oneself adequately to complete tasks

✓ **Procrastination**; missing deadlines and due dates

✓ **Poor study skills or habits** that significantly affect classwork and homework success

5. **DEFICITS IN EXECUTIVE FUNCTION, SELF-MONITORING, AND METACOGNITIVE SKILLS OFTEN RESULT IN:**

✓ **Poor planning and monitoring** in mathematical problem solving: not realizing that the answer is not close to estimate and requires readjusting or trying another strategy

✓ **Poor reading comprehension:** lack of self-monitoring for understanding while reading

✓ **Difficulty with written expression and fluency:** generating, planning, and organizing ideas; keeping the intended audience in mind and writing with a clear purpose; developing ideas and making revisions; appropriate sequence, flow, and coherency

✓ **Inefficient learning strategies:** note taking, test taking, study skills

✓ **Being unaware of grades** and how well they are performing; poor self-evaluation

6. **POOR MEMORY (ACTIVE WORKING MEMORY, SHORT-TERM MEMORY) OFTEN RESULTS IN:**

✓ **Difficulty recalling information**

✓ **Forgetfulness:** homework assignments; turning in completed work; following directions

✓ **Math weaknesses:** difficulty remembering information long enough to work through multiple steps of a problem; learning and retrieving basic facts, such as multiplication tables, quickly and accurately; remembering procedures and algorithms

✓ **Written language problems:** difficulty with spelling; letter/sound association and patterns; keeping ideas in mind long enough to manipulate and get down on paper; recalling and retrieving vocabulary and grammatical rules

✓ **Reading comprehension difficulties:** forgetting what was read to be able to accurately summarize or recall details

7. **SLOW PROCESSING SPEED OFTEN RESULTS IN:**

✓ **Slow, tedious written output and production**

✓ **Difficulty processing information** and being able to respond correctly to questions without sufficient "wait time"

✓ **Taking significantly longer to do class and homework assignments** than the average student: sometimes hours to complete what most classmates can do in 20 minutes

8. **POOR VISUAL MOTOR, FINE MOTOR, AND SPATIAL ORGANIZATIONAL SKILLS OFTEN RESULT IN:**

✓ **Poor handwriting skills;** struggling with and avoiding paper and pencil tasks

✓ **Written work that is messy and difficult to decipher**

✓ **Poorly organized and spaced written work**

✓ **Math computation errors:** due to misalignment and organization of numbers on a page when setting up and solving problems

✓ **Difficulty copying from board or book to paper**

9. **POOR LANGUAGE PROCESSING AND COMMUNICATION SKILLS OFTEN RESULT IN:**

✓ **Poor listening skills**

✓ **Poor turn taking in conversation;** being off-topic

✓ **Poor pragmatic skills:** using appropriate language at appropriate time

✓ **Difficulty processing language** involved in mathematical word problems, reading comprehension, and expressive writing

Additional information is available in in Appendix A.

CHAPTER 4

Basic Instructional Strategies and Accommodations for Challenging AD/HD Behaviors

Sandra F. Rief, M.A.

These intervention strategies and accommodations support and enhance learning for those who struggle with problems related to their AD/HD. (Adapted from *How to Reach and Teach Children with ADD/ADHD: Practical Techniques, Strategies, and Interventions, 2nd edition, The ADHD Book of Lists: A Practical Guide for Helping Children and Teens with Attention Deficit Disorders, The ADD/ADHD Checklist: An Easy Reference for Parents and Teachers,* and *How to Reach and Teach All Children in the Inclusive Classroom, 2nd edition*)

Sustained Attention, Memory, and On-Task Behavior

✓ **Require student to repeat directions,** share with a partner, or other technique before beginning tasks.

✓ **Use a timer and rewards,** such as points or tokens, to motivate and reinforce working productively for short time intervals.

✓ **Provide differentiated instruction** to boost interest and motivation: varied formats groupings, choices of activities, or questioning strategies.

✓ **Give multisensory instruction/lesson presentations,** utilizing auditory, visual, and tactile-kinesthetic techniques.

✓ **Use novel, engaging, high interest activities** and strategies to get and maintain students' attention.

✓ **Use active learning and high response strategies** and opportunities: think-pair-share, total physical response, unison response to signals, or recording answers on dry erase boards.

✓ **Give environmental and learning style accommodations or adaptations:** seating to avoid distractions, and materials and work areas to optimize attention to task and work production.

✓ **Use visual prompts, cues, and redirection** to task frequently.

✓ **Teach mnemonic devices, association strategies, melody, rhythm, or other memory strategies** to aid memory and recall of information

✓ **Provide written or pictorial directions** (and task cards) to accompany oral directions.

✓ **Use tools or aids to compensate for memory difficulties:** multiplication charts, vocabulary or word walls, or sticky notepad to jot down ideas before forgetting.

✓ **Label, highlight, underline, and add color** to important parts of a task.

✓ **Increase use of partners or buddies** to help focus attention to task, clarify directions, assist with recording of assignments in planner, and practice or review material.

Writing, Output, and Processing Speed

✓ **Provide graphic organizers** to plan and structure written work.

✓ **Use modeled and guided writing** to build expressive writing skills and scaffolds and support throughout the writing process

✓ **Allow other output modes to demonstrate learning:** oral reports and hands-on projects.

✓ **Teach keyboarding skills and encourage the use of computer** and other assistive technology for written assignments.

✓ **Provide special tools** (pencil grips) and materials (graph paper for math computation).

✓ **Reduce requirements to copy** and recopy. Allow print rather than cursive if easier.

✓ **Provide a minimum of five seconds wait time** (for example, think-pair-share before whole group discussion).

✓ **Allow student to dictate or tape record responses** if writing is a struggle.

✓ **Modify assignments** to compensate for length of time it takes to complete.

✓ **Give extended time** on tests.

Organization, Time Management, and Study Skills

✓ **Explicitly teach and provide tools for organization and effective study habits.** Require the use of binders, backpack, planner or assignment calendar, and color-coding strategies.

✓ **Organize the classroom environment.** Designate areas for storing materials and trays or files for turning in work. Provide assistance with organizing the student's notebook, desk, or locker or filing important papers.

✓ **Provide structure and support with time management on assignments,** particularly long-term projects.

✓ **Teach, model, and consistently use daily assignment sheets or planners.** Support families to ease the homework hassle.

Learning Strategies and Metacognitive Skills

✓ **Explicitly teach learning strategies** (for example, how to use resource or reference materials or take notes) and metacognitive strategies, such as journal responses and reading logs, that engage the learner in thinking about their learning, responding, and monitoring their own comprehension and production.

✓ **Build in goal-setting and self-evaluation** in assignments or projects.

✓ **Use graphic organizers** to aid in planning, organizing, and comprehension of reading or writing assignments.

✓ **Teach active reading strategies,** such as SQ3R, summarization, identifying the main idea, and story grammar skills.

Inhibition and Self-control

✓ **Anticipate and plan for problems** that can arise from lack of structure, unclear expectations, or environmental triggers.

✓ **Utilize auditory and visual techniques** to signal transitions or changes of activity.

✓ **Provide more frequent monitoring, feedback, and reinforcement.** Use positive and negative consequences that are meaningful to the student as well as shorter time intervals.

✓ **Allow alternatives to sitting** in a chair or at a desk.

✓ **Provide music, relaxation strategies, and access to a designated location** to calm and prevent escalation of behavior.

✓ **Individualize behavioral supports and interventions** and provide careful structure for cooperative group activities.

✓ **Teach and reinforce positive listening behaviors,** such as eye contact and not interrupting.

Additional information is available in in Appendix A.

CHAPTER 5

Creating a Positive Learning Environment

Sandra F. Rief, M.A.

The best classroom management involves anticipating potential problems and avoiding them through careful planning. The following are the key components and strategies for effective classroom management and preventing or reducing behavioral problems. (Adapted from *How to Reach and Teach Children with ADD/ADHD: Practical Techniques, Strategies, and Interventions, 2nd edition, The ADHD Book of Lists: A Practical Guide for Helping Children and Teens with Attention Deficit Disorders,* and *How to Reach and Teach All Children in the Inclusive Classroom.*)

A. Proactive Classroom Management

RULES AND BEHAVIORAL EXPECTATIONS
✓ **Limit the number of rules and behavioral standards** to four or five.
✓ **Make sure behaviors are observable.** For example, "Keep hands, feet, and objects to yourself." "Be on time and prepared for class."
✓ **Define concretely** what the behaviors should "look like" and "sound like."
✓ **Discuss, model, role-play, and practice** those desired behaviors and expectations.
✓ **Post them in words or pictures,** and refer to them frequently.
✓ **Reward students for rule-following behavior.**

TEACH PROCEDURES AND ROUTINES
✓ **Decide upon specific classroom procedures** and write them down for clarity.
✓ **Teach and practice procedures** until they become so well-established and automatic that they become routine. Plan procedures for the start of the school day or class period all the way through dismissal at the end of class or day.
✓ **Monitor, review, and reteach** as needed throughout the year.

TEACHER PROXIMITY AND MOVEMENT
✓ **Circulate and move** around the room frequently.
✓ **Use physical movement, proximity, and positioning** to manage disruptive students. Seat them closer for easy eye contact and close cueing or prompting (for example, to place a hand on their shoulder or point to a visual reminder on the desk). Walk or stand near students who are prone to misbehave.

USE SIGNALS AND VISUAL PROMPTS
✓ **Establish visual and auditory signals** to get students to stop what they are doing and give you their attention or to transition from one activity to another. For example, flash the lights, use a clapping pattern, play a bar of music, call out a signal word, or hold up a hand.

✓ **Post pictures or icons of behavioral expecta-tions,** such as "in seat" and "raise hand," on the wall, taped to the students' desks, or both. Point to or tap on the picture prompt as a reminder.

✓ **Post a time on the board or set a timer** to signal when work time has started.

MONITOR STUDENT BEHAVIOR

✓ **Scan the room frequently and remain aware** of what students are engaged in at all times. Positively reinforce students who are engaged appropriately. For example, "I see Karen and Alicia busy on their assignment. Thank you."

✓ **Address inappropriate behavior when scanning** with a gentle reminder, eye contact, or "the teacher look."

✓ **Redirect students** by mentioning their name, getting eye contact, and using a calm but firm voice.

PROVIDE POSITIVE ATTENTION AND REWARD APPROPRIATE BEHAVIOR

✓ **Increase the immediacy and frequency of** positive feedback and encouragement.

✓ **Focus attention on the student** when he or she is engaged in appropriate behavior (rather than caught in a rule violation).

✓ **Give at least three times more positive attention and comments** to students than negative or corrective feedback.

✓ **Use a high degree of positive verbal reinforcement** for appropriate behaviors and sincere praise that is specific about the behavior exhibited. For example, "Great job cooperating with your group and finishing the assignment on time." "I'm glad you chose to_____. That will help you_____."

✓ **Frequently acknowledge and recognize** good work, behavior, and social performance.

✓ **Establish positive reinforcement systems** for classroom management. (Read more about this in subsequent sections.)

✓ **Collaborate with the class** to create a *menu of possible reinforcers* or *rewards* that can be earned.

NEGATIVE CONSEQUENCES

✓ **Back up behavioral limits with fair and reasonable consequences** for misbehavior.

✓ **Specify consequences in advance.** Let students know what will happen if a behavior continues.

✓ **Set a beginning and end** for negative consequences.

✓ **Enforce with consistency and predictability** in a calm, nonemotional manner.

✓ **Handle inappropriate behavior as simply and promptly** as possible.

✓ **Deliver consequences using as few words** as possible. Act without lecturing; discussions about behavior can occur later.

IGNORE SOME BEHAVIORS

✓ **Choose to ignore minor inappropriate** behavior that is not intentional. Not every behavior warrants teacher intervention.

✓ **Be tolerant and flexible with students with AD/HD.** Allow extra movement or fiddling with objects, particularly for behaviors they have significant physiological difficulty controlling, such as motor fidgetiness.

POSITIVE TEACHING BEHAVIORS

✓ **Model respectful** language, tone of voice, and body language.

✓ **Provide effective and respectful** requests, redirection, and corrective feedback.

✓ **Use humor** to de-escalate potential problems.

✓ **Avoid lecturing, nagging, criticism, and sarcasm.**

✓ **Do not take a child's inappropriate behavior personally.**

✓ **Be well-planned and organized.**

✓ **Discuss inappropriate behavior** with students in private, when possible.

EFFECTIVE TEACHING STRATEGIES

Effective classroom management goes hand in hand with good teaching and instruction. Even students with the tendency for significant behavioral challenges generally demonstrate appropriate behavior when teachers provide:

- ✓ **Engaging, meaningful, high-interest learning activities or instruction;**
- ✓ **Differentiated instruction and pacing** to avoid frustration and boredom; and
- ✓ **Lessons that are well-planned, and class periods that have little lag time** (when students are unoccupied and waiting to find out what they are expected to do next).

The key to effective classroom management is *building positive relationships and rapport with students and making a connection on a personal level.* This requires teachers to be understanding, flexible, patient, and empathic. Children typically work hard and will want to cooperate and please adults whom they like, trust, and respect.

PREVENTING PROBLEMS DURING TRANSITIONS OR CHANGES OF ACTIVITY

Students with AD/HD typically have the greatest behavioral difficulties during transitional times of the day in the classroom and other school settings that are less structured and supervised, such as the playground, cafeteria, hallways, and bathrooms.

- ✓ **Prepare for changes in routine** (for example, assemblies, substitute teachers, field trips) through discussion and modeling expectations. Avoid catching students off guard.
- ✓ **Maintain a visual schedule** that is reviewed and referred to frequently. Point out changes in the schedule in advance.
- ✓ **Communicate clearly** when activities will begin and when they will end.
- ✓ **Give specific instructions** on how to switch to the next activity.
- ✓ **Be sure to clearly teach, model, and have students practice and rehearse all procedures** that will occur during a change of activity. This includes such things as the students' quick and quiet movement from class to class or from their

desks to the carpet area, and putting away and taking out materials.

- ✓ **Use signals for transitions:**
  - Have an opening desk or board assignment at the start of every class.
  - Review homework assignments just before pack-up.
  - Play a bar of music on a keyboard.
  - Flash lights.
  - Ring a bell.
  - Begin a clapping pattern.
  - Use prompts such as "1,2,3…eyes on me."
- ✓ **Reward smooth transitions.** Many teachers use free time at the end of class and individual points or table points to reward students, rows, or table clusters who are ready for the next activity.
- ✓ **Be organized in advance** with materials prepared for the next activity.

B. Environmental Supports

ESTABLISH A CLASSROOM ENVIRONMENT THAT:

- ✓ **Is calm, predictable, and well-structured** (for example, clear schedule, routines, rules, and behavioral guidelines);
- ✓ **Is well-organized** (for example, materials, furniture, physical space);
- ✓ **Builds a sense of "community,"** teamwork, and interdependence;
- ✓ **Is flexible** enough to accommodate the individual needs of students; and
- ✓ **Is emotionally, as well as physically, safe.** Students who are not fearful of making a mistake or looking or sounding foolish are willing to take the risk of participation.

STUDENT SEATING

- ✓ **Physically arrange the classroom with options for seating.** For example, offer single desk options instead of two-person desks or tables for students who need more buffer space. More optimal desk formations for students with AD/HD are U-shapes, E-shapes, and rows (straight or stag-

5

gered) rather than table formations with desk clusters facing each other.

✓ **Students with AD/HD are usually best seated:**
  – Close to the center of instruction;
  – Surrounded by and facing positive role models and well-focused students;
  – Within teacher cueing and prompting distance; and
  – Away from high traffic areas and distracters, such as noisy heaters or air conditioners, doors, windows, and pencil sharpeners.

✓ **Consider other alternatives to sitting in one's seat to work.** For example, allow a child to stand over his desk, kneel on his chair, or sit on a beanbag chair with paper attached to a clipboard to increase productivity and motivation.

SPACE, MATERIALS, ADJUSTING FOR ENVIRONMENTAL DISTRACTIONS

✓ **Designate physical boundaries** with colored tape on the carpet, floor, or tables.

✓ **Store materials in clearly labeled** bins, shelves, tubs, trays, or folders.

✓ **Reduce visual distractions,** such as unnecessary writing on the board, and minimize auditory distractions whenever possible.

✓ **Permit students to use earphones** to block out noise during seatwork, test taking, or other times of the day.

✓ **Provide "office areas" or "study carrels"** for seating options during certain times of the day as needed. These should be encouraged and experimented with by all students in the class so seating in these areas is never viewed as punitive or for students with special needs only.

✓ **Purchase or construct privacy boards** to place on tables while taking tests or other times of the day to block out visual distractions and limit the visual field.

✓ **Turn off the lights** at various times of the day for calming, particularly after P.E. and recess.

✓ **Allow students to work in or move to a quiet corner** or designated area of the room when needed.

C. Strategies to Address the Antecedents of Misbehavior and Consequences

COMMON TRIGGERS OR ANTECEDENTS TO MISBEHAVIOR

Students misbehave for many reasons. Certain conditions, times of day, settings, activities, events, and people can trigger misbehavior. By being aware of common triggers or antecedents to problematic behaviors, teachers can be proactive and make adjustments that can prevent or significantly reduce many behavioral problems. Again, the best management involves anticipating potential problems and avoiding them through careful planning.

1. **Environmental:** Uncomfortable conditions (too noisy, crowded, hot, or cold); certain settings (hallways, cafeteria, playground); when there is a lack of structure (organization, predictability, clear schedule, visual supports)

2. **Physical:** When the child is not feeling well (ill, overly tired, hungry, thirsty); medication-related factors (for example, short-acting medication is wearing off, change of prescription or dosage, forgetting medicine)

3. **Related to a Specific Activity or Event:** Certain subjects; change of routine without warning; large group discussions; independent seat work; cooperative learning groups and sharing of materials; tasks that the student perceives as boring, lengthy, or frustrating

4. **Related to a Performance or Skill Demand:** Speaking in front of the class; staying seated; reading out loud or independently; writing a paragraph; writing in cursive; waiting patiently for a turn; hurrying to complete a task; any behavioral or performance expectation that is a struggle for the student

5. **Related to a Specific Time:** First period of the day, before or after lunch; transition times of day; late afternoons

6. **Related to a Specific Person:** In the presence or absence of administrators or a particular teacher or

staff member; social problem with a classmate, peer, or group of students; a problem with parents

7. **Other:** When given no choices or options, when embarrassed in front of peers; when having difficulty communicating; when given no assistance or access to help on difficult tasks; when teased by classmates

ANTECEDENT STRATEGIES

Be proactive in identifying and altering the antecedent conditions to support students with behavioral challenges. Many of the strategies mentioned in sections A and B address management tactics and environmental accommodations that are preventive strategies.

Watch for warning signs of the student with AD/HD becoming overly stimulated, upset, frustrated, agitated, or restless or beginning to lose control, and INTERVENE at once.

✓ **Provide a cue or prompt.** For example, stand near the student and place a gentle hand on his or her shoulder.

✓ **Use a prearranged private signal,** such as a nonverbal cue, as a reminder to settle down. Divert the student's attention, if possible.

✓ **Redirect to a different location or activity.** For example, send the student out of the room on an errand. Provide cueing or signaling.

✓ **Change the activity or expectations.**

✓ **Lend direct support.**

✓ **Employ calming techniques** and remind about rewards and consequences.

✓ **Provide a calming area** in the room or other location where a student can go to briefly as a preventive, not punitive, measure to regroup, regain control, and avoid behaviors escalating to a higher level.

✓ **Build in numerous opportunities for movement** in the class.

✓ **Allow students to doodle, draw, color, and touch or hold objects** in their hands while listening. Oftentimes, students are better able to remain seated, pay attention, and control behavior.

✓ **Make sure independent seatwork is developmentally appropriate** and within the student's capability of completing successfully without assistance. Provide access to peer assistance as needed.

✓ **If a student is taking medication, be very aware and observant of changes** in behavior and factors, such as time of day, when he or she is experiencing more difficulty or complains of hunger, fatigue, or other ill feelings. Communicate your observations or concerns to parents, the school nurse, or a physician.

✓ **Teach social skills and strategies** for anger control, relaxation, conflict resolution, dealing with frustration appropriately, thinking and planning before acting, and other self-management skills for life. Talk about and model these strategies in various situations and contexts, and practice them frequently.

COMMON ANTECEDENTS OF MISBEHAVIOR

A common antecedent for misbehavior among students with AD/HD is being given work that is tedious or boring, offers little student choice, and is perceived as irrelevant and nonmeaningful. Even students with severe AD/HD generally exhibit minimal behavioral problems during lessons or activities that are interesting, keep them actively involved, and incorporate a variety of engaging, multisensory strategies. Teachers who have the most success with ALL students are those who: 1) pace their lessons to maximize attention and interest, 2) tap into the needs of students to utilize and showcase their strengths; and 3) encourage both working and social interactions with peers. See Appendix C.7 for more information on behavioral assessment.

FACTORS CONTRIBUTING TO MISBEHAVIOR

When students misbehave, it helps to understand that there are motivators to behavior — functions, goals, or needs that are being met by demonstrating those undesirable behaviors. Determining which of the student's needs are being fulfilled as a result of the misbehavior allows the teacher to make changes that reduce inappropriate behavior.

5

The main functions or goals of student behavior are:

✓ **To get or obtain something** (attention, power, revenge, stimulation) and

✓ **To avoid or escape something** (failure, fear, embarrassment, effort, blame, punishment, pain).

BEHAVIOR IS SUSTAINED BY REINFORCEMENT

Teachers need to be aware of the immediate consequences of a student's misbehavior. For example, the student is sent out of the room, adult attention is given, or peer attention or laughter occurs. Be careful that the consequences do not inadvertently reinforce the student's inappropriate behaviors. Instead, meet the student's needs proactively, which may include the need for attention, stimulation, or escape from failure. Provide many opportunities for the student to receive positive attention from peers and adults for appropriate behavior and performance, access to more stimulating activities, and materials, assistance or accommodations to prevent misbehavior.

D. Behavioral Interventions and Accommodations

Children with AD/HD have significant difficulty regulating their behavior without immediate reinforcement. To manage the behavioral challenges of students with AD/HD, teachers must be knowledgeable and skillful in using behavior modification techniques effectively. The following strategies can be used classwide to positively reinforce and motivate appropriate behavior of all students. In addition, some individualized behavioral programs that use research-validated interventions are highlighted for teachers to use to support the behavioral success of one or two students with AD/HD in the classroom.

CLASS (GROUP) BEHAVIOR MANAGEMENT SYSTEMS

A few examples of classroom incentive systems include:

1. **Table or team points.** Points are given for specific behaviors, such as quick and smooth transitions, cooperation and teamwork, and on-task behavior. Some teachers reward tables or teams that earn a certain number of points. Other teachers reward the one or two tables that earn the most points at the end of the day or week.

2. **Marbles in a jar.** Teachers (usually in primary grade classrooms) catch students engaged in appropriate behaviors. They call attention to the positive behavior of the individual student, group of students, or the whole class. Then, the teacher reinforces the positive behavior by putting a marble or other object in a jar. When the jar is full, the class earns a reward.

3. **Chart moves.** A chart is created for the class or group. The class advances one space on the chart each time they meet a set goal. When the chart is full, the whole class earns the reward.

4. **Token economy system.** Students can earn tokens, points, tickets, or class money, redeemable for privileges or at a class store, auction, or raffle. A menu of rewards is developed with corresponding price values attached.

REWARDS OR REINFORCERS

Students should be involved in identifying a menu of rewards that would be motivating and fun to work towards earning. Below are some examples of social, activity, and material rewards or reinforcers that students can earn in group incentive or individual programs:

1. **Social Rewards**

✓ **Positive phone calls, notes, or e-mails** to the student or parents

✓ **Earning a class privilege** or social status (for example, teach a class or be a team captain or class messenger)

✓ **Choice of seating,** such as near friends or in the teacher's desk or chair, for the period, day, or week

2. **Activity Rewards and Privileges**

✓ **Lunchtime activities or privileges,** such as choice of seating, eating in special location, or special games

✓ **Extra time in class** to catch up on work with teacher or peer assistance

✓ **Breakfast or lunch** with a teacher, administrator, or other staff member

✓ **Ice cream, popcorn, or pizza party** for the class or group of students achieving a certain goal

✓ **Free or earned time** (individual or class) for activities of choice, such as games, listening to music, drawing, working on a special project, and accessing learning or interest centers

✓ **Computer or Internet time** alone or with a friend

✓ **Extra time or access** to the gym, library, computer lab, or music room

✓ **Responsibilities or privileges that are desirable**

   – Homework pass excusing them from one assignment

   – Tutoring or mentoring to a younger or less able student

   – Taking care of class pet

   – Assisting another teacher or staff member

   – Operating AV equipment

3. **Material reinforcers**

✓ School supplies, such as special pencils, pens, erasers, and folders

   – Stickers, stars, badges, and certificates

   – Class money, tickets, or points redeemable at auctions, lotteries, or class stores

✓ **Selecting items from the class store or treasure chest**

INDIVIDUALIZED BEHAVIORAL PROGRAMS

Home Notes and Daily Report Cards

Home notes and daily report cards (DRCs) are excellent tools for tracking and monitoring a student's social, academic, and behavioral progress at school. They are highly effective for communicating between home and school and forging a partnership to motivate improved performance of children and teens with AD/HD.

Home notes and DRCs involve selecting and clearly defining one or more target behaviors to be the focus for improvement. The expectations are clearly defined and a chart is made with time frames broken down by periods of the day, subjects areas, or short time intervals. The teacher is responsible for observing and rating the child's performance on the target behaviors on a daily basis, and sending the note or DRC home at the end of the day or week. Rewards are provided accordingly at home, school, or both, based on the child's performance on the DRC. Detailed guidelines for developing a school-home daily report card are available from: 1) *How to Reach and Teach Children with ADD/ADHD: Practical Techniques, Strategies, and Interventions, 2nd edition* and 2) The Center for Children and Families at the State University of New York at Buffalo *Summer Treatment Program* website, http://www.wings.buffalo.edu/adhd. See Appendices C.1, C.2, and C.3 for sample reports.

Contingency Contracting

This is a written agreement typically developed and signed by the teacher, student, and parent. The contract clearly specifies the behaviors that the student is required to perform and the rewards that the student earns when he or she succeeds in meeting that behavioral goal. Sometimes the contract includes the negative consequence that follows the student's failure to perform the required behaviors. All parties sign the contract and follow through on their end of the agreement. See Appendix C.4 for a sample contract.

Token Programs

Token programs use secondary reinforcers, or tokens, to provide students with immediate reinforcement for appropriate behavior, which is necessary for motivating children with AD/HD to sustain the effort for behavioral change. The student earns a designated number of tokens, which can be exchanged for a primary reinforcement, such as a privilege, treat, or desired activity. These programs typically utilize points, tokens, plastic chips, moves or stickers on a chart, class money, or something tangible as an immediate reward for demonstrating the target behavior. These points or tokens can then be redeemed for a more valued and motivating reward at school, home, or both.

5

Chart Moves

Individual student charts are commonly used. One or a few specific target behaviors are identified for the student to improve. A chart of some type is developed (for example, one with boxes for placing stickers, stars, stamps, or teacher initials). Each time the student demonstrates the target behavior, a box on the chart is filled or a move is made on the chart. When the chart is completed or the student achieves a certain number of points on the chart, a reward is earned. Students respond positively when their behaviors are plotted on colored graph paper and they can see their own progress.

Response Cost

Response cost programs work by giving the student a designated number of tokens, points, or coins that the child tries to keep. One or two undesirable or inappropriate behaviors are targeted for improvement (for example, reduction of times the behavior occurs), and the number of tokens provided depends on the frequency of the baseline behavior. During specific time periods, the teacher monitors the student for those target behaviors, removing a token for each occurrence (for example, out of seat or talking without permission).

If the student has at least one token or point remaining at the end of the time interval, the student earns a reward, such as a sticker on his or her chart.

Although emotionally fragile kids may get upset with fines or deductions, it is a technique known to be effective for children or teens with AD/HD. When using a token program that combines positive reinforcement and response cost, it is very important that the student has far more opportunities to earn points or tokens than to lose them.

During the early stages of implementation, it can be helpful to allow students to correct misbehavior to re-earn points. Also, response cost programs fail if they become punitive (student never earns points or loses all points for one infraction) or the targeted behaviors are unrealistic. It is best to start small and then increase expectations when students begin to show success. By expecting too much too soon, students can get discouraged and disengage from the process. See Appendix C.6 for a sample form for counting points.

E. Positive Behavioral Supports: A Continuum of Interventions

The University of Oregon has taken a leadership role in designing and conducting much of the national research on positive behavioral support practices in schools. The Effective Behavioral Support model was developed by George Sugai, Ph.D., Robert Horner, Ph.D., and other researchers at the University's Center on Positive Behavioral Intervention and Support (PBIS) and was funded by the U.S. Department of Education Office of Special Education Programs (OSEP). This model is very useful in describing the varied levels of students' behavioral needs and establishing a continuum of supports for each of the levels — from schoolwide prevention efforts to interventions that address the needs of students who are moderately and highly at-risk. Many schools have chosen to implement this program because results show:

✓ Higher student grades
✓ Higher test scores
✓ Increased school attendance

✓ Decreased referrals to special education for evaluation

✓ Decreased disciplinary referrals

✓ Decreased suspensions and expulsions

Illinois, in particular, has demonstrated impressive results after implementing this program in elementary schools statewide. Updates are published regularly through their *EBD/PBIS Network* newsletter. The state is now working on strategies for implementing PBIS in middle and high school. For more information, visit their website at http://www.ebdnetwork-il.org.

In addition, researchers at the University of Oregon's Institute on Violence and Destructive Behavior (IVBD), under the direction of Jeff Sprague, Ph.D., have developed a comprehensive schoolwide prevention model known as B.E.S.T. (Building Effective Schools Together), which incorporates three levels of intervention: universal interventions (primary prevention), selected interventions (secondary prevention), and intensive, targeted interventions (tertiary prevention).

These models show that approximately 80 percent of students DO NOT have serious problematic behavior. By far, most students are able to be managed and function well with good "universal interventions." Basically, this involves *a school climate and culture that is positive and proactive with an environment structured for student success.* For example, positive outcomes are documented when schoolwide discipline is consistent and all staff knows the procedures, are able to "speak the same language," and reinforce schoolwide behavioral expectations. In addition, it involves effective classroom management practices. If this occurs in a school, approximately 80 percent of the population should be functioning well with regard to behavior and social skills.

In any school population, approximately approximately 15 percent of students are at risk for problem behavior. Many of our students with AD/HD fall within this category. These are the students who need additional and specialized interventions and supports. For example, these students need extra cues, prompts, monitoring, supervision, reinforcement, motivation, direct assistance, behavior modification, and closer

home and school collaboration. These are also the students who would benefit the most from their school's Student Support Team (SST) or Instructional Support Team (IST) process. Teachers should target this population of students for conferencing with their support team to discuss strategies and develop an action plan of appropriate instructional, behavioral, and academic interventions.

A relatively small number of students, approximately five percent of the school population, have chronic or intense behavioral problems. These students tend to consume the majority of time and resources of school staff, often depleting the energy of school personnel in the process. The needs of these students are intense and require more intensive classroom interventions and teacher strategies. These students also typically need medical and/or mental health treatment and services and close communication with parents, outside agencies, physicians, and treatment providers. Students with AD/HD and coexisting oppositional defiant disorder, conduct disorder, mood disorders, and other mental health disorders are commonly among this group of the school population.

INTERVENTIONS AT EACH OF THE THREE LEVELS MAY INCLUDE:

Universal Interventions (Primary Prevention)

✓ Teacher training in proactive classroom management strategies and differentiating instruction to effectively teach diverse learners

✓ Schoolwide commitment to and leadership in building a positive, prosocial climate and culture throughout the school

✓ Social-Emotional Learning (SEL), social skills, or character education programs that are taught, reinforced, and implemented schoolwide by all school personnel in all school settings

✓ Clear schoolwide rules and behavioral expectations, safety plans, procedures, and processes for teaching and reinforcing the expectations and for establishing and maintaining a safe and orderly environment

5

✓ Identifying specific locations or settings in the school that are problematic and providing more structure and support to minimize problems in these settings

✓ Establishing a schoolwide team to plan, oversee climate and problem prevention efforts, and monitor effectiveness of plans

Selected Interventions (Secondary Prevention)

✓ Teacher training and coaching in instructional and behavioral strategies that reach and teach students with learning, attention, and behavioral challenges

✓ Student Support Team (SST) process for effectively strategizing and planning for at-risk students (classroom strategies and accommodations and appropriate schoolwide safety nets or interventions). In schools with large populations or high numbers of at-risk students, a multitiered SST or restructuring for more than one team per building is recommended to increase the number of students being addressed through this process.

✓ Increased supervision, monitoring, and reinforcement

✓ Individualized behavioral interventions (daily report cards, home notes, contracts, or reinforcement plans)

✓ Use of functional assessment

✓ Self-management training

✓ Conflict resolution training

Intensive Targeted Interventions (Tertiary Prevention)

✓ Training educators about mental health disorders in children and strategies to help (for example, how to de-escalate situations with angry students)

✓ Crisis intervention training and skill development

✓ School case management practices for students with chronic or intense behavioral difficulties

✓ Functional Behavioral Assessments (FBAs) and Behavioral Intervention Plans (BIPs)

✓ Community, agency, and family linkages

✓ Wraparound services

Further information on behavioral issues is also provided in Chapters 8 and 11. See Chapter 11 and Appendix C.7 for more information on FBA.

Additional Information

For more information about PBIS, IVBD, and other research-validated behavioral interventions for school environments, visit:

✓ The OSEP Center on Positive Behavioral Interventions and Supports
 – Jeff Sprague, Co-director of IVDB
 – pbis@oregon.uoregon.edu or http://www.pbis.org

✓ The School Mental Health Project (SMHP) — UCLA Dept. of Psychology
 – http://smhp.psych.ucla.edu

✓ Violence prevention programs for preschool, elementary school, middle school, high school, and adults
 – http://www.unf.edu/dept/fie/sdfs/program_ inventory/VP.html

A broader range of resources is contained in Appendix A.

Establishing a Strong Foundation During the Early Years

Developmental and academic challenges, instructional strategies, social challenges, medication considerations, and suggested resources for these age groups are discussed in the next three chapters. Top challenges identified by classroom teachers for various age groups also are addressed.

Chapter 6: Impact of AD/HD on Preschoolers
✓ Overview
✓ AD/HD in the preschool years
✓ Unique challenges of diagnosing AD/HD in preschoolers
✓ Impact of AD/HD on parents
✓ Multimodal interventions
  – Proactive classroom management
  – Behavioral interventions
  – Social skills interventions
  – Academic interventions
  – Parent training
  – Medical interventions
  – Promising practices

SIDEBAR
✓ Top challenging behaviors in preschool

Chapter 7: Impact of AD/HD on Elementary Students
✓ Overview
✓ Impact of AD/HD on school performance
✓ Impact of delayed developmental skills
✓ Impact of executive function deficits
✓ Impact on social skills
✓ Unique challenges for girls
✓ Specific instructional strategies for common learning problems
  – General classroom management suggestions
  – Planning and use of class time
  – Preferential seating
  – Daily progress notes
  – Adapting the curriculum
  – Compensatory equipment
✓ Positive reinforcement
✓ Behavioral strategies
✓ Accommodations plans: IEPs and Section 504 plans

SIDEBAR
✓ Top challenging behaviors in grades K–2
✓ Top challenging behaviors in grades 3–5

Chapter 8: Advanced Strategies for Challenging Behaviors

✓ Inattention
✓ Noncompliance with rules: talking out of turn or being out of a seat
✓ Poor work completion
✓ Poor anger control: angry outbursts

CHAPTER 6

Impact of AD/HD on Preschoolers*

Adele Sebben, M.A.
Joan K. Teach, Ph.D.
Chris A. Zeigler Dendy, M.S.
Anne Teeter Elllison, Ed.D.

P reschool children with attention-deficit/hyperactivity disorder are characterized by their delayed development, or "immaturity," and, for many, higher activity levels. A few students exhibit extreme hyperactivity. In addition, these children often are unable to change their behavior easily, even with teacher instruction. They don't respond as well to rewards and consequences as other children. Because "normal development" varies widely across cognitive, language, motor, social, and emotional skills, diagnosing AD/HD in preschool can be difficult and at times controversial, even though researchers tell us that the majority of these children clearly show symptoms during the toddler and preschool years.[1]

Fortunately for children with attention deficits, the play-oriented preschool environment, which encourages movement and is tolerant of their lack of self-control and social skill deficits, can be an ideal setting for them. Typically, only the most severe cases of AD/HD are detected in preschool. However, the greater the demands placed upon the child to conform, comply with requests, develop language skills, and play cooperatively, the more likely the child will exhibit problems that result in referral for an AD/HD assessment.

Diagnosis in preschool is made more difficult because classic behaviors, such as a high activity level, impulsivity, not listening, talking a lot, daydreaming, blurting out, lacking social skills (difficulty waiting their turn and sharing), and being aggressive (hitting, biting or fighting), are not that unusual in many preschoolers. The key difference the teacher may see is that these behaviors are more frequent and are not as easily corrected with teacher management and redirection. Children who have persistent and severe management problems due to problems in self-control, hyperactivity, and inattention are likely to receive a diagnosis of AD/HD during their preschool or early school years.

Because of their impulsivity, these youngsters have trouble learning from their experiences and do not respond well to discipline or other efforts to control their behavioral excesses (temper tantrums, noncompliance, disruptive play). Therefore they often repeat misbehavior, much to the chagrin of teachers and parents alike. Contrary to popular belief, most children with AD/HD do not exhibit the classic "Dennis the Menace" type behaviors. Unlike "Dennis," these children are not plotting how they can cause problems for the teacher. Instead, the preschooler with AD/HD acts

* In most cases, AD/HD is used interchangeably throughout this Manual to describe both AD/HD predominately hyperactive-impulsive and AD/HD predominately inattentive. IDEA regulations refer to these two conditions as ADHD and ADD, respectively.

and reacts without any thought as to the reason for his actions or to the outcome. This chapter will explore early childhood history of AD/HD, typical problem behaviors, school interventions, and strategies for helping parents. For more information on preschoolers with AD/HD, Phyllis Anne Teeter, Ed.D., provides a very helpful overview of developmental expectations for the average preschool child in contrast to the child with an attention deficit.[2]

Peter Jensen, M.D., and other researchers advise that the earlier a child is identified and the sooner an intervention strategy is begun, the better the treatment outcome.[3] So the good news is that preschoolers with AD/HD can be successful if the proper treatment plan and school environment are created. By definition, the primary goal for most preschools is to create a loving and flexible school environment in which the child is encouraged to learn by moving freely and discovering and exploring his interests. Through this positive supportive process, the child not only begins to learn appropriate self-control and social skills, but also acquires basic academic facts, such as colors, shapes, numbers, and letters of the alphabet. Ideally, preschool classrooms should provide lots of supervised playtime, frequent physical activity time, and cognitive and academic stimulation with lots of hands-on learning opportunities. This stimulation should help children with AD/HD learn routines of the classroom and become engaged learners. During these years, basic hygiene and self-care skills may also have to be retaught.

AD/HD in the Preschool Years

Although Chapter 2 provides information on the diagnosis of both AD/HD, hyperactive-impulsive type and AD/HD, inattentive type, this overview is designed for preschool teachers. As discussed in Chapter 1, children with attention deficits may exhibit a 30 percent developmental delay. Thus, it is imperative that educators keep in mind the profound impact this delay has on the child's behavior and learning. These students act like children who are much younger, and many are unable to achieve expected age-appropriate developmental milestones.

INFANTS

When childhood history is taken for a youngster who has AD/HD-hyperactive/impulsive, mothers often describe the high activity level of their young child, even in the womb. Mothers often report excessive crying, drowsiness, and colic. In addition, the baby may have had trouble being soothed, been restless, and shown signs of an easily disturbed sleep pattern. Parents also report poor sucking and little smiling. Oftentimes, the early mother/child relationship suffers because of the infant's excessive crying and inability to be soothed, which is extremely frustrating for mothers. In contrast, parents of infants and toddlers with AD/HD inattentive often report a normal, uneventful early childhood.

TODDLERS

During the toddler years, some parents of children with AD/HD report excessive clumsiness with frequent falls and accidents. This is understandable when teachers consider that roughly 50 percent of children with attention deficits have significant problems with coordination.[4] The child may have difficulty playing alone and establishing common routines. The toddler may also have trouble paying attention and lack social readiness.[5] Parenting becomes challenging because of the child's high activity levels, noncompliance, and difficulty toilet training. The mother/child relationship becomes even more difficult and strained during these years. Many mothers feel isolated and unsupported and ultimately become depressed and feel inadequate as parents.[6]

PRESCHOOLERS

Between the ages of three and five years, many children are very active, even during structured activities. They may have difficulty in free play and move quickly from one activity to another, often failing to complete the first activity they started. Their lack of self-control and impulsive behavior can result in accidental injury, especially since some of these children can be fearless and reckless during play.

In the preschool classroom, delays in language development are obvious. According to Dr. Teeter, the development of language coincides with the development of increased self-control; speech becomes a substitute for actions.[7] Thus, misbehavior can occur because these children lack the language skills required to talk about their concerns. Instead of talking, they act. In addition, early language disorders, such as stammering, stuttering and poor pragmatics, are noted in more than 45 percent of the children. Pragmatics refers to the complexities of verbal communication, for example, understanding and properly using not only the meanings of words, but also the underlying subtleties of gesture, tone, and innuendo. In addition, "self-talk" that directs the child's thoughts and actions is not well-established.[8] Inattention and impulsivity interfere with success on academic tasks, and constant discipline for behavioral problems, such as placement in time-out, can reduce the opportunity to learn from play and other school activities.

Preschoolers who are pressured to perform academically, comply with requests, and sit quietly in their seats before they are developmentally capable have unhappy, difficult preschool years. Researchers have found that students with AD/HD exhibit more aggressive behaviors in programs where academics are heavily emphasized than in other preschool settings.[9]

Those children who are aggressive, don't take turns, and are unable to play cooperatively are often rejected by classmates. This rejection is often spawned by their development of basic social skills. The preschooler with AD/HD can be easily frustrated and is often described as strong-willed and intrusive. For some, the ability to settle down is difficult; for others, the distractions around them create too much stimulation; and for others, calming down and relaxing after being active is almost impossible. Seldom do they fall asleep for a daytime nap. At home, parents may report that the child has trouble falling asleep and waking up, and fights to avoid naptime and bedtime. Their driven, unrelenting motor activity is difficult to turn off.

In contrast, parents of children with AD/HD inattentive may not recognize the early signs that are associated with later academic problems. For many inattentive children, academic problems are not appar-

ent until first grade and, for some, even as late as middle or high school. These children may be daydreamers instead of the stereotypical "Dennis the Menace." The first hint of academic difficulty may not appear until they are asked to write stories, book reports, and class assignments. The student may also have problems with slow processing speed and fine motor coordination as evidenced by slow and laborious handwriting. Socially, these inattentive-type children can be more successful interacting with classmates because they are not aggressive and are more attuned to social rules and cues.

PREDICTORS OF SERIOUS BEHAVIOR PROBLEMS
A few children with attention deficits can have excessive rage reactions. Specific behaviors of concern include explosive temper tantrums, physical aggression, fighting, intentional destruction of property, and, in rare cases, cruelty to animals and fire setting. Early identification and intervention with children who exhibit these aggressive antisocial behaviors is critical. According to Hill Walker, Ph.D.,[10] children who have serious problems in preschool, left untreated, frequently have serious problems later in school and throughout their lifetime.

Dr. Walker's research has clearly shown that early intervention can prevent serious problems in later school years.[11] Teachers should trust their experience and instincts. Walker explains that 80 percent of boys who had been arrested could be predicted by 1) early teacher ratings of social skills, (2) total negative playground behavior, and 3) disciplinary contacts with the principal's office. Serious problems can lead to the student's suspension from school or expulsion from a private day care center. Schools should consider having at least one faculty member trained on Dr. Walker's *First Step to Success* program, a highly effective and nationally recognized violence prevention program.

Because these children are so difficult to raise, parents can struggle. They need help mastering strategies to address problem behaviors at home. Without help, many parents of these children use ineffective, inconsistent parenting strategies. So the message is clear; intervene early, offering help to both the child and parents.

6

Unique Challenges of Diagnosing AD/HD in Preschoolers

Diagnosis of AD/HD in preschoolers requires special considerations. Clare Jones, Ph.D., reminds us that AD/HD "affects children from the first months of their lives, through their school years and into adulthood."[12] With increasing research and knowledge about the symptoms of and the problems caused by AD/HD, physicians and mental health professionals are identifying and treating children at earlier ages. These professionals agree that many of the symptoms are evident at birth and will become more problematic as the child matures. In fact, the majority of children with AD/HD show symptoms during the toddler and preschool years. The official diagnostic criteria for AD/HD are available in Chapter 2.[13]

According to Dr. Jones, "physicians and mental health professionals are generally the first persons consulted when parents are concerned about the child's developmental issues. Most physicians will refer the parents for further testing and evaluation before making a diagnosis. Typical referral sources include educational psychologists, early childhood specialists, developmental pediatricians, and nurse practitioners. The professionals who are considering a diagnosis of AD/HD will understand normal age-appropriate development and should follow the guidelines of the Diagnostic and Statistical Manual (DSM-IV)."

Impact of AD/HD on Parents

Research shows that parent-child relationships for children with AD/HD are strained. Child noncompliance is often met with negative parent discipline and coercive family interactions. When parents learn that their child has AD/HD, they often begin the painful process of grieving for the loss of a perfect child. They may become angry, with each partner blaming the other for having "faulty" genes. Parents who believe it's their fault may have even greater feelings of helplessness. Denial may also be observed as family members look for other reasons for the child's behavior such as "poor parenting." Their anger may cause them to go from doctor to doctor in hopes of finding a different diagnosis, one they can more easily accept. Some parents may misdirect their anger at school personnel who "simply don't understand their child." Teachers can deal more effectively with this misdirected anger if they recognize that the anger is not personal. Parents are frustrated and frightened and don't know where to turn for help. As they move through the grieving process and into acceptance, parents may be more receptive and actually ask for assistance from the school.

Multimodal Interventions

AD/HD impacts all areas of development for the preschool child, including language, cognitive, social, emotional, and physical skills. As explained in Chapter 1, interventions are most effective when they are combined into a multimodal approach aimed at addressing all these key issues. Single interventions have only a limited effect in changing behavior. The greatest success comes when all parties work as a coordinated team on the child's behalf. The following sections will address key components of multimodal intervention: social skill development, behavioral interventions, academic strategies, parent training, and medical interventions.

GUIDING PRINCIPLES

The overriding principle for all interventions must be to provide a positive, supportive preschool learning environment that offers structure, consistency and adequate supervision. Children with AD/HD must have structure imposed on them. Unlike their peers, these children are not able to structure their own world and must have order established for them. The need for structure can be seen as the basis of their difficulty with executive function, which is so prevalent in older children with attention deficits.[14,15] Ultimately, this inability to transition well from one activity to another may be an early indication of the difficulty these children will have later in life as they try to manage time and information.

CONSISTENCY AND SUPERVISION

Consistency helps organize the environment of the preschool child with AD/HD and provides a dependable, reliable world. Closer supervision is also needed because of the impulsive and sometime dangerous risks that these children may take. Although all children must be guided and watched with care, the recklessness of some children with AD/HD requires special diligence. This recklessness usually results from their difficulty inhibiting dangerous behaviors, such as touching a hot stove or running into the street without looking.

PROACTIVE CLASSROOM MANAGEMENT

A proactive classroom management style, such as that described in Chapter 5, is basic to any successful preschool class. For example, teachers who provide structure and routine, clear rules, positive attention, signals and visual prompts, engaging and high-interest learning activities, brief activity time frames, and activities allowing movement are more likely to be successful with these students.

One classroom management strategy that teachers frequently use is the Rules/Praise/Ignore technique:[16]

1. Clarify rules in advance.
   a. Have only a few rules.
   b. Make them clear and to the point.
   c. Consider using pictures or illustrations for the rules.
   d. State the desired behavior by using positive phrasing rather than negative statements, for example, "keep your hands to yourself" rather than "don't hit."
2. Give praise; it is a powerful tool for change.
   a. Follow the recommended 3:1 ratio of positive statements to negative ones.
   b. Even in negative situations, maintain a calm, unemotional, and factual tone of voice.
3. Ignore or disengage from minor misbehavior.
   a. Ignore minor unintentional AD/HD behaviors, such as forgetfulness, disorganization, and fidgeting, when possible.

   b. Pick and choose your battles; target more serious behaviors for intervening.

Behavioral Interventions

Behavioral interventions offer the preschool teacher an avenue for teaching academic and social skills. However, utilization of behavioral strategies is often more challenging for children with AD/HD. These children don't learn as easily from punishment and rewards, and rewards must be much stronger, given more frequently, and changed more often. These students also don't learn as easily through modeling. Children with AD/HD can have difficulty seeing their own behavior as problematic and may even blame others for their own mistakes or misbehaviors.

Behavioral strategies can be effective if a few basic principles are followed. Children with attention problems need more frequent, immediate, consistent and tangible positive feedback.[17] Ideally, teachers should make three positive comments for every negative statement. Additionally, intervention must occur at the "point of performance," at the time the behavior is occurring.[18] Furthermore, the behavior should be dealt with in the classroom rather than by removing them to the office and giving them long lectures regarding their misbehavior.

Teachers should refer to Chapter 5 for more basics about behavioral strategies and Chapter 10 for more on the importance of intervening at the "point of performance." Additional resources are listed in Appendix A.

POSITIVE REINFORCEMENT

Understanding the proper use of positive and negative reinforcement is critically important. For example, behavior can be stopped by negative consequences, such as removal from the play group, but these consequences do not teach new or desired prosocial behaviors. In a situation where one child is hitting another, providing a negative consequence, such as a short time-out, may stop the behavior, but will not teach new behavior, such as sharing. New behaviors can only be developed by teaching the desired skill and providing positive consequences, such as rewarding a child with a smile or positive statement, such as "Good job!"

RESPONSE COST

A response cost program uses positive feedback paired with mild negative consequences. This strategy has been shown to be especially effective when children are oppositional.[19] (Additional information is available on positive and negative reinforcement and response cost programs in Chapter 5.)

Preschool reinforcers are often unique to each student and should be tailored to the needs of the child. Some common reinforcers for preschoolers are:[20]

✓ Giving small items or privileges, such as colored pencils or extra minutes in free play
✓ Choosing a game to play
✓ Choosing a book to be read aloud
✓ Having lunch or snack with a favorite adult
✓ Passing out snacks
✓ Being line leader
✓ Doing a special project
✓ Giving stickers or a hand stamp
✓ Taking home a favorite book or toy

(Other examples of reinforcers as well as a description of several behavior management systems for the whole class are available in Chapter 5.)

CHALLENGING BEHAVIOR

One effective strategy for addressing misbehavior is to redirect behavior to appropriate activities. For example, take a child who is misbehaving to the side of the room and quietly read to him for a few minutes until he calms down. Then make brief statements such as "We don't hit our friends. We might hurt them." Shortly thereafter, you can return the child to the group. You can also teach or model the appropriate behavior for sharing.

1, 2, 3 MAGIC

Another tried and true method for dealing with problem behaviors is *1, 2, 3 Magic,*[21] by Tom Phelan, Ph.D.

In this program, the teacher tells the child the appropriate behavior, then does not speak except to count slowly to three until the child complies. If the teacher reaches three without the child correcting his behavior, he may be placed briefly in time-out. Dr. Phelan suggests time-outs that last approximately one minute for each year of age (for example, a 6-year-old would sit for six minutes).

"ABC" STRATEGIES

Basic to any behavioral intervention for challenging behavior is the "ABC" mantra.

✓ "A" refers to the antecedent of any behavior. To begin a behavioral intervention, look first to what happens before the unwanted behavior begins.
✓ "B" is the behavior itself. The problem must be identified in observable behavioral terms (for example, "does not follow teacher directions" as opposed to "has a bad attitude").
✓ "C" is the consequence of the behavior. Respond in a manner that encourages the desired behavior.

According to the "ABC" mantra, if a child is increasingly active and has a meltdown at 11:00 each morning, a teacher should ask:

✓ What was his behavior earlier? Is he hungry or tired?
✓ Has his medicine worn off?
✓ What is the behavior? Is he fighting or wanting his blanket?
✓ What is the consequence of his behavior? Is he put down for a nap? Is he given lunch? Does he get more attention?

By critically examining the ABC's of a child's behavior, a plan can be developed to prevent the behavior from reoccurring. (Chapter 5 provides more information on developing a plan to prevent misbehavior. Additional information is also provided in Chapter 10 regarding a more advanced form of this strategy known as Functional Behavioral Assessment [FBA] and Behavior Intervention Plans [BIP].) See Appendix C.7 for an FBA checklist.

The Top Five Challenging Behaviors in Preschool

Joan K. Teach, Ph.D.

Since children with AD/HD lack self-control, they frequently have difficulty complying with classroom rules and expectations. Delayed social skills make these children appear somewhat immature and they may behave more like younger children. As the child nears kindergarten age, teachers should add more structure to the classroom routine in preparation for this transition. However, keep in mind that ensuring that these young children have positive learning experiences at school is the primary goal.

Below are the top five challenging behaviors that most teachers encounter in preschool children with AD/HD, as well as classroom interventions to help these children act more appropriately. (Chapter 5 offers additional suggestions for preventing or reducing behavioral problems by creating a proactive classroom and making changes to the environment.)

1. Delayed social skills:

Simple interventions, such as redirecting a student's interests to another activity, are best. Also, talk calmly and use only a few brief words to teach the desired social skills.

a. Waiting for a turn and sharing

- ✓ Redirect the child's interests. Rather than fighting over a doll, ask the second child to help by ironing clothes for the doll. Then swap activities; the first child irons while the second plays with the doll.
- ✓ Praise other children who are waiting their turn or sharing toys. "Thanks for sharing, Monica." "Wow! Jimmy is waiting his turn so patiently."
- ✓ Make a brief one-sentence statement about taking turns or sharing. "We take turns (share) with our friends at school."
- ✓ Praise the student when he does wait his turn or shares.
- ✓ Limit the number of situations in which students must wait for their turn or share.
  - Make numerous play centers available.
  - Provide duplicates of toys so the second child can play with the same toy.

b. Following directions

- ✓ Toss a fuzzy ball to a student who then repeats the directions or answers a question.
- ✓ Have everyone repeat the directions together.
- ✓ Play games that help with following directions such as stopping and starting.
  - *Simon Says*
  - *Red Light*
  - *Statue* or *Freeze*

c. Joining a group

- ✓ Practice skills that help students join in a group, for example, introducing oneself, greeting others, maintaining eye contact, and following the rules of the activity.
- ✓ Create a routine. When you enter the learning center, ask the student to introduce himself or herself.
  - Give special points or stars for each time a student complies with the greeting.
  - Encourage the student to greet other students in the corner by name.
- ✓ Use your telephone or housekeeping corner to practice common social skills.

CONTINUED NEXT PAGE

6

The Top Five Challenging Behaviors in Preschool, Cont.

d. Respecting boundaries: Make boundaries and limits visual. Help the student understand body space and orientation through these activities.

✓ Use tape lines. Mark three lines in rows on the floor in the group instructional area. Place circles or numbers evenly spaced along the line. Each child sits on an assigned circle or number.
✓ Use carpet squares. Students can sit on assigned carpet squares.
  • If carpet squares are not available for all students, the teacher can assign this student a carpet square or round pillow to define his or her space.
✓ Use tape to create boundaries.
  • Place tape on the floor to mark the space around the pencil sharpener.
    – To sharpen a pencil, you must be within that space. To wait, you must be outside the space.
    – When working at a table building a tower, ask the student to stay on his designated portion of the table.
✓ Give stretch breaks.
✓ Suggest an alternative behavior. Students can be taught to cross their arms when walking across the room or standing in line. This strategy can limit pushing, shoving, and taunting.

2. Adjusting to transitions: Changes in routine are very difficult for these children so build in additional time or activities to ease the transition.

a. Sing a song. Sing a song to "please join me" when children are asked to line up to leave the room. Children will gradually drift to the line. For any stragglers, insert their name into the song. "John, won't you please join me."

b. Call out students' names in the order they are to line up.

c. Make an announcement or give a signal before a change in activity or to get their attention.

✓ "You have five minutes before it is time to stop and clean up."
✓ Ring a bell three to five minutes before it is time to change activities, for example, to leave for lunch.
✓ Ask the student to clean up.
  • "First one to put everything away and sit with your head down" or "put your hands on your head."
✓ Start and stop music to signal the end of an activity.
✓ Clap your hands three times to signal that it is time to be quiet and listen for directions.

3. Aggressive behavior: Biting or hitting

a. Show the bite mark, and calmly explain, "You've hurt your friend and we don't ever hurt our friends."

b. If the biting continues, take the student aside, sit with them in a time-out area, and read a story. After a brief time, allow the child to return to the group with a reminder that we don't bite and hurt our friends.

4. High activity levels

a. Vary activities and include movement. Make movement part of the daily routine by offering several different activities for brief periods throughout the day:

✓ Take a movement break.
✓ Dance to music.
✓ Sing songs with motions.
✓ Become an animal, an airplane, or a clock that ticks and strikes three.

CONTINUED NEXT PAGE

RECORDING BEHAVIOR

If a child is really struggling, collecting more detailed information about the behavior on a simple chart should be helpful. A simple record can show the times of day or events that may be triggering problems. Typically, the teacher collects the following information:

1. Child's name
2. Date
3. Behavior of concern, such as hitting
4. Rating of the child's unwanted behavior on a scale of one to five for various 30-minute segments throughout the course of one day

---

The Top Five Challenging Behaviors in Preschool, Cont.

   c. Allow students to choose from a variety of activities. Some students are afraid of failing so ensuring successful participation in activities is very important. Some children are reluctant to engage in activities until they are sure what the activity is about. Allow the child to watch and participate when he is ready.

   d. Provide fidget toys. Allow the children to use fidget toys when they need to pay attention and listen, especially during "story time." This not only helps them pay attention and improves their patience with sitting still, but also keeps their hands busy and helps improve coordination.

5. Disrupting class: blurting out, making noises, and talking excessively. Ideally, preschool programs will involve frequent movement and activity, leaving little time to sit quietly or listen to one person talk at a time.

   a. Use simple positive strategies, such as redirection, ignoring comments, and praising those who are listening quietly.

   ✓ Use gestures, such as a finger across your lips and hand cupped behind your ear.

   ✓ Suggest an alternative behavior. Begin by saying, "Use your church (synagogue) voice. Whisper softly so no one can hear you. Remember, no talking out."

   b. Consider instituting a classwide behavior management program, such as *Change Your Clip* or *Red Light*. These two programs involve a three or four level color-coded behavior rating system. Green, yellow, orange, and red circles are mounted on magnets and placed on the board. Clothes pins with each student's name are clipped around the circle. Each student starts the day on the green circle.

   Put a positive spin on this strategy by saying that everyone is doing a good job listening, for example. If everyone's clip is still on the green circle, periodically spotlight three to five students, "Emily, Hunter, Nathan and Ashley are all working really hard, so their clips stay on the green circle."

   When a student acts inappropriately, the teacher can say, "Change your clip." The student then moves his clothes pin to the next circle. Most students comply with the teacher's requests more readily after the first clip move to yellow. The color rating scale and label for each circle is:

   i. Green = Great job

     • If everyone is on green at the end of the day, the teacher can give a treat like a few Skittles or M&Ms.

   ii. Yellow = Warning

   iii. Orange = Quiet or silent lunch

   iv. Red = Referral to the office or a telephone call to parents

6

5. Analysis of what else might have been going on when the behavior occurred, for example, the mis-behavior occurred just before lunch or naptime

To ease the use of the chart, remember to leave it in an easily accessible spot on top of the desk. This documentation can then be shared with parents, care-givers, medical providers, and counselors who can ben-efit from the information. Because these charts count the number of events and describe their severity, they help provide a more objective measurement of behav-ior to discuss with parents than generalizations, such as "your child is not getting along with other children at school." Another highly effective strategy is to invite parents to observe their child's behavior. The direct comparison to other children who are acting age-appropriately can be an eye-opener for the parents.

HOME-SCHOOL NOTES

Notes sent home from school each day can be very effective in improving the child's behavior, especially those who are 5-years-old or approaching kindergarten age.[22] Parents can provide rewards or consequences based upon their behavior. A sample school-home note (Daily Report Card) and additional tips are avail-able at The State University of New York, University at Buffalo, Center for Children and Families website, http://wings.buffalo.edu/psychology/adhd.

Social Skill Interventions

Teachers often report that one of the major challenges facing this group of children is the delayed develop-ment of their social skills. After all, 5-year-olds who act more like 3-year-olds present a major challenge to preschool teachers. Unfortunately, if these children have an undeveloped sense of the rules of social inter-actions, their negative impact on classmates creates dis-trust, dislike and distancing, which makes friendships difficult to develop. (Chapter 11 offers a broader dis-cussion of the social challenges present in all children with attention deficits.)

Key social skills. Important social skills that are emphasized in preschool include:[23]

✓ Taking turns, sharing, waiting, and following directions
✓ Joining a group using skills such as introducing yourself, greeting others, making eye contact, and going with the flow of an activity
✓ Understanding body space and orientation
✓ Communicating and conversing through asking and answering questions, staying on the topic, and using telephone etiquette
✓ Developing positive self-esteem by giving and receiving compliments, using positive self-talk, and learning to laugh at oneself

A few social skills programs, such as *Skillstreaming,*© are recommended. See the sidebar, *Top Five Challenging Behaviors,* for specific strategies for addressing social skill problems, such as sharing and taking turns.

Issues related to self-control are among the most challenging social skills for preschoolers. After all, most of the diagnostic criteria for AD/HD are linked to lack of self-control. Teachers who attempt to teach these skills must intervene at the "point of perform-ance." In other words, teaching a skill is best done in the actual setting when and where the skill is required. (Additional strategies for teaching skills are discussed in Chapter 11.) Ultimately, medication is one of the most effective interventions for improving overall behavior, including social skills, compliance with teacher requests, and reducing aggressive behavior or angry outbursts.[24]

If social skill problems reach the point where the child is rejected by his classmates and is acting impul-sively in ways that are dangerous, teachers may suggest that parents talk with their physician or counselor about an evaluation and intervention. For teaching mastery of social skills, lots of patience, practice, and praise is required.

Academic Interventions

From birth to two years, parents are the most appro-priate people to introduce learning activities to the child. Daily schedules for feeding and sleeping should be consistent and adapted to the child's needs. Avoiding loud and dynamic activity in the classroom may help the child. Physical distractions within the child's environment should be avoided if the child is sensitive to sensory overstimulation. Keeping in mind that the child's development may be delayed, the preschool teacher may consider the missed earlier developmental milestones and reteach some of these basic skills as needed.

During the preschool years of three to five, teachers can provide experiences for children with attentional difficulties that enhance and support their individual development. The classroom should be orderly, with a system for organizing materials, and learning activities should be brief and varied. Eye contact should be stressed and visual cues should be given whenever possible to increase the child's awareness of looking at and listening to the teacher. Skills such as following directions and being a contributing member of a class can be approached through simple childhood games. Learning sequential events, identifying simple shapes, colors, numbers and letters, learning to count, and singing songs from memory all provide a basis for later academic learning. When the child does not absorb these things readily, extra care must be given to ensure that he is attending, hearing, and learning what is presented in the classroom.

MOTOR SKILL DEVELOPMENT
Development of motor skills is delayed for roughly half of preschoolers with AD/HD.[25] Many also have poor fine motor coordination, making cutting and writing more difficult. Playing games that involve use of large muscles, such as soccer, running games like *Red Light,* and swimming can help overall coordination. Activities like the following increase practice of fine motor skills:[26]

✓ Use of finger paint, clay, and ball play with many sizes of balls and writing on chalk or dry erase boards.

✓ Trace and color within box lids to feel the shape and limits.

✓ Use a pencil or stick to draw in plasticine clay trays.

✓ Put a piece of coarse sandpaper on a clipboard, place paper on top, and write or draw with crayons or a pencil. The sandpaper creates a bubble effect.

✓ Buy special scissors that have two sets of finger holes so an adult can guide the cutting motion.

✓ Allow students to tear paper into pieces rather than cutting it.

(Several additional basic instructional strategies are discussed in more detail in Chapter 4.)

Parent Training
Parents and teachers must work together as partners to ensure a successful school experience for the preschool child with AD/HD. Teachers can be of greater assistance if they understand the most challenging parenting issues. CHADD has developed a model training program for educating parents known as *Parent to Parent.*[27] The course is designed to help parents understand their children better and learn effective strategies for home and school. Information regarding this training is available from the national CHADD office at 800-233-4050 or http://www.chadd.org. Local CHADD chapters may have certified instructors who can teach this course. Local school systems can send a teacher to special CHADD training to become a certified parent-teacher for this course. (A summary of the *Parent to Parent* program is provided in Chapter 13.)

Parent training in behavioral strategies with additional instruction for improving communication skills and consistency in parenting is very helpful. The *Triple P-Positive Parenting Program* has produced positive outcomes for children and parents.[28] Parents attending sessions on child management strategies and those receiving enhanced interventions (partner support and coping skills as described below) reported clinically significant improvement on child behaviors, marital relations, feelings of parent competency, relationship conflicts, and relationship adjustment.

Several components of the *Triple P-Positive Parenting Program* that appear to be effective use the following strategies:

1. STANDARD BEHAVIORAL FAMILY INTERVENTION (SBFI)

✓ Promotes child competence through quality parent-child time, talking, giving praise, giving attention, engaging activities, and behavior charts

✓ Manages misbehavior through rule setting, directed discussions, planned ignoring, clear and direct instructions, use of logical consequences, quiet time, and time-out

2. ENHANCED BEHAVIORAL FAMILY INTERVENTION (EBFI)

✓ Components of SBFI

✓ Positive partner support through improved communication skills, increased parenting consistency,

and increased coping skills to address parental depression, anxiety, anger, and stress

Both SBFI and EBFI showed positive short-term improvement in child behaviors, including an increase in compliance and a decrease in disruptive behaviors and oppositional defiance. While there was no change in inattention or conduct problems, mothers reported that they used fewer inappropriate parenting practices and increased their parenting skills. Both interventions increased parenting satisfaction, while EBFI was slightly better in decreasing parental conflicts over parenting practices. Long-term outcomes were equally promising. Positive gains were sustained for both interventions after one year.

Medical Interventions

While medication treatment of children with AD/HD under six years of age is not generally recommended, doctors may consider prescribing medication in cases where the AD/HD is more complex and the child is struggling at home and school, perhaps engaging in dangerous impulsive behaviors.[29] Typically children who receive an early diagnosis have more complex and challenging cases of AD/HD and roughly two-thirds also have a coexisting problem, such as a tic disorder, depression, or bipolar disorder.[30] If medication is prescribed, teachers are often the most accurate and helpful reporters of medication effectiveness. Teachers may be asked to complete a rating scale for doctors, indicating any changes they have observed in the student's behavior and performance.

Current research supports the prescription of medication in this situation and indicates that medication before the age of six years can make a positive difference for children with an early diagnosis of AD/HD.[27] Respected studies have found that children receiving medication before six years of age consistently show increased recall, attention, and self-control.[31] In 2002, researchers reviewed nine controlled studies of stimulant treatment and two controlled trials of stimulant side effects. For eight of the nine studies involving 206 preschoolers, results indicate treatment benefits for 86 percent of participants. (More detailed information on the impact of medication on schoolwork is available in Chapter 1 and for older students in Chapter 8.)

These studies also note that preschool children with AD/HD may experience slightly more and different types of stimulant-induced side effects, compared with older children. However, these side effects, which include social withdrawal, increased crying, and irritability, are reported as mild.[32] Ultimately, parents must discuss with their medical doctors the pros and cons of giving medication to their preschool child.

Currently, the National Institute for Mental Health (NIMH) is sponsoring the Preschool AD/HD Treatment Study (PATS), the largest multisite study investigating AD/HD and medication in preschool children. Children in this study receive extensive behavioral interventions, and those who do not show significant improvement are considered for medication trials. Initial reports suggest that medication can be effective and safe in preschool children with moderate to severe AD/HD.[33] Larry Greenhill, M.D., one of the senior scientists leading the investigation, suggests that parents undergo intensive parent training prior to using medication. While training helped only a minority of cases, it may help parents deal with behavior problems in their child. Dr. Greenhill also recommends that if one or both parents has AD/HD, they should seek treatment first or the child's treatment is unlikely to be successful.

Promising Practices

While research on interventions for preschool children is sparse, there are several new studies under way in addition to the aforementioned NIMH treatment study. George DuPaul, Ph.D., and colleagues developed a prevention program aimed at reducing the problems that young children with AD/HD experience in preschool and at home.[34] Based on his experience, Dr. DuPaul suggests that assessments identifying the function behind the problem is a powerful tool for this age group. Determining the "trigger" of the behaviors, for

example, the need to move, impulsivity, or attention seeking, and designing a behavioral intervention to reduce the behaviors (for example, allowing the child to stand, instead of sit, during circle time) appear to reduce serious behavioral problems.

The Center for Evidenced-Based Practice: Young Children with Challenging Behaviors is a multisite study focusing on teaching parents and teachers effective management techniques for preschool children at risk for AD/HD. These techniques include using firm, calm discipline practices, rewarding good behaviors, setting limits, handling anger, and understanding the child's needs. Dr. DuPaul suggests that these techniques can help preschool children adjust well to school and make friends, and may give them a chance to do well in elementary school without medication.[35] Although medication may be necessary at later stages, early identification and effective behavioral techniques can give preschool children at risk for AD/HD an excellent start to schooling. This program can provide an acceptable intervention alternative for parents who do not want to start giving their child medication at such an early age.

Dr. Teeter identifies several interesting research findings in her book, *Interventions for ADHD: Treatment in Developmental Context,*[36] and also suggests the following promising practices for teachers of preschool children:[34]

1. Clearly separate play and work areas in the classroom.
2. Use a step-by-step approach to organizing learning activities. For instance, place crayons out with paper and then remove them when coloring is done and story time starts.
3. Schedule activities in shorter time blocks, for example, two short circle sessions rather than one long one.
4. Use teaching strategies that are novel and stimulating.
5. Give clear directions. Single-step commands directed to the individual child may be needed.

CHAPTER 7

Impact of AD/HD on Elementary Students*

Clare B. Jones, Ph.D.
Joan K. Teach, Ph.D.

Adapted from *Practical Suggestions for AD/HD* and *Sourcebook for Children with Attention Deficit Disorder*

Overview

Elementary school, often referred to as the "building block of future learning," is where the child learns to behave and understand in a manner consistent with the social, cultural, and organizational requirements of a society. This six-year span from kindergarten to fifth grade is when children lay a critical educational foundation. Students begin learning the basic rules and regulations of attending school, the basis of social interaction, and the cognitive tools that enable them to pursue higher level education. This is a challenging learning process for most children. When a child brings the added complexity of AD/HD[1] to this developmental learning process, one can begin to understand the importance of offering interventions and strategies to support these students.

Impact of AD/HD on School Performance

During the developmental stages of elementary school, the problems most likely to be observed by teachers and parents are "continued difficulties with hyperactive–impulsive behavior joined by difficulties with goal-directed persistence (sustained attention)," according to Russell Barkley, Ph.D.[2] The teacher may observe the following characteristics:

✓ Difficulty with work completion and productivity
✓ Distraction
✓ Forgetfulness related to daily tasks
✓ Lack of planning
✓ Poor organization of work activities
✓ Trouble meeting deadlines associated with school assignments

Students with AD/HD face several significant challenges that interfere with their ability to succeed in school. Difficulties with executive functions, sometimes called executive skills, such as working memory, internalized speech, and verbal fluency, affect the acquisition of math, spelling, reading comprehension, and written language skills. Students may also have deficits in organizing events and objects.[3]

Poor fine motor coordination also manifests in many of these students. Their handwriting is often messy and difficult to read, and they can have difficulty mastering cursive writing, preferring to print even throughout their high school years.

Academic underachievement is frequently a hallmark of AD/HD. These students are at risk for serious problems during their school years, such as 1) undiagnosed coexisting learning disabilities, 2) deficits in executive skills, 3) failing a grade,

---

* In most cases, AD/HD is used interchangeably throughout this Manual to describe both AD/HD predominately hyperactive-impulsive and AD/HD predominately inattentive. IDEA regulations refer to these two conditions as ADHD and ADD, respectively.

The Top 11 Challenging Behaviors in Elementary School

Joan K. Teach, Ph.D.
Chris A. Zeigler Dendy, M.S.

Since many children with AD/HD lack self-control, they frequently have difficulty complying with classroom rules and expectations. In addition, the AD/HD diagnostic criteria of inattention, disorganization, incompletion of work, not listening, losing things, forgetfulness, excessive talking, and blurting out answers makes academic success extremely difficult, especially when the AD/HD is untreated.

Below are the top 11 challenging behaviors that most classroom teachers encounter in elementary school age children with AD/HD, as well as several classroom interventions to help these children succeed in school. The behaviors are divided into two lists: one for kindergarten through second grade and one for third through fifth grades.

Chapter 5 contains numerous suggestions for preventing or reducing behavioral problems by creating a proactive classroom or making changes to the environment. Chapters 4 and 9 offer additional high-interest instructional strategies that can be helpful to maintain a student's attention and assist with organizational and homework issues. Chapter 8 contains more advanced behavioral strategies for more challenging behaviors.

Kindergarten through Second Grade

Teachers of students in kindergarten through second grade are also encouraged to review the "Top Five Challenging Behaviors for Preschool Students" in Chapter 6 for additional ideas.

1. **Inattention; out of seat or designated area; not completing work.**

   ✓ **Use visual cues.** Use tape lines or carpet squares to visually show the child his space.
   ✓ **Set a kitchen timer.** Start out with small increments. Work 10 minutes, then get water. Work 15 minutes, then sharpen a pencil. Work 20 minutes, then spend time drawing.
      • When more than one task is assigned, set the timer for a designated time. When the timer goes off, the child should move on to the next task.
   ✓ **Draw a picture of appropriate behavior.** When a kindergarten child was unable to stay in her seat in the cafeteria, talking and punishing didn't work so one teacher drew a picture of the child sitting the proper way at a table in the cafeteria. After that, the student remained in her seat during lunch.
   ✓ **Assign two workstations.** Designate a work area in addition to the student's desk where he or she can move to after sitting for a while. Perhaps have the student change after completion of each subject.
   ✓ **Allow the student to sit on his or her knees or stand.** One student was always moving and sometimes sat on her knees or stood leaning on her desk. The student was completing her work regularly and participating in class discussions so the teacher seated her at the back of the room to avoid distracting others and allowed her to sit or stand as needed.

2. **Difficulty following directions and staying on task.**

   When students appear noncompliant, the underlying problem may be that they cannot pay attention, have problems with listening comprehension, have limited working memory capacity, or simply do not understand the directions.

   ✓ **Designate someone** — a "shepherd" or friend — to check that the directions are followed, assignments are written down, and completed work is submitted the next day.
   ✓ **Allow the use of fidget toys** as described in the "Preschool Top Five Challenges."
   ✓ **Use high-interest teaching strategies** to maintain attention.

CONTINUED ON PAGE 64

4) dropping out of school, 5) school suspensions, and 6) for a few, expulsion.[4]

The challenges these students face at school can be overwhelming at times. Some do not persist in their efforts, reporting great frustration and giving up more easily. These students often put forth a great deal of effort that does not "pay off" for them.[5] They learn that no matter how hard they try, they will not be successful.

Students with AD/HD inattentive particularly can have difficulty processing language tasks quickly, including the encoding (oral and written expression) and retrieval of information.[6] They may also sit quietly, daydreaming as they stare into space. For more information, teachers of students in grades K–3 may find it helpful to read Chapter 6 and those teaching students in grades 4–5 are referred to Chapters 9 and 10. Chapters 3–5 are also important companion guides to this section. Additional resources are listed in Appendix A.

Impact of Delayed Developmental Skills

Dr. Barkley reports a 30 percent developmental delay in these students in key academic skills, social skills, self-care, and control of emotions.[7] Consequently, these students can appear less mature than their peers. When viewed from this developmental perspective, a 10-year-old student may act more like a 7- or 8 year-old. Dr. Barkley further notes that social promises or commitments to friends are now combined with the impulsive, heedless, and disinhibited behavior that was initially seen in the child during preschool. The result of this continuing behavior challenge is that the elementary teacher will note difficulty with students not raising their hands in class discussion, their lack of turn taking and their lack of self-regulation.

Impact of Executive Function Deficits

The elementary age child with AD/HD experiences an immaturity in the development of skills that most elementary children have begun to establish. This absence of these skills can have a definite impact on the child's overall personal conduct, self-care skills, and ultimately the child's self-esteem. While the student's

peers are beginning to develop these adaptive and formative skills and feel successful with them, the child with AD/HD begins to fall significantly behind. Their off-task behaviors alert teachers and parents that the student is not producing at a rate commensurate with expected developmental levels.[8] When AD/HD and deficits in executive skills co-occur and the student's verbal language skills are impaired, he or she is at higher risk for having serious problems with aggression and antisocial behavior.[9] (Additional information about the impact of AD/HD, the 30 percent developmental delay, and executive skill deficits on school performance is available in Chapters 1, 3, 6, and 8.)

Impact on Social Skills

Some of these children, especially those with AD/HD combined type, may be socially rejected by peers. This social rejection is most often linked to their aggressive behavior.[10] As a result, they are more likely to be described as irritating, annoying, domineering, and rigid in social situations.[11] They often have difficulty accepting responsibility for their own behavior and may not adapt well in a win-or-lose situation. They can also have trouble joining clubs and participating in sports and other extracurricular activities.[12] Additionally, they are more likely to receive negative attention from both parents and teachers. When defiance and aggression are present in elementary school, they may portend serious behavior problems in the future. (Specific suggestions for reducing this unwanted behavior are discussed in Chapter 6. Additional information on social skills is provided in Chapter 12.)

Unique Challenges for Girls

Since girls with AD/HD are often more compliant and eager to please than boys, they are unlikely to present discipline problems at school. Thus, they can be overlooked until later on in their school years. Misdiagnosis of anxiety or depression can also delay a proper diagnosis. Although these girls don't present major discipline problems, the problems they face are just as serious as boys' problems. Girls with attention deficits are more likely than boys to struggle with impaired social skills, be emotionally reactive, or at

The Top 11 Challenging Behaviors in Elementary School, Cont.

3. Disrupting class; blurting out; talking excessively.

✓ **Use simple positive intervention strategies,** such as redirection, ignoring comments and praising those who are listening quietly.
  • Use gestures, such as a finger across your lips and hand cupped behind your ear.
✓ **Consider instituting a classwide behavior management program,** such as *Change Your Clip* or *Red Light*. These two programs involve a three or four level color-coded behavior rating system. Green, yellow, orange, and red circles are mounted on magnets and placed on the board. Clothes pins with each student's name are clipped around the circle. Each student starts the day on the green circle.

Put a positive spin on this strategy by saying that everyone is doing a good job listening, for example. If everyone's clip is still on the green circle, periodically spotlight three to five students, "Emily, Hunter, Nathan and Ashley are all working really hard — so their clips stay on the green circle." If everyone is on green at the end of the day, the teacher can give a treat, like a few Skittles, M&Ms, or raisins.

When a student acts inappropriately, the teacher can say, "Change your clip." The student then moves his clothes pin to the next circle. Most students will comply with the teacher's requests more readily after the first clip move to yellow. The color rating scale and label for each circle is:

1. Green = Great job
2. Yellow = Warning
3. Orange = Quiet or silent lunch
4. Red = Referral to the office or a telephone call to parents

Allow students to earn back the right to return to the green circle. "John, when you get three checks for following my directions and working, I will put your clip back on the green circle."

4. Difficulty getting along with peers; annoying others.

Unfortunately, there are no magic answers for enhancing social skills in students with AD/HD. Some students with AD/HD lack basic social skills, making it difficult to make and keep friends and possibly offending other students inadvertently. As a result, they are sometimes bullied or they become the bully themselves.

Some researchers recommend implementing a social skills curriculum. However, this program has a major flaw; these students do not always use their training when it is needed. Because of the deficits related to their AD/HD, these students have great difficulty generalizing the learned behavior into new settings. Having stated the obvious drawbacks, teachers nonetheless are still encouraged to teach social skills, while remaining realistic in their expectations for the results of the training. Chapter 11 provides a discussion on this topic, as well as strategies for enhancing training effectiveness and specific curricula that can be helpful.

✓ Consider implementing a social skills curriculum.
  • Creative Coaching: A Support Group for Children with AD/HD (for elementary and middle school age students)
  • Skills Streaming (for children)
  • The Walker Social Skills Curriculum: The ACCEPTS Program
✓ Implement an individual behavior management system utilizing a behavior chart. See Appendix C.11 for a sample Getting Along form.
✓ Consider implementing a bullying prevention program. This program can reduce bullying, teach students new communication skills, make them aware of what constitutes bullying, and teach students how to respond to bullying. The Olweus Bullying Prevention program is discussed in Chapter 12.
✓ Consider medication. Medication enables students to use the social skills they know, thus making it easier for these children to get along with others.[a]

CONTINUED ON PAGE 66

times be underreactive. Unique issues facing girls are discussed in more detail in Chapters 2 and 9.

Specific Instructional Strategies for Common Learning Problems

Effective classroom management and education of these children is a multistep process. Skillful teachers must be willing to shift focus from global performance to specific tasks, by breaking lessons into smaller segments and then teaching basic skills.[13] Given the nature of AD/HD, the hallmark of intervention is to make the task interesting and the payoff valuable. According to Sydney Zentall, Ph.D.,[14] Professor of Special Education at Purdue University, the educational environment for children with AD/HD must be structured to allow them to talk, move, and question. Such a program allows students to start, stop, and engage in tasks in a nondisruptive fashion.

Active learning strategies, such as the "start, stop think model," and other tips discussed in the chapter, *Managing and Educating Children with AD/HD,*[15] offer the teacher strategies for helping the student stay alert and focused. Additional instructional and behavioral strategies are discussed in Chapters 4, 5, 10, and 11.

Here are several important intervention strategies:

1. GENERAL CLASSROOM MANAGEMENT SUGGESTIONS

✓ Well-organized routines and methods for returning and retrieving materials are critical. Storage and classroom materials need to be arranged effectively for easy management.

✓ Buddy systems, in which classroom partners monitor one another, help students check homework assignments in schedule books and the returning of papers. Later, the teacher can check that assignments are recorded and new instructional information is understood.

✓ Students who move frequently and have difficulty organizing their papers can benefit from using a clipboard, which provides a sturdy format for papers and a structure for internal organization.[16]

✓ The child with AD/HD benefits from being placed away from distractions in the room, such as doors to the hallway, pencil sharpeners, and computer areas.

✓ Since children with attention deficits often have difficulty with organization and tend to lose supplies such as pencils and paper, extra supplies should be available.

✓ Making time, an abstract concept, visible through the use of a regular timer or a colorful one can be effective. Time Timer© offers timers that can be set for a specific time, which is visualized by a red area that gets smaller as time elapses (http://www.timetimer.com).

2. PLANNING AND USE OF CLASS TIME

Children with AD/HD benefit from having daily schedules available in list format within the room and within their work area. Consider color-coding this list for easy recall. Here are a few tips for improving use of class time:

a. Students with AD/HD have difficulty settling down to start an activity and moving from one activity to the next, so consider structuring and minimizing daily transitions. Offer an activity that aids in transitioning and helps the child move from an unstructured activity to a formal one by slowly adding more structure.[17] Examples of this process include:

- Clapping hands in a beat or pattern
- Giving verbal cues: "Eyes up here"
  - "Clap your hands once if you hear me. Clap your hands twice if you hear me. Clap your hands three times if you hear me."
- Holding up the material to be used in the next assignment
  - Book, paper, pencil
- Verbally prompting students what is to be done
  - "Take out your math book, a piece of paper, and a pencil, and turn to page 15."
  - Write the page number on the board
- Giving verbal directions for the assignment
- Asking students to parrot directions as a rehearsal

The Top 11 Challenging Behaviors in Elementary School, Cont.

5. Aggressive or emotional "blow-ups."

Sometimes aggressive or explosive behavior is linked to frustration related to the inability to be successful in school (adapted from *Teaching Teens with ADD and ADHD*).

✓ Ensure that hidden learning problems are identified and accommodated when needed.
✓ Ensure that assignments are appropriate, not too long and not too difficult.
✓ Suggest that parents talk with their doctor to ensure that medication levels are appropriate.
✓ Use language and actions that de-escalate anger.
  • Lower your voice and stay calm.
  • Be nonthreatening. Give students physical space. Don't touch them or get in their face.
  • Ask the student to step out of the room to give him or her time to cool off.
  • Listen, reflect feelings, and be understanding.
✓ Offer sympathy and understanding. "Something must be very wrong because this is unlike you to be so angry."
✓ Teach anger management, including alternative behaviors to aggression.
✓ Develop a prearranged crisis plan, such as the "Cool-off" pass system described in Chapter 8.
✓ Prevent a reoccurrence by conducting a Functional Behavior Assessment to identify the antecedent or "trigger" for the emotional blow-up. See Chapters 5 and 11 for more details on assessing behavior problems.

6. Poor handwriting; poor fine motor coordination; graphomotor problems.

Some students with AD/HD have severe writing problems. One parent described the writing process as being physically painful for her child.

✓ Refer to an occupational therapist for an evaluation.
✓ Vary traditional writing activities such as practicing spelling words with Scrabble letters instead of writing them five times each.
✓ Provide activities that strengthen fine motor coordination skills.
✓ Allow use of a computer as early as possible.

Third through Fifth Grades

Teachers of students in grades 3–5 are also encouraged to read the "Top Six Challenging Behaviors" for secondary students in Chapter 9 for additional ideas. Several effective strategies are listed here:

1. Difficulty paying attention and staying on task.

The hallmark characteristic of AD/HD is inattention. Medication can be helpful in increasing attention.[b] Teachers can also utilize several instructional strategies that are listed in Chapter 4. Briefly, they include:

✓ Use visual cues, prompts, and redirection to a task.
✓ Increase time on task by using timers and rewards.
✓ Use novel and engaging high-interest activities and strategies.
✓ Consider active-response strategies, such as writing on dry erase boards, replying in unison, and paired learning. For more information, see Chapter 10.
✓ Give task or job cards. Include pictures.
✓ Vary your voice. Be British, Southern, loud, soft, high, or low. Become an actor.

CONTINUED ON PAGE 68

– Saying "The first problem is on page 6." Or "Take out your math book, turn to page 29, and do problems 6 through 10"

b. Encourage the student to use a daily agenda, assignment book, or weekly calendar. Model how to use these tools and frequently check to see if the student is using the tool.

3. PREFERENTIAL SEATING

Preferential seating in the room, with direct view of the teaching area and away from a distracting neighbor, can increase compliance and decrease disruptive behavior. Researchers report that among children with behavioral and/or learning problems, on-task behavior doubles when a child's seat changes from desk clusters to rows. Row seating gives the child an island of isolated space and avoids the feeling of sensory overload and invasion of space. The rate of disruptions has been reported as three times higher in the desk cluster seating arrangement.[18]

4. DAILY PROGRESS NOTES

Research indicates that notes sent home from school are beneficial for children with AD/HD. These colorful notes are placed in a notebook, book bag, or planner on a daily basis. Creative communication tools of this decade now include e-mail and fax notes. Researchers consistently report that the daily note report process improves behavior and target academic performance.[19,20,21]

The teacher or parents should talk with the student before any notes are sent home. Since some students are be fearful of any notes sent home from the teacher, their purpose should be explained in positive terms. The child should be given some honest praise in the first note home, then, if possible, provide at least one positive comment in subsequent notes sent home. Faxing notes to parents also helps them be aware of the child's good days. Parents can greet him or her at the door with praise to reinforce the good behavior. See Appendix C.1 and C.2 for sample Daily Report forms.

5. ADAPTING THE CURRICULUM

Making thoughtful adjustments to instructional activities, often referred to as *diagnostic teaching,* benefits the unique qualities of each student. The curriculum should have age-appropriate expectations and be developmentally appropriate. The following accommodations are helpful for elementary school age students with AD/HD:

✓ **Break tasks into segments.** When long-term projects are assigned, separate the projects into short manageable parts with separate due dates. The teacher should check back with the student prior to each due date to ensure compliance and increase the possibility of success.

✓ **List activities.** Use a list of activities or items to be completed during a section of the day. This list is generated at first by the teacher and eventually by the student. As items are completed, they are crossed off the list. A complete list is rewarded with a predetermined reward.

✓ **Use mnemonics.** The use of mnemonic strategies, which are tricks and devices of learning, helps improve memory for rote facts and figures and recall of information. Acronyms, acrostics, rhythm, or chants can be helpful. Encourage students to create their own mnemonics.

✓ **Use other tools.** Grid charts containing multiplication facts or other information are effective. Graphic organizers also aid memory by organizing information in a manner that is easier to remember.

✓ **Use visual cues.** Visual models and diagrams of key material are helpful. For example, give the student a "job card" that lists the steps for completing a task. Posting key information on wall posters and using PowerPoint or overhead presentations are effective strategies.

✓ **Use manipulatives.** Manipulatives can be effective for memory work. For example, use a device that twists and shows correct multiplication table answers or craft sticks or other concrete objects for demonstrating simple math problems.

7

The Top 11 Challenging Behaviors in Elementary School, Cont.

✓ Move around. Variation is the key.

✓ Allow the use of fidget toys as described in the "Preschool Top Five Challenges" in Chapter 6.

2. **Not completing and submitting homework.**

Many students with attention deficits don't submit completed work in a timely manner. They forget to do their work or they complete it but lose it before reaching class to submit it. Their grades can fluctuate from one extreme to another, from zeros to 100s. They can also have difficulty understanding the directions for an assignment. Because of their forgetfulness, disorganization, and executive function deficits, these students often require extra supervision to ensure homework is submitted.

a. **Work not submitted due to disorganization and forgetfulness**

✓ *Post homework assignments* on the board.
✓ *Appoint "row captains" or a "homework buddy"* to pick up homework and check that assignments are recorded.
✓ *Intervene at the "point of performance."* At the end of the day, review homework assignments before students leave class and remind them which books to take home.
✓ *Provide an extra book or set of textbooks for home.*
✓ *Determine whether homework assignments are too long.* Provide accommodations, such as extended time or shortened assignments.
✓ *Use weekly or daily reports as needed.* See Appendices C.1, C.2, and C.3 for sample weekly reports and C.4 for a Classroom Behavior Rubric.
✓ *Communicate regularly with parents of struggling students via:*
  • Homework "hotlines"
  • Teacher websites
  • E-mail or ask parents to e-mail the teacher
  • Weekly reports
  • Teacher phone calls or conferences
✓ *Encourage parents to establish a homework routine.* When homework is completed, put it back into the notebook and backpack. Place the backpack in a routine place each night.
✓ *Give "free homework" coupons.* Students earn a "free or reduced homework" coupon when submitting all their homework for one week. Students who earned these coupons actually showed improvements in overall organization and grades received on notebooks. Students also work to improve their behavior if the amount of homework is reduced.
✓ Medication has been shown to be extremely effective in improving academic performance: for example, increasing the amount of work completed and the student's compliance with teacher requests.[c]

b. **Work not submitted due to not fully understanding directions**

✓ *Ensure that assignments are understood.*
  • Review the directions and then model how to complete the problem correctly.
  • Leave a sample problem on the board.
  • Incorporate color to highlight directions and delineate sections of the assignment.
    – Ask students to highlight the directions or the + and - signs for math assignments.
  • Teach students to write notations on their work.
    – Circle words that cue addition, subtraction, greater than, less than, and how many.
    – Ask the student to follow action directions: underline, circle, and cross out. Highlight the first action to be taken, then complete that step.

CONTINUED ON PAGE 70

✓ **Use organizational strategies.** Teach organizational techniques such as webbing, mapping, or use of graphic organizers to support writing assignments and note taking.

✓ **Give extended time.** Give the opportunity for untimed writing assignments.

✓ **Ignore poor handwriting.** Motor skills may not be fully developed in these students, so look at the content and accept what has been written. Have the child describe what he wrote if it is intelligible.

✓ **Adjust grading techniques.** Adapt standards on some writing assignments and grade written assignments with one grade for content and one for mechanics. Average both for a final grade on the paper.

✓ **Mark correct work.** Mark the student's papers for correct performance, not the mistakes.

✓ **Sequence tasks.** Give two tasks, with a preferred task to be completed after the less preferred task.

✓ **Give choices.** Give two parallel assignments and allow the child to choose the way the assignment will be done. For example, allow the student to do a project such as making a mobile or designing a book cover.

✓ **Incorporate color.** Use color to highlight directions and sections of the worksheet. For example, highlight the + and − signs in different colors on a math paper. The effective use of color to draw attention to relevant, discriminative stimuli has been well-documented.[22,23,24] Color accents can add key features to repetitive tasks, perhaps increasing interest and motivation. Color can make the important stimuli in an activity look more intriguing.

Additional suggestions for adapting the curriculum are provided in Chapters 4 and 10.

6. COMPENSATORY EQUIPMENT

Students with AD/HD can use various tools to support their efforts in compensating for their challenges. Some tools include:

✓ Tape recorder, digital if possible, to record teacher lectures or assignments

✓ Computer software, such as *Kidspiration* or *Inspiration* (http://www.inspiration.com), to develop their writing skills

✓ Written and spelling prompters, such as Wynn, Kurzweil,© or Write Out Loud© and Co-Writer®

✓ Handheld spell checker and dictionary

✓ Triplicate carbonized (NCR) notebook paper for taking notes in class

✓ Voice-activated software, such as Write and Speak and Dragon Naturally Speaking®

✓ Handheld daily organizers and minute minders that hold three minutes of tape for tape-recording assignments instead of writing them

Positive Reinforcement

Positive reinforcement is critical to recognizing the child's strengths and efforts. Teachers can support this by:

✓ Calling attention to the child's strengths by allowing for a consistent time each day or week when the child can display his or her talents

✓ Recognizing that excessive activity can mean increased energy and productivity when it is channeled positively

✓ Recognizing that bossiness can translate into leadership potential, so providing positive leadership opportunities is critical

✓ Recognizing that attraction to novel stimulation can lead to creativity

✓ Recognizing that this student must be actively involved in every aspect of learning; he is not a passive learner

✓ Understanding that these students have a natural playfulness that can be redirected in a positive manner and used to develop skills

Ultimately, teachers who work with students with AD/HD should attempt to make each student feel comfortable and successful with his or her disorder.

Behavioral Strategies

The classroom teacher can target specific behaviors within the regular classroom and in accordance with an individualized educational plan (IEP) or 504

The Top 11 Challenging Behaviors in Elementary School, Cont.

    c. **Work not submitted due to assignments that are too long or difficult.**

    If students are struggling with weak written expression, slow processing speed, reading comprehension, limited working memory capacity, or fine motor coordination problems, they may need extra time on assignments and tests. Chapter 9 gives a few suggestions for determining whether assignments are too long, as well as additional intervention strategies.

    ✓ Ensure that the length of assignments is appropriate by giving extended time or shortening writing assignments, if needed.

3. **Disorganization.**

As teacher expectations for completing work independently increase, several problems begin to surface: disorganization, difficulty getting started, difficulty completing assignments promptly, and difficulty planning ahead. Because of the developmental delays and disorganization related to their executive function deficits, these students need more supervision and support than their peers. Chapters 4 and 9 contain several helpful recommendations including the following:

✓ Provide additional support and supervision to improve organizational skills.
- Teach organizational and study strategies by using binders, planners, or assignment calendars and color-coding strategies.
- Organize the classroom area by setting up files or trays for returning work and designating areas for select tasks or materials.
- Provide assistance and teach skills by practicing organizing notebooks, lockers, and important papers.
- Tape a card to the child's desk with each class assignment listed in order. Mark off completed tasks.
- Designate a colored folder for all assignments.
- Monitor the planner or assignment book. Ask "row captains" to check planners and pick up homework.

4. **Difficulty with written work.**

Many students with AD/HD have great ideas but can't get them written down on paper. These children can seldom sit down with their thoughts well-organized and produce a written story or report. Some fail miserably in spelling and organizing the content material. Other students can explain their material verbally but fall apart when they try to put their ideas on paper. Deficits in executive function, especially limited working memory capacity and the ability to problem solve and reorganize and sequence information, result in serious problems with written expression and rapid completion of multistep math problems.

✓ **Provide organizational support.** Use organizational techniques such as webbing, mapping, or sticky notes to support writing assignments and notetaking.
- *Dictate ideas* to a scribe, student, or parent.
- *Tape-record the initial draft* of an essay or report.
- *Brainstorm creatively* with Mindmapping© or sticky notes.
- *Create an outline of essay components* for essays. Fill in labeled organizers or charts to show: who, what, when, where, and why.

✓ **Modify teaching strategies.** Several instructional strategies discussed in Chapters 4 and 9 are effective with these children. For example, give visual cues, reduce demands on memory, and use direct instruction.

CONTINUED ON PAGE 72

Plan. The following *behavior techniques* should be considered when designing classroom-based management systems.

1. **Encourage strengths.** Find what the child does well and build on those strengths. Reinforce what these children can do, not what they cannot do. In math, count the number of correct answers, not mistakes. Have students record their number on a chart. Reward students for having more correct answers as the week progresses. For improving writing proficiency, record the number of sentences written by the student, regardless of the number of errors.

2. **Use positive rewards.** Provide positive rewards, including praise and primary reinforcers (like stickers and tokens), for on-task and appropriate behaviors. When the child with AD/HD is performing, let them know immediately that they are doing well. Respond to the child's need for variety and change rewards often.

3. **Use redirection.** This strategy allows the child to quickly refocus on a new activity. The child is distracted from the current behavior and then quickly moved to another acceptable behavior.

4. **Ignore misbehavior.** At times, it may be appropriate to ignore minor misbehavior. The child with AD/HD often needs to touch, fidget, manipulate objects, or doodle to focus better. Respect this need for stimulus and avoid making it a reason for arguments.

5. **Allow the use of fidget toys.** Allow students to hold a fidget toy in their free hand when working. Fidget toys such as Wikki Stix, stress balls, and Koosh balls® are helpful. Standing during class or writing on a lapdesk also changes focus and interest. Sitting on a flexible cushion allows the student to wiggle or squirm when needed.

6. **Implement a point system.** Offer a point system in which children earn points for appropriate behavior, turning in papers, or compliance. Show the child how to keep a tally or score sheet and provide an easy system for recording information. Allow the child the opportunity to earn lost points for specific behaviors on a daily basis.

7. **Review the schedule daily.** Provide a well-organized daily plan. Involve the child in reviewing the plan and noting when responsibilities occur on the plan. Teach list making and crossing off completed tasks as a personal organizational strategy.

Positive reinforcement and additional behavioral strategies are discussed in Chapters 5 and 11.

Accommodation Plans: IEPs and Section 504 Plans

Some students with AD/HD can be successful in school with basic supports or accommodations that teachers often provide just because the child needs a little extra help. These strategies are often labeled "good teaching strategies." Other students who are struggling require services under Section 504 or IDEA (Individuals with Disabilities Education Act). Many students can be served successfully under Section 504, but others with more challenging struggles require support pursuant to IDEA. If the multidisciplinary team decides that the student would benefit from services afforded by the IEP process, the child will probably qualify under the Other Health Impairment (OHI) category. (IDEA and Section 504 are discussed in more detail in Chapter 14.)

EDUCATIONAL PLANS

Teachers can develop an informal educational plan for students who are struggling. On a more formal basis, IEPs and Section 504 plans are developed for eligible students. IEPs and some 504 plans:

✓ describe the disability

✓ detail how the services will be provided

✓ list who will be responsible for each task

✓ list the recommended accommodations

All team members as well as parents often have input on the educational plan. Parent input is mandated for IEPs and is often solicited for 504 plans as a matter of best practice principles. Everyone at the team meeting signs and receives a copy of the final educational plan. A copy is kept in the student's cumulative record

The Top 11 Challenging Behaviors in Elementary School, Cont.

✓ **Introduce technology to provide assistance.**
 • *Use computer programs* like *Kidspiration or Inspiration* to organize ideas and material.
 • *Use a computer writing assistant program* such as *Write Out Loud, Co-Writer, and Dragon Naturally Speaking*®.
✓ **Modify grading.** Give two grades, one for content and one for mechanics; then average the score.
✓ **Use color to highlight directions or key details.** For example, in social studies, highlight people in blue, happenings in yellow, dates in red or pink, and places in green.

5. Not completing long-term projects.

✓ **Modify assignments.**
 • Break down long-term assignments into two or three segments.
 • Give multiple due dates and grades.
✓ **Provide organizational support and increased supervision.**
 • *Prompt the child* about getting started on the project and monitor progress.
 • *Notify parents of the due dates.*
 • *Involve parents in monitoring.* Ask parents to initial the assignment book.
 • *Have the student record reminders* in the assignment book and request the parent to initial the assignment book when it arrives home and is understood.
 • *Check progress regularly.* Check back with the student prior to each due date.
✓ **Provide a job card that outlines the project.**
✓ **Show completed model projects or reports** to improve the overall quality of reports.
✓ **Provide a graphic organizer for the project** as described in Chapter 10.

6. Difficulty memorizing rote information.

✓ **Use mnemonic strategies** (tricks and devices of learning).
✓ **Use manipulatives** (objects that can be physically manipulated to aid in learning).
✓ **Use color-cuing or hands-on activities.** Moving objects and arranging items requires greater involvement of the learner and is sometimes necessary to encourage understanding and memorization.
✓ **Create a rap or rhyme for hard-to-remember multiplication facts.** For example, "7 times 8 is 56, I ate a grape and it made me sick."

for future reference, and the plan is modified and changed as skills are mastered and obtained.

ACCOMMODATIONS

Typical accommodations that are provided to students with AD/HD include:
✓ Preferential seating
✓ Reduction of copying or written tasks, including homework assignments
✓ Support in recording homework assignments in a plan book
✓ Use of compensatory tools in the classroom, for example, a computer or calculator
✓ Advance notice sent to parents of due dates, especially on long-term projects
✓ Daily note sent home

✓ Additional copies of textbooks for home use
✓ Supplementing verbal instruction with visual information
✓ Alternative testing measures, including oral testing, or support on bubble sheet scan tests such as using a ruler to keep the row in line or writing answers directly on the test copy to later be transferred to the bubble sheet by an aide
✓ Breaking tasks into shorter chunks or segments
✓ Additional time for timed tasks or eliminating the time factor entirely

Teachers may also receive consultation or assistance from a school psychologist or other professionals who are familiar with AD/HD to implement the educational plan.

CHAPTER 8

Advanced Strategies for Challenging Behaviors

Sharon K. Weiss, M.Ed.
Terry Illes, Ph.D.

Children with AD/HD are often overwhelmed by the challenges of the school day. Sometimes, just the demands of the day — sharing teacher attention, sitting quietly for extended periods, organizing materials, managing time, following multi-step directions, and completing seatwork independently — are beyond the child's capabilities.[1]

Unfortunately, students who are overwhelmed may misbehave. Teachers can handle most problems but occasionally some AD/HD-related misbehavior is especially challenging. As teachers develop intervention strategies to address these behaviors, they should keep in mind that students cannot change a behavior unless they are aware that it is inappropriate. None of us can.

Teachers are more successful in changing behavior when they provide a supportive structure that encourages the desired change. Many of the approaches suggested in this chapter are based on establishing a structure that reminds students of what is expected and provides a prompt for that behavior. The primary goal is to provide a cue so that the teacher does not have to be the reminder. Educators need to always ask themselves: "What do I want them to do instead of what they are doing? How can I use visual cues to prompt appropriate behaviors so that I don't have to continually provide a reminder?"

This structure includes clearly defining and reviewing the expected behavior changes, then practicing the target behaviors to make certain that students can consistently perform them. Practicing this behavior in advance increases the chances students will use the correct behavior when needed. Another tip for maximizing the effectiveness of behavioral strategies with students with AD/HD is to intervene at the "point of performance," as described in Chapter 11. In other words, intervene at the point in time when the child must use the new skill.

Several challenging behaviors that may require more intensive interventions are targeted in this chapter. If the basic intervention strategies suggested in earlier chapters don't work, these suggestions may be effective. Of course, the most effective strategy is the combination of medication and behavioral interventions.[2] Generally speaking, implementing the strategies in this chapter may require a greater time investment and closer monitoring by the teacher, teacher's aide, or a classmate. Some strategies, such as response cost and chart moves, are discussed in more detail in Chapter 5. Additional resources are listed in Appendix A.

8

ISSUE: Inattention

SOLUTION: Help students stay on task

✓ **Set interim deadlines.** Before handing out the assignment, determine a specific time when students must complete smaller segments of classwork, such as a row of problems or two questions. Mark the paper to remind the student of how much work must be completed within the time limit, so that the teacher does not need to provide a verbal reminder.

    In addition, consider using a timer, such as a *Time Timer,*© that you can set for 15 minutes so students can "see" how much time they have left to complete the assignment.

✓ **Use headphones with a "beeper tape."** This aid produces a bell sound on a random schedule, which can be heard by both the teacher and students. If students are on task when the beeper sounds, have them record this on a self-monitoring chart. Ask students to chart their daily progress. A simple bar graph that plots the number of times that they are on task when the tone sounds works well.

    If they are willing and won't be embarrassed, post the chart on the classroom wall at the end of the week. Students should be rewarded or given positive reinforcement as their performance improves. Often students improve without using further rewards. Do not expect perfection — that they will always be on task. Teachers can create their own tape or purchase the *Listen, Look and Think Program,*© which provides all the resources needed to implement this strategy. See Appendix C.11 for a record keeping form.

> ### "The students who are the most 'unlovable' are the very ones who need love the most.
>
> ### • Glenda Liddle, media specialist

✓ **Use a response cost program in combination with a beeper tape.** Divide the day into monitoring intervals, for example, 30 minutes. For each monitoring session, provide students with a predetermined number of tokens. If students are off task when the tone sounds, the teacher, aide, or student removes a token. If students have at least one token left during the monitoring session, award a point or "chart move." Repeat the monitoring sessions throughout the day, and if they earn enough points or chart moves during the day, provide a reward. Typically a response cost program is used in situations where there is a high rate of inappropriate behavior and traditional reward programs have been ineffective. Response cost programs provide both rewards and consequences for behavior and are explained in greater detail in Chapter 5. See Appendix C.7 for a Response Cost Form.

ISSUE: Noncompliance with rules (talking out of turn or being out of a seat)

SOLUTION: Increase students' awareness of their behavior

Begin by clearly defining the rule and behavior of concern. "Not raising your hand" is not as specific as "calling out." Similarly, "raising your hand and waiting quietly to be called on" more specifically and accurately describes the desired behavior.

✓ **Self-Monitoring Chart.** Use a self-monitoring chart where students can record the number of times they blurt out or leave their desk without teacher permission. Provide a reward as the behavior improves. Gradually increase goals or standards of improvement and reinforce the student as he achieves each benchmark of fewer interruptions or decreased out-of-seat behaviors. Provide a reward such as those listed in Chapter 5. Instructions for increasing the use of hand-raising through self-monitoring strategies are provided in *The ADHD Handbook for Schools.*[3] See Appendix C.9 for a Hand Raising Form.

✓ **Response Cost Program with Visual Prompts.** Use a response cost program that provides visual prompts for the appropriate behavior. For example, provide students with a predetermined number of tokens and place the tokens on their desks. Divide the day into monitoring intervals, such as 30-minute sessions. Remove a token each time students talk out of turn or leave their desks. If students have at least one token left during the monitoring session, they earn one point or make a "chart move." If students earn sufficient points by the end of the day, provide a reward.

✓ **Cue Cards.** All of the suggested strategies in this section can be enhanced by using visual "cue cards" to prompt the appropriate response. Cue cards are pictures of the appropriate behavior, which are given to students to encourage the desired behavior. These cards can easily be made using graphics programs, such as *Clip Art*. For example, you can print a picture of a student raising his or her hand in class, tape the picture to card stock, and laminate the card. Students keep the picture at their desk as a reminder of the appropriate behavior. When students wish to ask a question or permission to leave their desks, they quietly hold up the appropriate laminated card.

✓ **Token Program.** Use a token program to reinforce appropriate target behaviors. The program should be implemented for short periods of time (for example five to ten minutes) several times per day (for example, 10 times). Provide students with a token or chart move for each five to ten time period in which they remembered to raise their hands before talking or leaving their seats. That is, students receive a token for not committing any rule violations during the monitoring period. When students earn a predetermined number of points, an individual or group reward is provided. A sample token economy form is available in Appendix B.

✓ **An Answer Journal.** Establish a behavior or procedure that students can use instead of calling out, such as having them record ideas and thoughts on a sheet of paper or journal on their desk. Clarify behavioral expectations and tell students what you want them to do instead of what they're doing wrong: "Each time you think of something you want to say or add to the class discussion, write it in the journal." To make it easier for younger students, ask them to write a word or make a hash mark. Provide positive feedback when the desired behavior occurs.

Students earn "credit" for each entry if they also refrained from calling out the information in class. Credit is also given even if the same information was given by another student. Credits can translate to privileges, bonus points for a class participation grade, or a note sent home documenting the success. The teacher agrees to review and sign off on the journal or paper each day. The goal is for students to sit quietly. Whether they write down original ideas or record what others say, as long as they sit quietly, they have met the goal of the program.

ISSUE: Poor work completion

SOLUTION: Break up the work into several sessions

A common teacher complaint is that children with AD/HD often fail to complete their classwork. Some teachers withhold recess time as a consequence for incomplete work and require the student to complete the assignment during this time. This strategy is generally ineffective because it fails to change the behavior that interferes with work completion. Children with AD/HD often do not complete their work because they are unable to consistently sustain effort during seatwork time, they have slow processing speed or poor time management skills, or homework assignments are too long. The following protocol will help a student with AD/HD manage time more effectively:

1. Provide the student with a digital timer.
2. Break down work sessions into small units of time, for example five to ten minutes for younger children.
3. Assign a small part of the assignment to be completed within this time limit.
4. Make sure that the student has all of the materials needed to complete the work.
5. Start the timer.
6. After time has expired, check to see whether the student has completed the assigned work.
7. Use a chart to keep track of whether the student "beat the clock." See Appendix C.10 for a "I Beat the Clock" form.
8. Repeat the timed sessions several times throughout the day, for instance, 10 sessions per day. When students beat the timer a predetermined number of times per day, they earn a daily incentive. Make sure that the requirements to earn a reward are attainable, even if there is an occasional failure. That is, if you are timing the student 10 times, a reward may be provided if the student beats the clock seven times. As the student progresses, the duration and frequency of the timings can be extended.

ISSUE: Poor anger control and angry outbursts

Solution: Teach anger management and strategies to avoid outbursts

Many of the students who exhibit poor anger control are easily overwhelmed and frustrated but lack the skills to deal with their feelings effectively. As Anne Teeter, Ed.D., explains, aggressive behavior can also occur because these children lack the verbal skills to express themselves and ask for what they need.

✓ **Teach the appropriate behavior.** Teachers often focus on eliminating angry outbursts rather than teaching the child more appropriate ways of expressing anger. Unless students know what they can do to release anger, telling them what they cannot do is unlikely to be effective. In other words, students must be offered appropriate ways to express anger to replace the inappropriate expression of anger. Perhaps a "safe" place can be designated in the school, such as the guidance counselor's or school psychologist's office, where students can more openly display anger. It is also important to teach students appropriate ways to verbally express anger. This might include how to identify and verbalize feelings as well as how to appropriately make requests of others. Suggestions for addressing anger management are provided in *Teaching Teens with ADD and ADHD*. See Appendix A for a list of resources on anger and anger management.

✓ **Cool-off Pass System.** Students can use a pass to go to a cool-off area before a behavioral outburst occurs. They receive credit for every pass they use and double credit for every pass they do NOT use. Credits can be cashed in for privileges that are available on a weekly basis. Daily rewards may be

One Child's AD/HD Story

Mark, a 13-year-old seventh grader with AD/HD, was struggling terribly in school. In the first two months of school, he received six discipline notices for misbehaviors such as disrupting class, disregarding authority, tardiness, and writing in the pencil tray of a school desk. In addition, he has had two after-school detentions and two suspensions from school. The student was not currently on medication. These misbehaviors occurred even though there was a Section 504 plan in place. The parents were extremely concerned and requested a 504 meeting. What can teachers do to help this child be successful in school?

Objectives: Initially the school established these objectives, but of course objectives alone won't help the student successfully comply with them. What would you do to provide the necessary supports to ensure that Mark could comply with these objectives?

Mark will...

Behavior Issues

A. Walk to class without bothering others
B. Arrive on time to class
C. Stay in his seat when appropriate
D. Wait to be called upon
E. Control his emotions.

Academic/Homework Issues

F. Write down homework assignments
G. Turn in homework on time
H. Complete assignments correctly
I. Avoid careless errors
J. Get teachers to sign his behavior chart in each class.

Possible Interventions: An effective intervention should include supports and accommodations provided at school plus parental support at home. Medication should also help improve Mark's ability to concentrate, complete work, and control his emotions.[a] *Giving a reward* after mastery of each skill will also be helpful. Initially teachers may pick three or four issues as priorities and work on those first. Remember that students whose academic performance improves also show positive behavior changes. Here are some strategies teachers could use to help Mark succeed.

Select the options that best address each individual child's specific situation.

Teachers can address these issues by...

A, B: Arrive in class on time without bothering others.

1) Model the proper way to walk from class to class.
2) Send an escort of Mark's choice to walk with him.
3) Double check his class routes to ensure that they are the most direct routes between classes.
4) Determine if Mark has time to stop at his locker between class or needs to carry more books with him.

(Some students, particularly middle schoolers, overwhelmed by attending a larger school, can get disoriented and may have an impaired sense of time. In addition they may also have a poor sense of direction that prevents them from selecting the shortest route between classes.)

CONTINUED ON PAGE 78

8

One Child's ADHD Story, Cont.

C: Stay in seat.

1) Assign tasks that are not too difficult for Mark to complete.
2) Give clear directions.
3) Develop a signal Mark is to give the teacher when he needs help.
4) Give Mark legal reasons to move, such as taking a messages to the office or collecting papers.
5) Assign two work stations, a desk and perhaps a table at the back of the room.
6) Consider creating a "stand-up" desk area.

D: Listen and wait to be recognized.

1) Teach "shaping" strategies that break down listening and waiting to be called upon into several steps, and reward mastery of each step: a) sits quietly without blurting out (even if just daydreaming); b) sits quietly and looks at teacher (even if not listening); c) sits and listens to teacher (no blurting); d) sits, listens, and raises hand (even if still blurts out); and d) sits, listens, raises hand, and waits to be called upon. Reward mastery of each step achieved regardless of how small. "That's great, Mark! You raised your hand! You waited 30 seconds before you talked. You're making progress. Next time, can you make it a whole minute?" Call on him more quickly, and then reinforce his behavior.
2) Give Mark three to five cards or tokens, one for each time he is allowed to speak. When the tokens are gone, he must record his comments in writing.

E: Control emotions.

1) Medication will help Mark stop and think before speaking and make it somewhat easier to control his emotions.[b]
2) Give him an alternate behavior to use when he feels angry and out of control. "When you feel angry, would you like to count to ten or walk back and forth at the back of the room?" Praise him when he does this successfully.
3) Give Mark an "escape valve," such as an open pass to go to the guidance counselor's office anytime he feels as though he may totally lose his temper or control of his emotions.
4) Invite Mark to participate in an anger management class.

F, G, H, I: Successfully complete homework.

Specific strategies for helping students complete homework are provided in "Top Five Challenging Behaviors in Middle and High school."

J: Get teacher signature on behavior chart.

1) Build in a prompting system whereby the teacher or another student reminds Mark to get the note signed.
2) Consider eliminating having the chart signed and sending compliance notes home by e-mail.

Parents can help by...

A. **Conferring with their doctor about the student's academic performance and behavior.**
   a. Follow up with a doctor's appointment and discuss the possibility of medication.
   b. For a child who is already on medication but doing poorly, the teacher can complete a behavior rating scale that can then be discussed with the doctor.

B. **Providing structure during homework sessions.**

C. **Monitoring homework completion and establish a routine to ensure its return to school each day.**

D. **Rewarding improvements on Mark's academic achievement and behavior chart.**

> "Education is a partnership formed on behalf of the child. You can't have a real partnership without good communication between parents and educators."
>
> • Sharon K. Weiss, M.Ed., behavioral consultant

best used for younger students or those having daily outbursts.

1. **Identify a cool-off area.** Identify an area where students can go when they are upset. This may need to be a place outside the classroom. Get input from students on activities or options that should be available in the cool-off room.

2. **Provide students passes.** Begin by taking a baseline count of the number of outbursts that occur in a day or week. Students begin with as many passes as there are outbursts. Over time, the number of passes gradually decreases. Provide students with a card that indicates the number of passes they have in a day or week. Initially, the teacher holds the passes.

3. **Discuss the plan with the student.** Have at least two planning conferences with students before implementing the system. Choose a staff member with whom students have a good relationship to discuss the plan.

4. **Practice the strategy.** Allow students to practice receiving a pass or handing in a pass and going to the cool-off area. These practice sessions should occur at different times of the day and with all teachers who have direct contact with them. It is important for students to practice the system several times when they are calm.

5. **Monitor implementation of the plan.** Once the program begins, meet with students on a regularly scheduled basis to review progress.

6. **Phase out the program over time.** Part of the review should include discussing the possibility of decreasing the number of passes. As the number decreases, the credits for passes used without an outburst should increase. The double bonus for unused passes stays in effect. Eventually, students earn credits for days or weeks without an outburst.

Keep in mind that even after the program is phased out, students may still need a pass to go to a cool-off area during a major crisis. Russell Barkley,[4] Ph.D., reminds us that when some behavioral programs are withdrawn from these students, problem behaviors return.

✓ **A Peer Contract.** Another strategy that can decrease negative behaviors as well as provide a model of appropriate behavior is having students take data on each other. See Appendices C.5 and C.6 for sample contracts.

1. Pair peers who may be a positive influence on each other, for example, students who like or respect each other.

2. Define the behavior of concern, such as making off-task or negative comments in response to teacher directions.

3. Determine a specific length of time that the program will run, for instance, a week, one class period, or one day.

4. During that timeframe, each student records data on the other student's performance.

5. Criteria for success can be one or several periods of time or a percentage of time in which students do not make any negative comments. When the team is successful, they both earn the reward.

8

Avoiding the "Brick Wall" in Middle and High School

Parents of children with an attention deficit often say,
"It's like my son hit a brick wall when he entered middle school."

• *Chris A. Zeigler Dendy, M.S., former teacher and school psychologist*

Developmental challenges, academic challenges, instructional strategies, social challenges, unique challenges for girls and medication consideration are addressed in the next three chapters. Resources are listed in Appendix A. Tips are also given for addressing the top challenges identified by classroom teachers of middle and high schoolers.

Chapter 9: Impact of AD/HD on Middle and High School Students

✓ Developmental challenges
✓ Academic challenges
✓ Social challenges
✓ Unique challenges in middle school
✓ Unique challenges facing teenage girls
✓ Unique medication challenges for teenagers
✓ General suggestions for middle and high school teachers

SIDEBAR
✓ Top challenging behaviors in middle and high school

Chapter 10: Specific Instructional Strategies for Common Learning Problems

✓ Effective teaching strategies for middle and high school students
 – Modify teaching methods
 – Modify assignments
 – Modify testing and grading
  • A parent's perspective on homework
 – Increase support and supervision
 – Increase use of technology
✓ Effective classroom accommodations for middle and high school students

Chapter 11: Effective Behavioral Strategies for Middle and High School Students

✓ Utilize positive behavioral strategies
✓ Utilize a variety of effective behavioral strategies
✓ Provide increased "developmentally appropriate" supervision
✓ Conduct a Functional Behavior Assessment
✓ Develop a Behavior Intervention Plan
✓ Teach skills and compensatory strategies
✓ Consider implementing a school–wide positive behavior program

CHAPTER 9

Impact of AD/HD on Middle and High School Students*

Chris A. Zeigler Dendy, M.S.
Ann B. Welch, Ph.D.

Joan Helbing, M.S.
Kathy Hubbard Weeks, M.S.W.

Adapted from *Teaching Teens with ADD and ADHD* and *A Bird's-Eye View of Life with ADD and ADHD*

Overview

Most teachers recognize that students with attention deficits are unique — each one has different strengths and challenges. Furthermore, teachers will also be interested to learn that these students can have mild, moderate, or severe AD/HD, and two-thirds have at least one other coexisting condition, such as a learning disability, anxiety, or depression. For some students with a mild to moderate attention disorder, medication seems to work extremely well. But most others who have more complex cases of AD/HD and coexisting conditions — 67 percent — require significant support and accommodations.[1]

Since the *greatest academic challenges often occur when these students enter middle and high school,* having teachers at the secondary level who understand AD/HD is critical. Although teachers may not realize it, many of the common problems experienced by these students, such as not turning in homework and disorganization, are linked to their attention disorder. Of course the AD/HD should not be used as an excuse, but teachers may have to use different strategies to successfully teach these students. Several factors that contribute to the increased difficulties at the secondary level are discussed in detail in this chapter.

Academic deficits are often the underlying cause of behavior problems in students with AD/HD, as explained in Chapter 1. Consequently, providing interventions to address learning problems is critical. Researchers have found that interventions that focus primarily on improving learning are more likely to improve behavior and academics than interventions that target behavior problems only.

Middle and high school teachers across the country identify the following issues as the most common challenges facing these students:

1) Failure to complete and submit school and homework on time
2) Forgetting homework assignments
3) Chronic disorganization
4) Difficulty getting started and persisting with work
5) Specific academic problems
   a. Poor reading comprehension: difficulty remembering what was read
   b. Weak writing skills: difficulty getting ideas down on paper; limited working memory capacity; difficulty organizing and sequencing; difficulty finishing the work
   c. Difficulty memorizing rote information, including multiplication tables and understanding abstract math concepts (Algebra)

* In most cases, AD/HD is used interchangeably throughout this Manual to describe both AD/HD predominately hyperactive-impulsive and AD/HD predominately inattentive. IDEA regulations refer to these two conditions as ADHD and ADD, respectively.

6) Difficulty planning ahead: difficulty with long-term projects

7) Being disruptive: acting impulsively; blurting out; talking excessively

8) Misunderstanding expectations with regard to assignments or behavior in the classroom: difficulty following directions

Before getting into the details of the impact of AD/HD on academic performance and strategies to address these issues, here is an overview of typical expectations of this age student.

Developmental Expectations for Teenagers and Preteens

During the middle and high school years, teenagers and preteens undertake several important developmental tasks such as discovering their identity, establishing independence, maturing and accepting more responsibility, seeking acceptance from peers, adjusting to hormonal and sexual growth spurts, dating, and planning for a career. Cognitively, the student may begin to engage in abstract thinking, develop hypotheses, and problem solve solutions. Since middle and high school teachers are aware of these traditional developmental stages, they expect teenagers to exercise increased self-control and act more maturely and responsibly.

In addition to increased teacher expectations, academic and executive function demands also expand significantly. Students with AD/HD face more difficult subjects, more classes, more teachers, greater demands for memory and organizational skills, and expectations for exercising self-control and completing work independently. The ability to juggle these complex demands is dependent on strong executive function skills — skills that are often lacking in these students.

Unfortunately, at a time when academic demands and expectations for working independently are increasing, these students are also experiencing a *significant developmental delay of four to six years* that makes it almost impossible for them to master these expected developmental tasks concurrent with their peers. Many of these students were moderately successful in elementary school because teachers provided the much-needed higher levels of supervision and guidance. However, once that "valuable safety net" is removed in middle school, many students with AD/HD flounder, due primarily to developmental delays and lack of management and organizational skills linked to the executive function deficits.[2]

Further compounding their academic problems, students must also cope with the primary characteristics of AD/HD and, in many cases, coexisting conditions. Deficits in social skills are another challenge that often plague students, especially those with AD/HD combined or hyperactive-impulsive types.[3] Some face painful peer rejection, teasing, bullying, or exclusion from social activities. (Social skills are discussed in more detail in Chapter 12.) Occasionally, teens who are struggling academically act out, rebelling against teachers or parents. As these teenagers assert their independence and sometimes make impulsive decisions, behavioral problems can arise or accidents can occur. For example, these teens are more likely to have auto accidents and receive speeding tickets than their peers. These young teens may also engage in risky behaviors — sexual activity, drug use, or delinquent acts — in hopes of winning the approval of their peers. All these challenges combined make it difficult, if not impossible, for these children to be successful in school without proper treatment and the understanding and support from their teachers.

A. Developmental Challenges

1. IMPACT OF AD/HD AND COEXISTING CONDITIONS ON SCHOOL PERFORMANCE

Academic underachievement, a hallmark of attention deficit disorder, becomes even more apparent during middle and high school. As explained in Chapter 1, according to research from the National Institute of Mental Health, over two-thirds of students with AD/HD have a least one other coexisting condition, such as a learning disability, anxiety, depression, or bipolar disorder. These combined conditions often have a profound impact on the school performance of these students.

In addition, many of these students experience *executive function deficits* that impair organizational skills, time management, and academic skills. The true complexity of AD/HD is graphically portrayed in the drawing of the "ADD/ADHD Iceberg" (Table 1).[4] Just as a large portion of an iceberg is hidden, most of the complexities of AD/HD lurk beneath the surface. Remember, however, every student with AD/HD goes not experience all the challenges described in this chapter.

Typically, the more coexisting conditions a student has, the more difficulty a student experiences in school. When these conditions are not treated properly, students with attention deficits are at risk for a multitude of problems, including school failure, suspension, or dropping out of school. Many of these problems can be avoided — or their negative impact lessened — by knowledgeable educators and parents intervening early and providing appropriate classroom accommodations.

2. IMPACT OF EXECUTIVE FUNCTION DEFICITS ON SCHOOL PERFORMANCE

Leading researchers on AD/HD like Russell A. Barkley, Ph.D.,[5] and Tom E. Brown, Ph.D.,[6] have identified a combination of critical skills known as *executive functions* that influence a student's ability to succeed in school. As explained in Chapter 1, executive function has been likened to the conductor of an orchestra and the CEO of the brain. Students with AD/HD typically have deficits in these executive skills that interfere with their ability to do well in school. Practically speaking, many of the so-called "AD/HD behaviors" that teachers observe in the classroom, including forgetfulness, disorganization, and weak time management skills, are all linked to executive function deficits.

✓ **Deficits in working memory.** Students may have a limited capacity for holding information in mind, manipulating it, and then reorganizing it. This is a skill that is essential for writing essays or solving complex math problems.

✓ **Difficulty activating and maintaining effort.** Students may have difficulty getting started on tasks and sticking with them until the task is finished.

✓ **Impaired sense of time.** Students cannot accurately judge the passage of time. They may be late to school or class or unable to estimate how long a task will take to complete. Consequently, any assignment or long-term project with a due date in the distant future creates a disabling situation for these students.

✓ **Poor regulation of emotions.** Students may be more emotionally reactive so they are less likely to stop and think before they act or speak. Thus, they may impulsively talk back to teachers or get into fights at school. They have difficulty sticking with a task, especially if they become bored, and may give up more easily that their peers.

✓ **Difficulty using "self-talk" to control behavior.** Internalized speech is often delayed, which means these students are less likely to use self-talk to direct their behavior to complete future tasks or control their own behavior. They have trouble following rules, don't learn as easily from past mistakes, and often repeat misbehavior.

✓ **Difficulty analyzing, reconstituting, and problem solving.** Students may have problems with the complex problem solving required for critical tasks

9

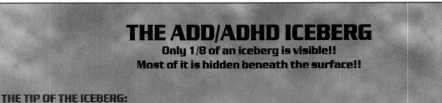

THE ADD/ADHD ICEBERG

Only 1/8 of an iceberg is visible!!
Most of it is hidden beneath the surface!!

THE TIP OF THE ICEBERG:
The Obvious ADD/ADHD Behaviors

IMPULSIVITY
Lacks self-control   Difficulty awaiting turn
Blurts out   Interrupts
Tells untruths   Intrudes
Talks back   Loses temper

HYPERACTIVITY
Restless   Talks a lot
Fidgets   Can't sit still
Runs or climbs a lot   Always on the go

INATTENTION
Disorganized   Doesn't follow through
Doesn't pay attention   Is forgetful
Doesn't seem to listen   Distractible
Makes careless mistakes   Loses things
Doesn't do school work

HIDDEN BENEATH THE SURFACE:
The Not So Obvious Behaviors!!

**NEUROTRANSMITTER DEFICITS
IMPACT BEHAVIOR**
Inefficient levels of neurotransmitters,
dpamine, norepinephrine, & serotonin,
result in reduced brain activity
on thinking tasks.

WEAK EXECUTIVE FUNCTIONING
Working Memory and Recall
Activation, Alertness, and Effort
Internalizing language
Controlling emotions
Complex Problem Solving

IMPAIRED SENSE OF TIME
Doesn't judge passage of time accurately
Loses track of time
Often late
Doesn't have skills to plan ahead
Forgets long-term projects or is late
Difficulty estimating time required for tasks
Difficulty planning for future
Impatient
Hates waiting
Time creeps
Homework takes forever
Avoids doing homework

SLEEP DISTURBANCE (56%)
Doesn't get restful sleep
Can't fall asleep
Can't wake up
Late for school
Sleeps in class
Sleep deprived
Irritable
Morning battles with parents

**30 PERCENT
DEVELOPMENTAL DELAY**
Less mature
Less responsible
18 yr. old acts like 12

**NOT LEARNING EASILY FROM
REWARDS AND PUNISHMENT**
Repeats misbehavior
May be difficult to discipline
Less likely to follow rules
Difficulty managing his own behavior
Doesn't study past behavior
Doesn't learn from past behavior
Acts without sense of hindsight
Must have immediate rewards
Long-term rewards don't work
Doesn't examine his own behavior
Difficulty changing his behavior

COEXISTING CONDITIONS
2/3 have at least one other condition
Anxiety (34%)   Depression (29%)
Bipolar (12%)   Substance Abuse (5-40%)
Tourette Disorder (11%)
Obsessive Compulsive Disorder (4%)
Oppositional Defiant Disorder (54-67%)
Conduct Disorder (22-43%)

SERIOUS LEARNING PROBLEMS (90%)
Specific Learning Disability (25-50%)
Poor working memory   Can't memorize easily
Forgets teacher and parent requests
Slow math calculation (26%)
Spelling Problems (24%)
Poor written expression (65%)
Difficulty writing essays
Slow retrieval of information
Poor listening and reading comprehension
Difficulty describing the world in words
Difficulty rapidly putting words together
Disorganization
Slow cognitive processing speed
Poor fine motor coordination
Poor handwriting
Inattention   Impulsive learning style

LOW FRUSTRATION TOLERANCE
Difficulty Controlling Emotions
Short fuse   Emotionally reactive
Loses temper easily
May give up more easily
Doesn't stick with things
Speaks or acts before thinking
Concerned with own feelings
Difficulty seeing others perspective
May be self-centered
May be selfish

* * * * * * * * * * * * *
ADD/ADHD is often more complex than most people realize!
Like icebergs, many problems related to ADD/ADHD are not visible. ADD/ADHD may be mild, moderate, or severe.
is likely to coexist with other conditions, and may be a disability for some students.

A Bird's Eye View of Life with ADD & ADHD   www.chrisdendy.com   © 2006 Alex Zeigler

Reprinted with the permission of Alex Zeigler and Chris A. Zeigler Dendy from *A Bird's Eye View of Life with ADD and ADHD.*

at school and in life. For example, their verbal fluency and ability to communicate clearly with others, write essays, sequence information, organize ideas, and solve complex math problems is often impaired.

Impairments in organizing, planning, and sequencing are especially noticeable in the school environment. These deficits create some of the most significant and least understood obstacles to successful school performance for students. While students may not have difficulty understanding the material or concepts presented, they can have great difficulty showing what they know or producing the work necessary to complete an assignment satisfactorily. Regardless of how smart the student is, these difficulties are common, often resulting in a poor work product.

Students with AD/HD may also lack basic academic skills. For instance, passive and inefficient study habits are common among these students.[7] These teens often experience problems in studying, memorizing, reading comprehension, paying attention to details in assignments, and writing in a clear, concise, and organized manner.

In addition, educators and parents must be alert to the danger of attributing these problems to the transition to middle or high school rather than to executive function deficits. Time eases many of the stresses associated with a new environment, but executive function deficits require proactive accommodations and instructional intervention. A particularly damaging assumption is reflected in the often-heard statements that students "should be able to do this by now" and "need to take more responsibility for their actions." Certainly, students with attention deficits must learn to take more responsibility, but this learning must occur in the context of their own developmental timetables. If students are not yet able "to do this by themselves," IDEA (Individuals with Disabilities Education Act) and Section 504 mandate the provision of supports and accommodations for eligible students.

Deficits in executive function may explain the often-heard lament from teachers and parents about these students: "He has such a high IQ. He could do better in school if he would just try." However, *having a high IQ score alone is not enough to succeed in school!* Hopefully, this information will help dispel the "laziness myth" that sometimes casts doubts on the good intentions of students with attention deficits.

Dr. Barkley provides us with both good and bad news about the development of these skills: executive functions don't fully mature until the student's early thirties. Although executive function does improve with age, the student's delays at the middle and high school levels are often too profound to overcome without help and understanding from teachers.

3. IMPACT OF DELAYED DEVELOPMENTAL SKILLS ON SCHOOL PERFORMANCE

Developmentally, teachers expect most teenagers to remember assignments, complete homework, submit it in a timely manner, and juggle long-term semester projects without frequent monitoring. Unfortunately, these youngsters experience a 30 percent delay in developmental skills, including executive functions that interfere with their ability to perform these developmentally appropriate tasks in a timely manner.[8] For teenagers, this delay often translates into a four to six year developmental lag that can adversely impact their ability to manage critical academic tasks. Although these teenagers can look and seem mature in some areas, their ability to organize, remember things, manage time, act responsibly, use self-care skills, use good social skills, and be self-aware typically are not as well-developed as in other students the same age.

Unsuspecting and uninformed teachers and parents are often dealing with the equivalent of a 9- or 10-year-old child in a 14-year-old freshman's body. Furthermore, the 11-year-old sixth grader who is trying to survive the transition to middle school is often more like a 7- or 8-year-old. This means that teacher expectations and the student's abilities are frequently on a collision course fraught with conflicts, incomplete work, and failing grades. Fortunately, more and more teachers and parents are recognizing that they must provide more supervision, not less, to middle and high school students who have attention deficits. After all,

9

The Top Five Challenging Behaviors in Middle and High School

Adapted from *Teaching Teens with ADD and ADHD and A Bird's Eye view of Life with ADD and ADHD*

Chris A. Zeigler Dendy, M.S.

The primary underlying causes of the academic struggles faced by students with AD/HD are often the very behaviors that comprise the official diagnostic criteria: inattention, disorganization, not completing work, not listening, losing things, forgetfulness, and, for some, talking a lot and blurting out answers. Not all students with attention deficits struggle with each of these challenges, but teachers should consider these issues when a student continues to struggle academically or behaviorally.

Below are the top five problems that middle and high school students with AD/HD face and intervention strategies to address them. Difficulty completing assignments in a timely manner is one of the most frequently heard teacher complaints. Parents express concerns about "zeros" received for incomplete homework, time impairment, and late evening announcements that a long-term semester project is due the next day.

Fortunately, academic and behavioral interventions that can help these students succeed in school are provided in Chapters 10 and 11. Chapter 10 provides more detail on the strategies included in this section. Chapter 5 also contains numerous suggestions for creating a proactive classroom or making changes to the environment to prevent or reduce behavioral problems. Several resources are listed in Appendix A that will help teachers implement these suggestions.

1) Not completing homework; forgetting assignments and projects

These students often forget assignments and books, to return completed work, to get papers signed, or to attend meetings or detention.

- ✓ *Post homework assignments* on the board.
- ✓ *Monitor an assignment book.*
- ✓ *Appoint "row captains" or a "homework buddy"* to pick up homework and check that assignments are recorded.
- ✓ *Intervene at the "point of performance."* Meet the student at the locker after school to ensure that assignments and the appropriate books are taken home.
- ✓ *Provide an extra book or set of textbooks for home.*
- ✓ *Determine whether homework assignments are too long.* Provide accommodations, such as extended time or shortened assignments.
- ✓ *Communicate regularly with parents of struggling students via:*
  - Homework "hotlines"
  - Teacher websites
  - E-mail or ask parents to e-mail the teacher
  - Weekly reports (See Appendices C.1, C.2, C.3, and C.4.)
  - Teacher phone calls or conferences

2) Not completing long-term projects

Students often forget about these assignments until the night before they are due. See resources for graphic organizers in Appendix A.

- ✓ *Modify assignments.*
  - Break down long-term assignments into two or three segments.
  - Give separate due dates and grades.
- ✓ *Provide organizational support and increased supervision.*
  - Notify parents of due dates.

CONTINUED ON PAGE 90

from a developmental perspective, *students with attention deficits actually **require more** supervision than their peers!*

The combination of the symptoms of AD/HD, executive function deficits, and developmental delays contribute to problems in these key areas:

✓ **Disorganization.** Students with attention deficits report having more difficulty keeping track of multiple things at the same time or prioritizing a list of various activities. The rapid movement of ideas throughout their brains is difficult to manage and coordinate into productive action. The disorganization can manifest in a messy desk or bedroom and often impacts all of their activities, including handwriting, planning, sequencing tasks, personal hygiene, and thinking.

✓ **Lag in maturity.** Students with attention deficits are challenged to make age-appropriate transitions at a socially acceptable pace. The inability to "act their age" can impact social relationships, their emotional well-being, and behavioral self-control.

✓ **Difficulty with self-monitoring.** This critical skill is needed to respond to social interactions with peers and adults. Students with attention deficits may not be able to accurately reflect upon their own behavior or make quick adjustments and change their behavior in difficult situations. This skill is one of the most difficult for these students to master and requires much practice over extended periods of time.

✓ **Accident-prone.** While half of all students with AD/HD have good motor skills, others struggle with impaired coordination that makes them appear clumsy. They are less likely to enjoy and succeed at sports and may be teased at school because of their awkwardness.

Teachers and parents alike want students to be more responsible and work well independently. But these students must be taught missing skills or compensatory strategies on a level that is commensurate with their younger developmental age.

4. IMPACT OF SLEEP PROBLEMS ON SCHOOL PERFORMANCE

Researchers tell us that teenagers need more sleep than any other age group — an average of 9.5 hours each night. Yet their innate tendency is to go to bed and get up later. Obviously, teens who are sleep-deprived can be more irritable and have greater difficulty concentrating in class.

Further compounding this already problematic situation, 56 percent of youngsters with AD/HD also have sleep disturbances — difficulty falling asleep and difficulty waking up.[9] So even when teens with an attention deficit go to bed on time, they may be unable to fall asleep easily. Dysfunction of the neurotransmitter serotonin is the suspected culprit for their sleep problems. In addition, teenagers with attention deficits often fail to get restful sleep; 55 percent wake up tired even after eight hours of sleep. Nationally, some school systems are *implementing later start times* to accommodate the unique developmental needs of teens.

Parents often complain that waking up their teen is a major source of conflict each morning. Regrettably, this can set the tone for the day — angry yelling followed by an irritable, frustrated teen rushing to get to school, hopefully, on time. Consequently, teachers face frustrated, irritable, sleep-deprived students who have already started their day on the "wrong foot." Unfortunately, many parents are unaware of the AD/HD link to sleep disturbances and instead blame laziness and irresponsibility for their morning confrontations. Even parents who understand the link become frustrated with the constant battle to get their teen up and out the door each morning.

Of additional significance, two experts on learning, Mel Levine, M.D.,[10] and Don Deshler, Ph.D.,[11] tell us that important information is often consolidated into memory during sleep. Lack of sleep impairs memory and the ability to concentrate so the profound importance of resolving any sleep issues for students should be apparent. By making parents aware of the link between attention deficits and sleep

9

The Top Five Challenging Behaviors in Middle and High School, Cont.

- List parental notification as an accommodation in the IEP or 504 Plan.
- Provide a graphic organizer that outlines the task.

✓ *Show completed model projects or reports.*

✓ *Teach skills, such as time management and organization.*

- Introduce a four-step planning process: plan, prioritize, schedule, and follow the plan.
- Teach students to develop graphic organizers.

3) Chronic disorganization

Students often lose their homework and other possessions because they are disorganized and forgetful.

✓ *Teach self-management skills,* such as compensatory strategies, problem solving, study skills, test taking strategies, anger management, and self-advocacy.

✓ *Teach organizational skills,* such as organizing schoolwork, notebooks, backpack, or locker.

- Use graphic organizers that outline academic tasks.
- Provide job cards to guide tasks.

✓ *Use technology,* such as a computer, PDA (Personal Digital Assistant), calculator, or spell and grammar checker.

4) Academic challenges

Twenty-five to fifty percent of students with AD/HD have learning disabilities that are often linked to their executive function deficits, especially limited working memory capacity. Specific teaching strategies are discussed in Chapter 10.

✓ *Provide direct instruction or teach compensatory strategies for academic deficits commonly found in these areas.*

- Written and verbal expression: difficulty writing essays and answering questions concisely in class
- Math computation: difficulty automating math facts such as multiplication tables
- Slow processing speed
- Slow retrieval of stored information
- Poor reading comprehension
- Poor spelling

✓ *Determine whether "limited working memory capacity" presents problems for the student.* A deficit in this area makes it extremely difficult for the student to hold information in mind while manipulating it for problem-solving purposes. Students often struggle with impaired written expression and lack problem-solving skills for complex math like Algebra. In addition, memorization of rote facts such as multiplication tables can be extremely difficult.

- Reduce memory demands.
  - Give visual cues and hands-on activities.
  - Break down tasks into smaller segments.
  - Provide a notetaker.
  - Reduce the amount of written work required, for example, by shortening assignments.
  - Use an overhead projector or Powerpoint for teaching.
  - Use supportive technology, such as computers or calculators.
- Provide organizational supports.
  - Use graphic organizers that outline the task.
  - Provide step-by-step job cards.
  - Use computer software such as Inspiration.

CONTINUED ON PAGE 91

The Top Five Challenging Behaviors in Middle and High School, Cont.

- – Provide teacher aides or peer tutors.
- – Monitor assignments more closely.
- Teach memory strategies.
  - – Use mnemonics, visual cues, hands-on activities, and color cues.
- Externalize prompts.
  - – Use visual posting: post key facts in large print on colorful poster board on the walls. Remove the information on test day.[a]

5) Impaired sense of time

Many students cannot accurately judge the passage of time. Consequently, they are often late to school or class. They also have difficulty estimating the time required to complete assignments. See time management resources in Appendix A.

- ✓ *Teach compensatory skills and externalize prompts.*
  - Make time, an abstract concept, concrete either visually or audibly.
    - – Use timers, wrist watch alarms, computer alarms, "talking timers," Time Timers© (portray the passage of time visually), sticky notes, and personal reminders.
- ✓ *Teach skills.*
  - Teach time management.
  - Use a timer to practice estimating the time it takes to complete homework. First, estimate the time it will take to complete. Then record the actual time required for completion.

problems and suggesting that parents talk with their physician, educators can often help families resolve this major roadblock to academic success. Suggestions for addressing this sleep problem, such as establishing a good sleep routine, drinking milk, taking a hot shower, and listening to music, are provided in *Teenagers with ADD and ADHD* and *A Bird's-Eye View of Life with ADD and ADHD*.

In summary, *the increased demands* at the middle and high school level often make the student's AD/HD, executive deficits, coexisting conditions, and developmental delays more obvious during the teenage years. These students have more classes, more teachers, more challenging academic work, increased homework, and increased demands for strong executive function skills, such as being organized and working independently. The demands often feel overwhelming to the student with an attention deficit who is lagging behind his peers developmentally.

Furthermore, if educators observe students who are receiving treatment for their attention deficit disorder yet are still struggling, the overall treatment and academic plans are not working properly and must be revised. Researchers suggests educators and parents investigate these common culprits:

1) Unidentified executive functions deficits
2) Unidentified coexisting conditions, such as a learning disability, anxiety, depression, or sleep disturbances
3) Medication doses that are too low or occasionally too high to provide peak academic performance

Schools can identify learning disabilities or executive function deficits but must encourage families to speak with their family physician about coexisting disorders or proper doses of medication. Chapter 1 provides additional information on these important issues.

B. Academic Challenges

1. COMMON LEARNING PROBLEMS

Middle and high school students with attention deficits often experience the greatest impairment in several key areas: *a) written expression, b) math computation, c) working memory, d) memorization, e) time management and time estimation, and f) organizational skills and planning ahead.* Additional information on common learning problems among students with AD/HD and intervention strategies are discussed in Chapters 3 and 4.

Specific Learning Disabilities. Research has shown that 25 to 50 percent of students with attention deficits meet the criteria for a specific learning disability.[12] Several other learning disabilities can coexist with the attention deficit: *spelling (12 to 27 percent); reading (8 to 39 percent); and math (12 to 30 percent), especially with math calculation and fluency with math facts.*

Also of interest to educators, roughly 50 to 65 percent of students with AD/HD and SLD have written expression problems.[13] Impairments in working, short-term, and long-term memory can interfere with their written expression skills. Writing tasks require attention to a myriad of issues, such as handwriting, spacing, spelling, punctuation, and grammar, which are often dependent on strong executive function skills. Students must also formulate their thoughts into complete sentences, keep those thoughts in mind while they struggle with the mechanics of writing, and organize their ideas to form coherent paragraphs and longer reports. The cognitive demands of attending to all these details can be overwhelming for a student with an attention deficit.

These students can have wonderful ideas but tend to have great difficulty getting those ideas on paper. Brief responses of only a few sentences may be common when writing an essay or answering essay questions on tests. Responses may also contain disorganized, unrelated, and unfocused ideas in one paragraph. Obviously, these students may have greater difficulty and require more time for reports, essays, or essay exams. However, simply giving these students more time may not be sufficient. They may also need more structure than their peers.

2. COMMON REASONS FOR SCHOOL FAILURE

Several key reasons for school failure, including failure to complete homework and long-term projects, were listed at the beginning of this chapter. Many of these academic struggles are related to executive function deficits and, for some students, slow processing speed, which manifests in slow reading, writing, and test completion. Because of their many learning challenges, some students lack confidence and experience test anxiety that further undermines their test performance.

Unfortunately, some teachers are unaware of the complexity of attention deficit disorder and the serious learning challenges middle and high school students face when completing seemingly "simple" school work. The student's need for extra support is often difficult to accept, even for teachers who are familiar with the challenges of attention disorders. Teachers may wonder whether they are doing students a disservice by "coddling" them. But in reality, these students must have these extra supports if they are to be successful. Unfortunately, middle and high school teachers feel the pressure of preparing students to enter the "real world" in only a few short years and are often overburdened with the responsibility of teaching 120 to 150 students per day.

Parents, teachers, and students must work together to balance the push for greater independence with the need for instructional and environmental support. Over time, some supports can be phased out, as the student matures and masters more skills. However, unlike other students, these teenagers may always need supports to address a few AD/HD-related issues that do not improve significantly with time, for example, extended time on tests or shortened assignments to accommodate their slow processing speed and limited working memory capacity.

C. Social Challenges

According to researchers, roughly 50 to 60 percent of children with AD/HD have difficulty with peer relationships. Students with AD/HD inattentive often have fewer problems maintaining friendships. Students with AD/HD often have difficulty making and keeping friends due to their lack of basic social skills.[14] Some students with AD/HD impulsively say or do things that cause other students to dislike or avoid them. Teaching social skills to most of these students is very difficult because they don't always use the skills when they are needed. This type of training may be more helpful to students with AD/HD inattentive who are shy or anxious. Specific strategies for improving social skills are provided in Chapter 12.

Unfortunately, these social problems can get worse in middle school, where students are also struggling with hormonal changes and increased teacher expectations. In addition, other developmental challenges are occurring: establishing relationships with members of the opposite sex, avoiding the temptation to experiment with illegal drugs, and learning to drive safely. In truth, problems with social skills are a lifelong challenge for many individuals with AD/HD.

The more complex environment of middle and high school can also be challenging. Just understanding how to fit in and be accepted by other middle school students is difficult. Students with attention deficits may be targeted by bullies or excluded from social events or teams. Students must adapt to multiple teachers, who may have different rules and expectations. In addition, some middle schools lack the carpeting that softens noise levels in elementary schools, thus increasing environmental distractions.

A true middle school places students and teachers in teams to ease the transition for all students. However, even a team of four teachers and a hundred students can be overwhelming for students with attention deficits. Visiting the new school during the summer helps familiarize students with the layout of the school, the location of their classes, and perhaps the names of a few teachers, easing the transition to middle or high school.

D. Unique Challenges In Middle School (Ann B. Welch, Ph.D.)

Although middle and high school students with attention disorders share some common academic challenges, there are also significant differences. Often the first hint of major academic problems among students with attention deficits occurs when they enter middle school. In fact, parents often say, "It's like my child hit a brick wall in middle school." The transitions to middle and high school are challenging for almost all students, but the challenge is magnified for students with AD/HD. Prior to that time, some of these students have been sheltered from the more negative consequences associated with the disorder by elementary school teachers who provided needed structure, encouragement, and support.

As they enter middle school, some students whose attention disorder has not yet been diagnosed become obvious. Bright students or students who are especially eager to do well in school (frequently girls) may have worked hard to compensate and had extra support from parents so they were able to make it through elementary school undetected. But the demands beginning in middle school are often too much for them to overcome and expose the previously undiagnosed attention disorder. Additionally, increased demands for strong social skills in middle school expose another weakness for children with AD/HD.

Middle school is the first year of their exposure to increased demands for academic performance, using complex executive function skills, working independently, changing classrooms, and working with several teachers with different personalities, expectations, and teaching styles.

Teachers must also take into consideration that an 11-year-old sixth grader with an attention deficit can be more like a 7- or 8-year old when it comes to executive functions, especially key organizational skills. This discrepancy is frustrating for students as well as teachers. For example, the student reads on grade level but has trouble finding his classroom. Physically, he looks mature but still exhibits chronic disorganization.

9

Common middle school fears, such as being unable to open a locker or remember a lunch code in the cafeteria, are exacerbated for these students. One mother discovered much to her horror that her son had not had lunch in weeks because he forgot his lunch code.

E. Unique Challenges Facing Teenage Girls (Joan Helbing, M.Ed.)

AD/HD is often overlooked in girls because they are less likely to be discipline problems at school. Unfortunately, they can be misdiagnosed with anxiety or depression. Although girls may not cause as many discipline problems as boys, the problems they face are just as serious. Girls with attention deficits are more likely than boys to struggle with impaired social skills, be emotionally reactive, or at times underreactive. In addition, girls are often faced with the roller-coaster symptoms of PMS. They may be emotionally intense, "throwing tantrums," having "meltdowns" and refusals at a much higher rate than their peers. Girls must also juggle societal expectations that they should be compliant, controlled, passive, dressed neatly, and sensitive to feelings of others. Experts tell us that failure to comply with societal expectations and misbehavior in girls are viewed more negatively than the same behavior in boys. As a result of these demands, girls can experience significant self-blame, low self-esteem, demoralization, anxiety, and depression. If girls are to grow up and reach their full potential, early diagnosis and treatment are critical.

IMPACT AT SCHOOL AND HOME

AD/HD in girls impacts every aspect of their lives. At school, many of these girls are eager to please and may appear to "keep things together." Since research is lacking, our best information about girls comes from Patricia Quinn, M.D., and Kathleen Nadeau, Ph.D., who offer several important observations about girls based upon their extensive clinical experience.[15] For example, girls typically work harder to hide their academic difficulties and to conform to teacher expectations. They may put in long hours to complete work that other students can complete in 30 minutes to an hour. At home, they can be overreactive to parents and siblings.

Studies conducted on girls with AD/HD show these young women have greater intellectual impairment but lower rates of hyperactivity and externalizing disorders, such as oppositional defiant or conduct disorder, compared to boys with AD/HD.[16] Because of these differences, girls may not be referred for AD/HD assessment when problems do exist. Finally, when problems are severe, parents may seek advice from a professional outside the school.

Girls with more serious AD/HD combined type who are referred to clinics have similar problems as boys, including coexisting disorders, core AD/HD symptoms, impaired psychological functioning, and a family history of mental health problems, and do not differ on measures of inattention, internalizing problems, such as anxiety or depression, and peer aggression. Girls have more problems in reading and more difficulties with inattention than boys. Furthermore, referred girls were a more extreme sample than were the boys, with higher rates of AD/HD in the family. Stimulant medications work as well for girls as they do for boys. See Chapter 2, "More about AD/HD in Girls," for more information.

According to research conducted at Harvard, girls seen by pediatricians and psychiatrists are more likely to show conduct problems, mood and anxiety disorders, a lower IQ, and more impairment on social, family and school functioning than non-referred girls.[17] Girls in this study had high rates of substance abuse disorders, including alcohol, drug and cigarette use, and were at higher risk for panic and obsessive compulsive disorders than boys with AD/HD.

IMPAIRED SOCIAL SKILLS

While impaired social skills are not included in the official DSM-IV diagnostic criteria for AD/HD, it is one of the major challenges facing girls with AD/HD. Society demands that girls interact socially and be adept at the skills needed to initiate, develop, and maintain friendships. This pressure can cause more missed cues, especially when feelings are strong. Girls with attention deficits often report that they have a sense of "never belonging" because they are aware of their "different-ness" but are powerless to monitor it well or change it. The need for peer acceptance is so intense, girls may engage in dangerous or self-destructive behaviors. Some girls with AD/HD inattentive can be socially with-drawn while those with AD/HD hyperactive-impulsive or combined can be louder and bossier. These personal-ity traits are not conducive to healthy friendships. See Chapter 12 for more information on social skills.

ADDITIONAL CHALLENGES

Researchers report that girls with AD/HD had more depression and anxiety, lower self-esteem, and higher overall symptoms of distress and stress.[23] Girls in the study reported strained relationships with teachers, thoughts about committing suicide, and expressing their stress by engaging in episodes of self-harm. Com-pared to boys, girls reported higher rates of overall dis-tress, anxiety, depression, being controlled by the events of the moment, hyperactivity, conduct problems, and cognitive deficits. Girls feel and report more distress than boys because they "may be more affected by environmental factors than males with ADHD."[18] Girls in this study had higher rates of AD/HD predomi-nantly inattentive type.

Like boys, girls with AD/HD can be very disor-ganized, underachieve in school, experience sleep problems, and have poor motor coordination. Restless-ness during the teen years can take the form of gum chewing, sucking on candy, chewing ice cubes, and, playing with hair or jewelry. Some girls demonstrate compulsive behaviors around organization perhaps in part because of their high anxiety. In other words, they can be extremely compulsive in their efforts to bring some calm to their chaos. Several other areas that can pose significant challenges and impact their success at home and school and in the community include:

✓ **PMS.** Many girls with attention deficits experience a substantial increase in their hypersensitivity and emotionality before and/or during their menstrual period. These hormonal fluctuations can result in mood swings, extreme irritability, and emotional overreaction.

✓ **Emotional Lability.** Girls with AD/HD are often described as either overreactive or underreactive rel-ative to their emotional control. For many, their dis-appointments and frustrations are often internalized rather than acted out, and they may hyperfocus on their mistakes. Shame can become an emotion that is all too familiar relative to how they think of themselves, and girls with AD/HD are often viewed by parents and teachers as emotionally very needy.

An informal checklist developed by Drs. Nadeau and Quinn can be used as a way to gather information from girls. While this material cannot be used for diag-nostic purposes, it helps identify areas of difficulty and can lead to a referral to a professional for formal evalu-ation. The checklist is available on their website, http://www.addvance.com. Additional information is also available from the National Center on Gender Issues and AD/HD at http://www.ncgiadd.org.

The symptoms of AD/HD are chronic and severe for many girls but can wax and wane depending on other factors. The negative self-evaluation that many girls continually experience can produce social, emo-tional, and academic problems. These lingering nega-tive effects continue to grow and "take on a life of their own" as these girls get older. Providing a safe and nurturing school environment can help girls with attention deficits not only survive but also flourish.

F. Unique Medication Challenges for Teenagers

Although, professionally and legally, teachers should have no involvement whatsoever in medication issues, medication's profound impact on students' academic performance cannot be ignored. Teachers must have at least a basic knowledge of medication so that they can spot problems that could potentially interfere with learning. Stimulant medications that are prescribed for children are also effective for teenagers and adults with attention deficits. Typically, these medications are often the cornerstone of treatment regardless of the person's age. More detailed information on medications is available in Chapter 1.

9

Several unique medication challenges exist in middle and high school. For example, medication effectiveness often decreases due to growth and hormonal changes. Consequently, a change or increase in medication may be necessary. In addition, some teens refuse to take their medicine or forget to take their medicine, which is sometimes mistaken for medication refusal. Friends may also pressure these teens to "share" their medicine.

G. General Suggestions for Middle and High School Teachers

Teachers may find the following suggestions effective in helping students with attention deficit disorder succeed in school.

✓ Involve the teenager as a *respected partner* in the development of an educational plan and the learning process.

✓ *Provide AD/HD education* through books, videos, youth panel discussions, and individual and group discussions.
  – The students in one special education class in New Hampshire created their own book on AD/HD, complete with scientific facts, cartoons, and advice from students for problem solving. The finished book was distributed to all school administrators and teachers.

✓ Identify learning problems, including executive function deficits, and *provide accommodations*.

✓ *Adjust expectations* so that they are realistic for the student's four to six year developmental delay.

✓ Expect to *provide more supervision* than would ordinarily be provided for this age group.

✓ *Give parents permission to be involved* in the supervision of homework. When parents are interested and willing, teach them skills to coach their teenager and monitor school work when needed.

✓ *Don't be surprised* when these students forget assignments, books, or homework. Remember that forgetfulness is one of the diagnostic criteria for AD/HD. This is not to say these behaviors are acceptable and teachers should ignore them.

✓ *Teach students the academic and behavioral skills* they need to compensate or support them by giving prompts such as those described in Chapters 10 and 11.
  – Self-management skills such as time management, organizational skills, study skills, anger management, prosocial skills, self-advocacy, and social skills.
  – Self-monitoring strategies such as listening to a beep or tone and marking whether one is on task, which is described in Chapter 8.
  – *Teach students new skills* at the *"point of performance,"* or the specific situation where students actually need the skill.
    • Keep in mind that teaching these skills does not guarantee that the student will use them appropriately all of the time. Typically, failure to use these skills at appropriate times occurs not because they are choosing to be difficult, but because they lack the necessary executive function skills.
  – *Understand the impact of medication on school performance.* Students who forget to take their medication in the morning cannot concentrate in class. Some medications can take an hour to become effective, so if a student takes medication walking out the door to school, the medication may not take effect until halfway through first period. Conversely, medication may no longer be effective during the evening when students are attempting to do their homework.

The school years often represent the most difficult years for someone with an attention deficit disorder. But it is important to remember that the characteristics of AD/HD that may not be valued in school — when reframed positively as high energy, creative thinking, a sense of humor, and tenacity — are often valued in the adult work world. The ultimate goal for both teachers and parents is to help students maximize their talents, find their niche in our society, and enjoy happy, productive lives.

CHAPTER 10

Specific Instructional Strategies for Common Learning Problems

Chris A. Zeigler Dendy, M.S.

Adapted from *Teaching Teens with ADD and ADHD*

T he same teaching strategies that are effective for students with AD/HD are effective for all students. The use of teaching strategies that involve multiple senses, especially the provision of visual cues and hands-on activities and direct instruction in academics and organizational strategies, is more likely to help these students achieve academic success.

Researchers are increasingly recognizing the importance of addressing academic deficits to correct behavior problems. George DuPaul, Ph.D., a leading researcher on learning issues and AD/HD at Lehigh University, has found that focusing on learning improves both academic performance and behavior.[1] However, the converse is rarely true. So by focusing on academic issues first, teachers should see improvements in both schoolwork and behavior.

Academic achievement is also associated with positive relationships with peers, teachers, and parents.[2] According to Marc Atkins, Ph.D., of the University of Chicago, "academic interventions improve children's social and emotional function, often rivaling the benefits seen from psychosocial interventions like counseling and skills training."[3]

Specific teaching strategies for secondary students with attention deficits and multiple learning problems are discussed in this chapter. These suggestions include modification of teaching methods, assignments and testing and grading, provision of increased support and supervision, and increased use of technology. Age-appropriate suggestions for accommodations are also provided. The overview of effective intervention strategies and accommodations in Chapters 4 and 5 can also be helpful. Additional intervention strategies are available in the "Top Five Common Challenging AD/HD Behaviors" for this age group (Chapter 9). Several resources are listed in Appendix A that will help you implement these suggested intervention strategies.

Major deficits discussed in Chapters 9 to 11 should be noted in the student's IEP or 504 plan along with specific intervention strategies. This applies not only to deficits in academics, but also deficits in organization, time management, behavioral control, and social skills.

Arthur Robin, Ph.D., a psychologist specializing in treating adolescents with AD/HD, reminds us that finding a student's strengths and talents is also critical.[4] Building on these strengths is essential for both academic and behavioral interventions. Teaching key skills and compensatory strategies, providing encouragement and positive feedback, and believing in the student's ability to succeed are invaluable elements of an effective educational plan.

Effective Teaching Strategies for Secondary Level Students

1. MODIFY TEACHING METHODS.

Students with attention deficits often have *limited working memory capacity, difficulty storing and retrieving information from long-term memory, difficulty organizing and sequencing information, and difficulty planning ahead.* Several general principles can enhance the effectiveness of teaching this group of students.

✓ **Use visual cues and hands-on activities.** Teachers may find that by using more visual cues and hands-on activities, students are more likely to retain information, follow the rules, and meet teacher expectations.

✓ **Reduce demands on memory.** Since these students often have *difficulty analyzing, organizing and remembering information,* they may struggle with written essays, complex math problems, and long-term projects. So it is very important to *reduce demands* on their already limited memory capacity.

✓ **Provide assistance with organization and problem solving.** Two key deficits related to executive function also cause problems for this age student: a) disorganization and b) weak problem-solving skills necessary for analysis of an assignment and the subsequent sequencing and synthesis required for completion of the work.

✓ **Offer direct instruction.** In other words, *teaching specific learning strategies or skills* is essential to the academic success of many of these students. Don Deshler, Ph.D., gives excellent tips for teaching strategies for *reading, writing (including paraphrasing and summarizing), memory, test taking, notetaking, math, and social skills in Teaching Adolescents with Learning Disabilities*[5] These strategies are very effective — for example, the grades of students who are taught test-taking skills show, on average, a 10-point improvement in their grades. Direct instruc-

tion of organizational, time management, memory strategies, and study skills is also critical.[6,7]

✓ **Externalize prompts.** Russell A. Barkley, Ph.D., suggests *"externalizing prompts"* to help students compensate for their deficits in several areas: memorization, time awareness, written expression, complex problem solving, and disorganization. Several specific strategies based on these five principles can be helpful, including the use of graphic organizers, sticky notes, alarm watches, and personal reminders. When learning an abstract concept such as time awareness, the student can actually "see the passage of time" with an external prompt such as a timer or clock, especially a colorful one like the Time Timer©.

✓ **Other effective teaching strategies include:**

- *"Keeping the rules in view"* is a good example of providing visual cues.[8] Since students with AD/HD have deficits in "following the rules," anything that reminds them of a behavioral or academic rule or teacher expectations reduces the need to retrieve the rule from memory.

- *Leave written step-by-step problem examples on the board.*

- *Use an overhead projector.* This teaching tool allows the teacher to "model" a new skill, such as how to write an essay. Then students are asked to practice that same task for class or homework. Some teachers find it helpful to cover the unused portion of the transparency so as not to overwhelm or confuse students.

- *Use a pointer.* Using a pointer tool to emphasize important information can benefit students with AD/HD.

- *Cue the student on key points.* These students often have difficulty picking out key points so be direct. Tell the student, "This is important; write this down."

- *Use graphic organizers* that give both visual cues and organizational guidance.[9] For example, provide an outline of the major components of essay writing. A few sources for graphic organizers are listed in Appendix A.

- *Show model reports or projects.* The overall quality of long-term projects improves when students observe examples of excellent projects. Some teachers show examples of reports that earned grades of A, B, C, and F.
- *Provide job cards.* Some teachers give job cards that list the four or five major steps required to complete a task.
- *Break down tasks* such as essay writing into their component parts and *offer practice* opportunities until each skill is mastered.
- *Provide teacher aides or peer tutors.* These students tend to do well with one-on-one instruction.
- *Allow students to tutor other students.* Having the student explain the information to someone else is an excellent way to help him understand material.
- *Increase class participation* through different *group response* techniques, such as hand signals, response cards, and writing answers on dry erase boards so they can be displayed easily for the teacher.[10]
  - *Writing on dry erase boards* can also increase a student's willingness to attempt difficult work because mistakes can be erased quickly and easily.
- *Use color* to help students learn material and correct errors.[11] Some teachers report highlighting each step of a math problem in a different color can be helpful.
- *Teach self-management strategies.*
  - Introduce strategies for memorization. Dr. Deshler provides several suggestions for helping students memorize information and retain it in long-term memory more effectively:[12]
    1. Link episodic and semantic information. For example, link words with pictures or events, give visual cues, or provide hands-on activities.
    2. Connect new information to prior knowledge.
    3. Elaborate on new information.
    4. Learn mnemonics or memory tricks, such as music and rhyming phrases.
    5. Organize key information in a logical concise manner. For example, use graphic organizers or notes provided by the teacher.
- *Teach organizational, study, test taking, time management, and self-advocacy strategies.* Introducing traditional four-step time management skills similar to those of Stephen Covey can be very helpful.[13] Specific tips on teaching time management, which are provided in *Teaching Teens with ADD and ADHD,* include:
  - Plan, prioritize, schedule, and follow the plan.
  - Schedule work on a timeline, going backwards from the due date.

✓ **Teach the appropriate use of technology** as described in Section E.

✓ **Educate students about their AD/HD.** Books and videos, such as those in Appendix A, can be helpful.

2. MODIFY ASSIGNMENTS.

Students with an attention deficit can have difficulties with *verbal expression, slow processing speed, and fine motor coordination* that slow down the production of written work. These deficits have significant implications for notetaking and class and homework assignments. Many of these students cannot complete their work as quickly as their peers and ultimately *produce less written work* in the same period of time as their classmates! A student with AD/HD can spend an hour or more on assignments that other students complete in 30 minutes. Some students also have difficulty *listening to a teacher, identifying key points, and taking notes at the same time.* Those students with attention deficits who experience these challenges benefit from, having a notetaker, shorter assignments, and extra time to complete homework and projects.

Sydney Zentall, Ph.D., and Sam Goldstein, Ph.D., have found that most teachers underestimate how long students with learning problems take to complete homework.[14] For example, a teacher may assign home-work that requires 30 minutes to an hour to complete. For students with AD/HD, that assignment may require two hours — or more — to finish. These researchers also report that students often avoid homework because it is *1) too long* or *2) too difficult for their present level.* Drs. Goldberg and Zentall suggest this strategy to *determine whether the amount of homework is appropriate:* the teacher writes down how long the homework should take; the student and parents report back how long the assignment actually took to complete; and then the two times are compared. If there is a large discrepancy, then the assignments should be shortened.

Assigning reasonable amounts of homework is critical. Recommendations in a joint statement from the National Parent Teacher Association (PTA) and National Education Association (NEA) suggest that students in elementary and middle school spend *approximately 10 minutes per grade per night on homework* for all subjects.[15] Of course, the amount of homework in high school can vary by subject, but generally speaking, ninth graders should spend a total of roughly 90 minutes an evening on all their homework assignments.

Teachers can *reduce the amount of written work* in several ways without compromising the amount of academic material mastered:

✓ **Shorten class and homework assignments.** If assignments are not reduced to a reasonable length, students will begin avoiding homework.

✓ **Allow students to write down only the correct answers** (not the question).

✓ **Photocopy questions** and have the student write the answers on the paper.

✓ **Offer alternative activities involving other forms of expression,** such as recording a book report on video or audiotape.

✓ **Give tips on notetaking.** Teach students strategies for notetaking, such as taking notes in two columns. Draw a line down the page, dividing the paper into sections. Then write the main idea in the left-hand column and the supporting details in the right-hand column.

✓ **Teach shorthand.** Show students how to take notes in the form of shorthand, substituting symbols for some words. Unfortunately, this may not work for some students since memorizing the shorthand symbols can be difficult. However, all students should learn a few common abbreviations to facilitate accurate recording of assignments in their planners.

✓ **Provide a notetaker.** Sometimes teachers select a *notetaker* for several students, ask the notetaker to make copies of the day's notes, and then make notes available to any interested student. If the school provides NCR paper, the notetaker keeps the top copy, the second copy is kept in a class-room binder, available for viewing or copying by any student, and the third copy is sent to the special education department. Special education teachers can provide more effective support when they have access to the complete notes for each class. Some students with attention deficits pay attention better when they take notes as best they can, in addition to using the notetaker's class notes.

✓ **Offer outlines and study guides.** Some teachers give outlines, study guides, and long-term assignments in advance to parents of children who are struggling academically. Outlines and study guides help students clearly identify key information to study.

Long-term assignments are especially troublesome for students with AD/HD. Their *forgetfulness, impaired sense of time, limited organizational skills,* and *difficulty planning ahead* make it extremely difficult to complete these assignments in a timely manner. On researcher reports that the time lag between the assignment and due date creates a disability for these students.[16]

1. *Provide organizational support.*

   a. *Break down long-term assignments into two or three segments.* Some of these students are overwhelmed by long-term projects. By breaking the project into segments, the teacher provides the student with a better understanding of how to a) analyze the problem, b) know where to start, and c) identify the steps to complete a project.

b. *Give separate due dates and grades.* Students often lack the ability to estimate the amount of time required to complete a project and don't know how to schedule a timeline backward to know when they must begin working. As a result, they often put off the work until the last minute and are more likely to totally forget the project or complete it hurriedly in an unsatisfactory manner.

c. *Notify parents of due dates.* Parents often like to be *notified in advance of any major projects* so that their teenager doesn't come home on a Thursday night and say, "By the way, Mom, my semester project is due tomorrow."

   i. *List parental notification as an accommodation.* If the student has an IEP or 504 plan, advance notice of tests and long-term projects is a very helpful accommodation.

d. *Provide a graphic organizer.* Showing students how to use a *graphic organizer for a long-term project,* such as the one described in *Teaching Teens with ADD and ADHD,* provides important structure and guidance. In addition, teachers can also create graphic organizers that are appropriate for their specific subject matter.[17] (These resources are listed in Appendix A.) Once a student learns how to use any graphic organizer, providing the same organizer for a later assignment reminds students of the recommended or required structure.

   i. *Teach students to develop graphic organizers.* Some teachers have taught their students how to make their own graphic organizers.

3. MODIFY TESTING AND GRADING.

Some students with attention deficits experience serious learning deficits that interfere with their ability to 1) *complete class and homework in a timely manner* and 2) *accurately reflect their knowledge and skills on timed essays and tests.* For example, weak *verbal expression skills, slow processing speed, and poor fine motor coordination* often interfere with the ability to rapidly get ideas down on paper. Furthermore, limited *working memory* capacity makes it difficult for them to hold information (math facts or thoughts that must be organized into paragraphs) in their heads while problem solving or writing a composition. As part of their verbal expression deficits, these students can also struggle with *rapid retrieval of information* stored in long-term memory, such as grammar and spelling rules when polishing a final essay.

✓ **Give extended time on assignments and tests.** Students with attention deficits in middle and high school often say that *extended time on tests and some assignments* is one of the most helpful *accommodations* they receive. One student who completed a standardized test within the usual time limit said that just knowing extra time was available enabled her to complete the test within the usual time limit.

✓ **Modify test style.** Some students find that tests involving *recognition skills* rather than cold recall of facts can more accurately reflect their mastery of information — *multiple choice, true/false, fill-in-the-blank, and word banks* instead of essay exams. Those students with serious written expression problems may require oral exams.

✓ **Request accommodations on state tests.** Eligible students can also be given *accommodations during special testing* situations, such as state academic achievement tests, competency exams for graduation, and college entrance tests (SAT and ACT). Clearly, testing accommodations minimize the impact of the disability to "level the playing field," not simply to help a student perform better on the tests. The necessary accommodations should be stated in the IEP or 504 plan.

✓ **Adjust grading system.** Some teachers *adjust grading techniques* by allowing students to:

   • *Drop their lowest grade or earn extra credit,* especially when they are in danger of failing, yet seem to understand the material.

- *Submit homework late for credit*. If students turn in homework late, allow them to *do the make-up work for full credit.*
- *Reduce the amount of make-up work*. Some teachers allow students to do *reduced amounts of make-up work* until they are caught up. Otherwise, these students can become so discouraged and overwhelmed that they simply give up.
- *Implement a correction plan*. However, to ensure that homework is completed in the future, simultaneously *institute a plan,* such as using a *weekly report,* to monitor and correct the homework problem.

A Parent's Perspective on Homework. Parents often have serious concerns about just how far to push their frustrated, and sometimes depressed, teens to complete their homework. Data on suicide does give them pause for concern. In one study, 10 percent of youngsters with AD/HD attempted suicide while none of the non-AD/HD youth in this study ever made an attempt.[18]

Give parents some control. After many evenings of tears and screaming fights, one Texas parent and special education consultant came up with a unique solution to this problem. The parents and school agreed to include a statement in the teenager's IEP that parents would *"determine when enough homework was enough,"* even if the assignment was not complete. Anticipate occasions when these teens become so overwhelmed that they can be pushed no further.

4. INCREASE SUPPORT AND SUPERVISION.
The four to six year developmental delay often associated with AD/HD in middle and high schoolers necessitates *more supervision and support* than would ordinarily be expected for these students. If students are expected to cope successfully with problems related to executive function deficits, such as *disorganization, forgotten assignments, limited memory capacity, and incomplete homework,* extra support and supervision are critical. Utilization of effective classroom management strategies like those in Chapter 5 and those recom-

mended by others like Robert Reid, Ph.D., University of Nebraska at Lincoln, are also effective.[19]

✓ **Monitor an assignment book.** For some students with attention deficits, simply monitoring an assignment book on a daily basis corrects problems with homework completion. However, many others need additional support.

✓ **Recruit others to help.** Some teachers use creative strategies to increase supervision without making extra work for themselves. For example, teachers can recruit other students or adults to help these teenagers in a variety of ways.

- *Row captains*. As Clare B. Jones, Ph.D., suggests, teachers can appoint *"row captains"* who pick up homework each day and check that all students have written down their homework assignments.[20]
- *Homework buddy*. A "homework buddy" can check that the student has recorded homework correctly.
- *Organizational coach*. A close friend, peer tutor, or teacher aide can *meet the student* at the locker after school to ensure the student takes home assignments and the correct books. This intensive level of support is only used when a student is failing or consistently not turning in assignments. Later, after the student masters the skill, the level of supervision can be reduced.
  - One parent *paid a high school senior* to meet her freshman daughter at her locker each day to organize homework materials.
- *School counselors*. The student can *stop by the counselor's office* after school for a calendar check and possibly a reward.
- *Parents*. Parents can *monitor the assignment book and homework completion* on a daily basis.
- *Students*. Some students with attention deficits *carry everything in their backpacks,* preferring a heavy backpack to the dangers of leaving necessary materials in their lockers.

✓ **Hire a tutor.** All teenagers want to be less dependent on their parents. Some, especially those with AD/HD, can be resistant to parental "interfer-

ence" regarding homework. If homework battles erupt frequently, parents can consider *hiring someone else* to provide afterschool tutoring or homework supervision to remove the homework battle from the parent-child relationship.

School-Home Communication. Communication between school and home is essential to the academic success of these children. Several strategies can be helpful:

1. **Weekly reports.** Weekly reports monitored by both teachers and parents are extremely effective with these students. Daily reports may be necessary for some students. Home-school contracts may also be helpful in clearly stating expectations for the student, parent, and teacher.[21] See Appendices C.3 and C.4 for sample weekly reports. Detailed guidelines for establishing a school-home daily report card are available from the Center for Children and Families at the State University of New York at Buffalo *Summer Treatment Program* website, http://www.wings.buffalo.edu/adhd.

2. **Homework hotlines.** Schools may provide *homework "hotlines"* where teachers record the homework each day and any student can call in to get it.

3. **Teacher website.** Individual teachers can establish a website where the daily assignments are listed.

4. **E-mail.** Teachers can *e-mail updated information* to parents about assignment completion or better yet, ask parents to e-mail them each week so teachers only have to reply to the e-mail.

5. **Post assignments.** Teachers can *post assignments* for an entire week in a specific place at the front of the room.

   a. One teacher posted homework assignments in the *classroom window, facing out,* for a nearby student who chronically forgot his assignments.

6. **Extra books.** An *extra book or set of textbooks* at home can be the easiest way to ensure that students have the necessary materials.

7. **Electronic communication.** One innovative program, *MyADHD.com,* enables stakeholders, such as parents, educators, health care providers, and adults with AD/HD, to stay connected with one another. This website contains dozens of behavior rating scales (in English and Spanish) and history forms that can be completed electronically and stored in the subscriber's secure private account. A doctor, for example, can send a rating scale to a teacher via e-mail for completion and when filled out online the completed form is sent back to the doctor's private MyADHD.com account. The site also contains many tools for behavior management, family communication, study strategies, cognitive therapy, and management of ADHD symptoms in adults. If a student is struggling, teachers can suggest that parents talk to their treatment professional about MyADHD.com.

A membership fee is required for accessing services from MyADHD.com.

5. INCREASE USE OF TECHNOLOGY.

Technology is considered a lifesaver for many students with attention deficits. In fact, if a student has an IEP, the IEP team is required to consider whether assistive technology is necessary. Schools must remember that assistive technology is as important for students with learning and attention problems as it is for students with visual or physical disabilities.

✓ **Computers.** Computers are excellent tools for students with attention deficits. Having a copy of their work saved on the computer is helpful, considering their propensity to lose homework.

- Students can type up homework rather than labor with poor fine motor skills and slow processing speed.
    - *Keyboarding skills.* It is, however, important to evaluate a student's keyboarding skills, which may be weak. Because of their *slow processing speed, limited working memory capacity, and slow retrieval of information from long-term memory,* some students are unable to type rapidly. *Shortened assignments* in keyboarding classes can be essential for some of these students.
    - *Keyboarding software.* Software is available to provide keyboarding instruction, which

Photo: Leonard Kong and Green Lake Crew

should be provided as early as possible to avoid the development of ineffective "hunt and peck" strategies. One of these programs may be helpful: Type to Learn© or Mavis Bacon Teaches Typing for Kids.©

- Academic software programs for some subjects or organizational or time management are also available.
    - *Inspiration.*® Many educators have found that Inspiration software helps students improve their outlining, writing, and organizational skills.
    - *Dragon NaturallySpeaking.*® Users can dictate into most Windows-based applications at speeds of up to 160 words per minute and turn speech into text (http://www.scansoft.com).
    - *Spell and grammar checkers.* Spell checkers and grammar checkers also simplify writing tasks. Handheld spell checkers, such as the Franklin Speller,® are often beneficial.
    - *Organizational software.* Most computers are also equipped with software to assist with *time management and organization,* such as Microsoft's Outlook® and Apple's iCal.© Both have yellow "sticky notes" that can be posted on the screen as reminders.
    - *Earning make-up credits.* Some schools, such as Kenosha Unified in Wisconsin, use self-paced *computer software programs for students to earn make-up credits,* enabling them to graduate on time with their classmates.
- *Books on tape (audiobooks).* Some students have found that listening to *books on tape* while reading the material makes learning easier. Information on this free program is available from your local library.
- *Other electronic devices.* Other electronic devices can help students compensate for their *difficulty memorizing, retaining, and quickly retrieving information.*
    - *Calculator.* Many of these students can benefit from using calculators. It is not unusual

for even bright students with attention deficits to have difficulty memorizing basic math facts, such as addition or multiplication, and quickly retrieving the information.

- *Alarms.* Some students like to use *special watches or beepers,* such as *WatchMinder* (Patent #5,861,797), that have an alarm that beeps to remind them of important meetings, to stay after school, or to take medication. Often, alarms can be set to vibrate to avoid unwanted attention or disruption to other students. Computers also have alarms that can be set as reminders.

- *PDA.* Some students use *electronic calendars and schedules* on handheld PDAs, such as a Wizard, iPAQ,© or any Palm product to help them remember important assignments and meetings. Of course, students must learn to use these tools responsibly and not as toys.

Effective Classroom Accommodations for Secondary Level Students

Several excellent classroom accommodations were suggested in 1991 in a joint policy memo regarding students with attention deficits from the U.S. Department of Education and Office of Civil Rights. These accommodations, which are still relevant today, include:

✓ extended time on schoolwork and tests
✓ use of visual aids
✓ modified homework assignments
✓ notetakers
✓ tutors
✓ structured learning environment
✓ repeated and simplified instructions
✓ behavior management
✓ adjusted class schedules
✓ tape recorders
✓ computer-aided instruction
✓ audiovisual equipment
✓ modified textbooks or workbooks
✓ consultation
✓ reduced class size
✓ special resources
✓ classroom aides
✓ case managers to monitor student progress
✓ modified nonacademic times

ACCOMMODATIONS FOR STUDENTS IN PRIVATE VS. PUBLIC SCHOOLS

Private schools that receive any federal funds, except for those with a religious affiliation, are governed by Section 504 and/or the American with Disabilities Act (ADA). So technically speaking, students should be eligible similar accommodations in either public or most private school settings. Over the last few years, most private schools have made a special effort to expand their knowledge and expertise with students with AD/HD. In fact, some private schools now specialize in educating students with attention deficits.

A Few Closing Thoughts...

Because students with attention deficits often have subtle learning problems, teachers are more effective if they use multisensory teaching strategies such as those described in this chapter. At some point, it may be tempting to believe that *"I've done all I can do, so it must be the child's fault that he is not succeeding in school."* However, David Turner, a veteran educator and director of a model Section 504 program in Utah known as CLASS Act, made this observation:

> *"If you keep teaching the same way you've always taught and kids keep failing, who is the slow learner?"*

CHAPTER 11

Effective Behavioral Strategies for Middle and High School Students

Chris A. Zeigler Dendy, M.S.

Adapted from *Teaching Teens with ADD and ADHD*

11

The development of positive behavior intervention strategies is a major feature of recent revisions to IDEA (Individuals with Disabilities Education Act). The purpose of these strategies is to utilize positive interventions before the student's grades plummet or misbehavior escalates. Remember that academic interventions provide a double benefit by also bringing about positive behavioral changes. Several suggestions for middle and high schoolers can help teachers develop positive intervention strategies and inspire student cooperation. An overview of effective behavioral strategies, such as using positive statements in a ratio of 3 to 1 negatives, is provided in Chapter 5.

Initially, teachers can utilize some of the following behavioral strategies to address minor problems. If problems persist, however, they can implement a more advance intervention system by conducting a Functional Behavior Assessment (FBA) and developing a Behavior Intervention Plan (BIP). This process includes an assessment of the behavior, noting any antecedent events that can trigger misbehavior, and then implementing a more formal behavioral plan.

1. Utilize positive behavioral strategies

Behavioral strategies are more difficult to implement successfully with students who have AD/HD. However, there are several steps teachers can take to increase the likelihood of success.

a. Intensify positive interventions. To be effective, positive interventions must be given more frequently, include stronger rewards, provide attention for appropriate behavior, and include sincere praise.

b. Intervene at the point of performance. Russell A. Barkley, Ph.D., reminds us that one way to enhance the effectiveness of behavioral strategies is to intervene at the "point of performance."[1] This term refers to providing needed strategies or supports at the time when a student should actually practice the skill. Simply telling the student to remember an assignment, sending him to an organizational class, or punishing him is not an effective way to change behavior.[2,3]

By intervening at the *point of performance,* the behavioral intervention is more likely to be

tionally, a colorful Time Timer© clock can be placed nearby so the student has a visual cue to remind them of the passage of time and show them how long they have to complete the assignment.

d. **Consider a point system or token economy.** Point systems and token economies are more difficult to manage in middle and high school. These systems may require significant time and consistency and often are not as effective with these students. Many teenagers are eagerly seeking their independence and often resent "being manipulated" by adults. In addition, students with attention deficits are not as easily motivated by rewards and punishments as their peers.

However, *token economies* can be very effective when implemented with extra supports such as that offered through a university that is able to provide adequate staff and creativity in devising the reward system. One nationally recognized model program was developed by William Pelham, Ph.D., a professor at the State University of New York at Buffalo. Another program, Challenging Horizons (CHP), a multimodal afterschool treatment program for middle school students with AD/HD, utilizes a strong behavioral component. Challenging Horizons, which was developed by Steven Evans, Ph.D., is featured as a model program in Chapter 11.

successful. So, for example, asking a student to remember to take home all the necessary books and homework assignments in a 9:00 a.m. class is not nearly as effective as having someone — a teacher, aide, or friend — meet the student at the locker at the end of the day to gather materials needed to complete homework.

c. **Provide external prompts.** Because of their impaired memory functions, externalizing prompts as reminders for events or responsibilities is critical. For example, arrange for friends or aides to remind the student which books must be taken home each evening. Students can set a watch, computer, or PDA alarm to remind them of assignments. Addi-

e. **Consider a group reward system.** Sometimes a less complicated *group reward* can be effective. For example, when the whole class earns enough points for completion of homework by all students, the class can earn a five-point bonus on their final exam grade, a coupon to skip one homework assignment, or a pizza party. Teacher enthusiasm and creativity can engage students in earning unusual "rewards."[4] For example, one teacher rewarded students with vegetables from her garden.

f. **Use peer-mediated reinforcement.** Students' misbehavior is often reinforced by peers who laugh when they act out. Ann Abramowitz, Ph.D.,

Associate Professor at Emory University, has found that peer-mediated reinforcement in the classroom is effective in teaching students to ignore misbehavior.[5]

g. **Develop a contract.** Sometimes contracts between teenagers and teachers or parents can be effective. The student and his teachers can draw up an agreement that lists the specific things that each of them will do to correct a problem and clearly spells out expectations for all involved parties. For example, the student can agree to complete homework each night and turn it in daily, and the parents can agree to monitor homework completion each evening. Teachers must provide the supports and accommodations that will enable the student to be successful. For example, they can ask another student in the class to give a reminder about homework assignments. See Appendices C.5 and C.6 for sample contracts.

　i. *Words of caution:* signing a contract to change "AD/HD behaviors" provides no guarantee that the problem will stop. Students with attention deficits are not always able to follow through on their good intentions. The flaw in this intervention is that it is impossible to reinforce elements of the contract at the "point of performance." Daily supervision may be necessary to ensure compliance with the contract.

　ii. Remember that it is critical for the contract to state parent and teacher behaviors that will be necessary to support the student's behavior change. Otherwise, the "contract" can unintentionally become another opportunity to blame the student for failure to perform.

h. **Avoid humiliation.** Dr. Jones explains that "humiliation is not a behavior management strategy!" The "golden rule," however, is a good reminder: If a comment is not appropriate to make to an adult, it should be avoided for a teen. Following this rule can help parents and teachers phrase corrective feedback more productively.

2. Utilize a variety of effective behavioral strategies.

a. **"If you can't change the 'AD/HD behavior,' then change the environment."** Some "AD/HD behaviors," such as disorganization, forgetfulness, and impaired sense of time, may not improve significantly even with medication. For a student with a time impairment, give them a wristwatch alarm or have another student give prompts. Changing the environment or teaching students to compensate for these challenges is critical.

b. **Give students choices, but only two or three.** Students who are given choices produce more work and are more compliant and less aggressive. However, a student can become bogged down and unable to make a decision when too many choices are offered.

c. **Use depersonalization. Eliminate criticism and blame.** Teachers and guidance counselors have an opportunity to educate students about the characteristics of attention deficit by discussing them in a less threatening third-party context. "Many students with AD/HD have trouble (remembering their homework). Is that true for you? There are a few things we might do to help you (a friend may be asked to remind you). What would be most helpful to you?" Offer suggestions.

d. **Give "I" messages.** "You" messages are often negative and blaming. For example, "You really have been goofing off. You haven't done your homework in several days." Instead, try, "I am surprised and concerned that you didn't finish your homework. I know you want to do well in school. What can you do (or how can I help you) to get your work finished on time?" If the student has no ideas, then offer suggestions.

e. **Use "time-in" instead of time-out.** A school might establish a "time-in" program for students who have behaved inappropriately. Instead of sending a student to an in-school suspension, the student is sent to "time-in" where he is taught the skills he lacks and other prosocial skills.

11

> "Don't judge students by their 'best day ever.' I'd hate that pressure as a teacher to be judged by my 'best day ever.'"

f. **Use Grandma's rule or the "Premack Principle."** First we work and then we play. "When you finish writing your paragraph, you may work on the creative cover for your report." Assign the more difficult portion of the task first and then the easier, more interesting task to finish up.

g. **Use behavioral momentum.** Although this strategy is the exact opposite of Grandma's Rule, it can be more effective for some students with attention deficits. First, ask the student to do a couple of things they like to do; then ask them to do the less desirable activity.

3. Provide increased "developmentally appropriate" supervision.

a. **Provide increased supervision.** Because of their significant developmental delay, teenagers with attention deficits need more supervision than typically provided for their peers.

b. **Consider assigning a case manager.** Some teens with more complex cases of AD/HD face significant struggles in the transition to middle and high school. This has prompted some schools to assign case managers to assist with the transition. The case manager remains in close contact with students and their teachers to identify problems early.

4. Conduct a Functional Behavior Assessment (FBA).

When students are struggling, it may be a good idea to utilize information gathered via an FBA. FBAs are actually mandated by IDEA when eligible students experience continuing difficulties at school. Teachers and other school personnel can take the information gathered from the FBA, use it to develop a theory of why the misbehavior occurred, and then guide the development of the Behavior Intervention Plan. A good Functional Behavior Assessment answers several important questions:[6]

✓ What is the student's behavior of concern?

✓ When and where does the behavior occur?

✓ What is the antecedent or "trigger" for the behavior?

✓ Are there other contributing factors?

  • Were medications working effectively?

  • Have any unique upsetting situations occurred recently at home or school?

✓ What purpose or function does the behavior serve?

✓ What was the teacher's response?

✓ What was the student's response to the teacher?

✓ Why is the behavior continuing? What is maintaining it?

✓ What does the student view as a reward or positive reinforcement? Could this reward serve as an incentive for him to change his behavior?

✓ What interventions were tried previously? Which ones were effective?

5. Develop a Behavior Intervention Plan (BIP).

Each specific behavior or issue of concern should be identified and an intervention strategy developed for the BIP. For example, what should teachers do when the student is not completing his class and homework in Language Arts, a 1:00 p.m. class, yet is completing his work in Algebra at 8:30 a.m.? More information is available on FBA and BIP at http://www.pbis.org.

a. First, teachers and parents can determine whether learning problems, such as *written expression* or *slow processing speed,* are difficult for him, as they are for many of these students. If so, accommodations, such as using a computer, dictating some assignments, reducing written work, or providing some tutoring, can be helpful.

b. Teaching strategies, such as using *graphic organizers* or *overhead projectors,* that rely on visual cues are often effective.

c. Finally, teachers may find that for a few students misbehavior is linked to the time of day when *medication has worn off* and is no longer effective. For this student, the medication lost its effectiveness by 1:00 p.m. Parents can talk with their doctor to discuss changing the time of day the medication is administered or switching to a sustained-release medication.

6. Teach skills and compensatory strategies.

Teaching students the skills they lack or teaching them to compensate for problems that are linked to AD/HD is critical. Direct instruction is a key strategy for teaching self-management skills such as time management, organizational skills, study skills, note-taking, anger management, prosocial skills, and self-advocacy.

Students can also learn *compensatory skills* for many challenges through the use of technology, such as computers and electronic organizers. Teaching these students how to use PDAs or assignments books, create or use graphic organizers to manage more difficult assignments or projects, or use software programs such as Inspiration helps them become more independent. Furthermore, students who have been *educated about their attention deficit* and taught compensatory strategies are much more likely to have the necessary skills to take charge of their lives. Otherwise, students may come to believe they have problems in these areas because they are bad, lazy, or not trying.

Teachers should keep in mind, however, that even though needed skills are taught, the student may not always use them in the moment they are needed. These students often act before they think about the skills they learned in a class, which is why Dr. Barkley and other researchers put such an emphasis on using visual prompts as necessary reminders.

The task of teaching skills is always easier said than done. In some cases, formal curricula are available; in others, teachers have favorite strategies they have developed over the years. Some key skills and coping strategies are described in the following list. (See Appendix A for a list of resources to address these skills.)

✓ **Planning and problem solving**: Assigning a long-term project presents an opportunity to teach standard four-step planning like that of Steven Covey through the use of a *graphic organizer:*[7] plan, prioritize, schedule, and do it.

✓ **Time management**: Teach the student how to "externalize" time reminders using a watch alarm or a PDA or having a friend remind him. Make time concrete and visible with a Time Timer©, a special clock with a color inset that decreases in size as time passes, allowing the student to "see" time (http://www.timetimer.com).

✓ **Organizational skills:** Most students can learn how to use a school planner or a PDA to keep up with school assignments. One student who always lost his assignment book came up with a simpler solution that works well for him. Each day he writes his assignments on a 3x5 card that he carries in his pocket. Students can also be taught an efficient way to organize their lockers.

✓ **Anger management:** Educating students about anger, making them aware of the events that trigger their anger, and giving them alternative ways of handling anger are helpful strategies. For example, students can learn to talk about their anger in healthy ways, take deep breaths and count to ten, take a time-out to calm down, or talk to a friend. Effective medication levels can also reduce the student's level of anger.

✓ **Conflict resolution:** Conflict resolution involves learning problem-solving skills, how to talk about conflict in an objective manner, and good communication skills.

✓ **Self-advocacy:** Educating students about their AD/HD and teaching them how to advocate for themselves is critical. Encourage students to ask for help or the accommodations that they need. Some students actually chair their IEP meetings. Students interested in doing so should read *A Student's Guide to the IEP,*[8] published by NICHCY (National Dissemination Center for Children with Disabilities). Realistically, however, most students with attention deficits do not take the time to read this document so parents or teachers can read the document and teach the student the key steps recommended by NICHCY.

Teach students to recognize their challenges and to tell teachers when they are struggling with a task or having a bad day. But keep in mind, even if you teach all these skills, students may not be able to stop and think to use them because of the very characteristics of their AD/HD.

✓ **Decision-making:** Use prosocial strategies that teach responsible decision-making. For example, a teacher may ask a student who is not following rules, "Is that a good choice or a bad choice?" This question gives the student an opportunity to identify the misbehavior and correct it himself.

7. Consider implementing a schoolwide positive behavior program.[9]

Many schools are implementing schoolwide positive behavior intervention programs or PBIS. These programs create a schoolwide positive learning environment in which academic and test scores improve and misbehavior decreases. Consistent expectations and interventions for all students are reinforced. A description of this model program is provided in Chapter 5. Illinois has successfully implemented PBIS statewide in elementary and middle schools and has recently shifted the focus to implementation in high schools. Visit http://www.pbis.org for more information.

Key Issues Impacting Students with AD/HD

"One comment, right or wrong, can live with a student for the next 20 years of their life!"

• *Sherri Guenther, teacher*

Key issues of great importance to children with AD/HD are discussed in the next three chapters.

Chapter 12: Social Skills for Children And Adolescents
✓ Overview
✓ Underlying causes
✓ Impact on academic performance
✓ The importance of mastering social skills
✓ What must a student do to get along with others?
✓ Boys vs. girls
✓ Research on social skills training
✓ Five intervention strategies to improve peers relationships
✓ Assessing deficits
✓ Enhancing the effectiveness of social skills training
✓ Other intervention strategies

Chapter 13: Preparing for the Future
✓ Overview
✓ Educational needs after high school
✓ Technical, two- and four-year colleges
✓ Obtaining accommodations and services
✓ Choosing a college

Chapter 14: Educational Laws Regarding Students with AD/HD
✓ Overview
✓ Section 504
   – Who is an individual with a disability?
   – What are "major life activities"?
   – What does "substantially limits" mean?
   – What is necessary for a section 504 evaluation?
   – What services can eligible students receive?

✓ IDEA
   – What is OHI and why is it important?
   – What services can eligible students receive?
   – What should be included in an IEP or Section 504 Plan?
✓ Frequently asked questions (FAQs)
   – Are ADD or ADHD eligible disabilities?
   – What should a teacher do if ADD/ADHD is suspected?

- What are common ADD/ADHD behaviors indicating the need for an IEP or 504 plan?
- Can students with ADD/ADHD also have learning disabilities?
- Does a student have to be failing any classes to be eligible for services?
- What about children who are on grade level but are bright and not achieving up to their ability levels?
- Are children with a high IQ eligible for services?
- What should be done if a student has an IEP but continues to struggle?
- If a student has an IEP that requires accommodations, is a classroom teacher required to provide them?
- What are positive behavior supports?
- What are Functional Behavior Assessments and Behavior Intervention Plans?
- If a student with ADD or ADHD has been suspended for behavior problems, what interventions should the school provide pursuant to the IEP or 504 Plan?
- Why is it important to establish disability eligibility no later than high school?
- Conclusion

CHAPTER 12

Social Skills for Children and Adolescents

Chris A. Zeigler Dendy, M.S.

Accoding to researchers, roughly 50 to 60 percent of children with AD/HD have difficulty with peer relationships.[1] Specifically, these students lack basic social skills and have difficulty making and keeping friends.[2] To further compound their social deficits, these students experience a 30 percent developmental delay, which can make them seem less mature.[3] These students often have trouble reading the subtle details and cues that are so critical for successful social relationships. Some students may not recognize that they are being too loud, complain too often, are aggressive, bossy, insensitive, demanding or inflexible, or have said something offensive. Intrusion into the personal space of other students and overreacting angrily when things don't go their way are not uncommon occurrences. However, of even greater concern, these students may be totally unaware of their poor social skills.

Because AD/HD is an invisible disability, students who are socially unskilled can be viewed by others as rude, self-centered, irresponsible, lazy, or ill-mannered.[4] Consequently, these students may be rejected by their peers and viewed less positively by their teachers. Students with AD/HD or LD who lack social skills are more susceptible to bullying, more often as the victim but also as the perpetrator.[5] Their social problems often get even worse in middle school, since students are also undergoing hormonal changes and dealing with increased teacher expectations. Regrettably, problems with social skills are a lifelong challenge for many.

In contrast, students with AD/HD inattentive type are not as impulsive or aggressive as those with AD/HD hyperactive or combined type, so they may have better social skills and more friends. But for some of this subgroup of students, shyness, anxiety, and withdrawal can create a different set of social problems.[6] They may be ignored by other students.

Underlying Causes

Some researchers now believe that social skills deficits are linked to impairment of executive functions of the brain that contribute to their lack of self-control.[7] Ironically these students may know the proper social skills but typically lack the ability to use them at the appropriate time. *Social skills training alone is not enough.* While this training only teaches new skills, it does not ensure the *efficient use of existing skills.*

Impact on Academic Performance

Since AD/HD and learning disabilities often overlap as much as 50 percent, it is important to note that students with learning disabilities also experience problems with social skills. Some social skill deficits, such as misinterpreting social cues and difficulty interacting with friends, are similar for both groups. Researchers also tell us that social skill deficits can have a major impact on academic performance.[8] For example, these students can have *poor constructive communication;* that means they can have trouble asking questions and getting the information they need to complete a task. They can also struggle to recognize when characters in a story are making deceptive statements. Examples of important social skills in the school setting include:

✓ Giving and accepting negative feedback
✓ Making friends
✓ Giving positive feedback
✓ Explaining a problem
✓ Negotiating
✓ Asking questions
✓ Problem solving
✓ Following directions
✓ Resisting peer pressure
✓ Conversing
✓ Initiating or joining in on activities
✓ Using good manners

The Importance of Mastering Social Skills

One predictor of how a child with AD/HD will do in adulthood is how well he or she gets along with other children.[9] In the school setting, more serious social skill deficits are often linked to disciplinary problems, suspensions, school failure, dropping out of school, and, ultimately for some, delinquency. Additionally, researchers tell us that having a best friend can have a protective effect on children. Teachers and parents must help these children improve their social relationships with their peers.

What Must a Student Do to Get Along with Others?

To get along with peers and teachers, students must be attentive, responsible, and able to control their impulsivity.[10] "Highly likeable people" are considered to have the following characteristics: sincere, honest, understanding, loyal, truthful, trustworthy, intelligent, dependable, thoughtful, considerate, reliable, warm, kind, friendly, happy, unselfish, humorous, responsible, cheerful, and trusted.[11] Yet these characteristics are the very ones that can be absent in students with attention deficits. Since people with AD/HD may be considered "high maintenance" in relationships, anything adults can do to help students improve their likeability characteristics can also improve their friendships.

Assessing Deficits

Teachers can assess a student's skill deficits through informal observations or more formal measures. Below are three strategies for assessing social skills deficits.[12]

Typically, knowledgeable evaluators rate the behavior of the student on several key social skills. The scale can be completed again later to determine whether the student has shown any improvement. See Appendix A for more information.

1. **Social skills ratings scales.** Three examples of rating scales are:

   a. The *Walker-McConnell Scale of Social Competence and School Adjustment.* This scale takes teachers no more than 10 minutes to complete and provides scores by category. For elementary-aged children, there are 43 items under three categories: peer and teacher preferred social behaviors and school adjustment. For adolescents, there are 53 items under four categories: self-control, peer relations, school adjustment, and empathy.

   b. *Social Skills Rating System.* This scale rates social skills at school, home, and in the community in 15 to 25 minutes. Categories include self-control, empathy, cooperation assertion, responsibility, hyperactivity, and externalizing and internalizing problems. A student self-report version is also available.

   c. *The Tough Kids Social Skills Book.* Susan Sheridan provides helpful materials, including social skills inventories to help teachers assess social skills.

2. **Social status nomination.** Hand out a list of all students in the class and instruct the class to identify the three students who are most willing to volunteer to help classmates with assignments and the three students who are least likely to volunteer to help classmates. This information should give the teacher a good idea of the most well-liked and least-liked students in the class.

3. **Direct observation.** Make a list of basic social skills and record the number of times a student acts appropriately.

Boys vs. Girls

Understanding the differences in what boys and girls view as good social skills is very important.[13] Relationships between boys often revolve around activities, especially sports. Girls, on the other hand, view school as the center of their social life. Girls have their most meaningful interactions at school while boys have theirs after school and on weekends. Boys are much less likely to talk about personal, confidential, or sensitive topics. Girls also enjoy talking about other people's lives; boys do not. Girls spend a lot of time talking about the social and academics aspects of school; boys see school as an "interruption" of their social life. Boys don't require you to be friendly, but girls do. Girls who pass each other without speaking are considered "stuck-up" or "snobs;" not true for boys. Girls who are clean and dress fashionably are also more popular. Being trustworthy and responsible regarding care of property are highly respected by both boys and girls.

Based upon what we know about gender-related social skills, students with AD/HD must learn strategies to earn greater acceptance from their peers. Girls must learn to smile, make eye contact, and greet other girls in social situations. Girls can also practice good hygiene and dress more appropriately. On the other hand, boys can learn more about sports and stay informed about the current win-loss record of their favorite sports team. Computer and video games are also a great common ground for building relationships among boys. Teaching both boys and girls more about the favorite topic of the desired peer group can be helpful.

> **"Students know what to do but don't always do what they know."**
>
> • Sam Goldstein, Ph.D.

"Coping skills evolve slowly: expecting rapid, far-reaching change in behavior is about as reasonable and gratifying as trying to nail Jell-O® to a wall!"

• Janet Roper, M.S., guidance counselor

Research on Social Skills Training

Research regarding the effectiveness of social skills training is mixed. Most experts think this training holds promise but does not provide a magic answer for improving social skills. Intensive training programs have been shown to help children improve their knowledge of social skills and their behavior at home as judged by parents.[14] These programs are more likely to be effective with two subgroups of students: those who tend to exhibit the shyness and anxiety sometimes linked to AD/HD inattentive and those with conduct problems. Unfortunately, the major failure of these programs is that *positive changes do not always generalize to the school setting.*[15] In other words, even though the student may know what to do, he or she doesn't always use the proper skills.

Educators should avoid placing several students with aggressive, antisocial behavior in a group together since the group may inadvertently become a "deviancy training group,"[16] where they can learn undesirable behaviors from each other.

The bottom line is that the biochemical nature of AD/HD makes it very difficult for these students to consistently utilize appropriate social skills. Socials skills training does not work magic so teachers must have realistic expectations for what these programs can accomplish. The student may show some improvement at times, but typically the use of these skills is inconsistent, especially in the classroom or at recess.

Five Intervention Strategies to Improve Peer Relationships

Researchers suggest five forms of intervention that have been successful at improving peer relationships:

1. systematic teaching of social skills
2. social problem solving
3. teaching other behavioral skills often considered important by children, such as sports skills and board game rules
4. decreasing undesirable and antisocial behaviors
5. developing a close friendship

These interventions can be offered in several settings, including the classroom, small groups at school, afterschool programs, and summer camps. The components of effective programs are listed and described in subsequent sections. The intensive summer camp model established by William Pelham, Ph.D., is a nationally recognized program. All five forms of intervention are utilized in this six to eight week program that runs for six to nine hours on weekdays. Both academic and peer problems are addressed. Most of the day is spent participating in recreational activities, such as baseball or soccer, where skills, strategy, and rules are taught. Two hours are reserved for academics, including related skills such as organization.

Additional information on the summer camp model and two other model programs that teach social, academic, and life skills, *Challenging Horizons (CHP)* and the Irvine Paraprofessional Program (IPP), is provided in Chapter 15.

Enhancing the Effectiveness of Social Skills Training

Social skills training is effective only "when it is used with parent and school interventions and rewards and consequences to reduce disruptive and negative behaviors."[17] Reinforcing targeted social skills both at school and at home is critical. Effective social skills programs involve *instruction, modeling, role playing, instructive feedback, rewards and consequences, and practice.* The targeted skill must be clearly defined, for example, sharing or negotiating. Labeling the praise is also important: "I like the way you shared with John. That's a great way to make friends." More advanced social skills such as *negotiating, accepting the choices of others, and complimenting* should also be taught.

The program should also be offered in *real-world or natural settings* such as the school, rather than in an office or clinic[18] and teachers, other school personnel, and parents must also participate, always reinforcing appropriate social skills when they occur. Some programs like *Creative Coaching* target one social skill each week, and teachers and parents reinforce that specific skill in class and at home. Each new skill that is added is then reinforced on a regular basis. Booster sessions may be necessary to review and reinforce skills learned earlier in the program. See the list of Resources in Appendix A for more information.

Other Intervention Strategies

Several additional strategies that can enhance a student's social skills are:

✓ **Medication.** Medication is one of the most effective interventions available for improving behavior, academic performance, and interpersonal relationships. The student's self control and concentration improves so that he or she is more likely to use his social skills. However, medication alone is not sufficient to improve social skills.

✓ **Social and/or life skills curricula.** Brief descriptions of several social skills curricula are listed in Appendix A. The curriculum can include the following elements:

 • *Promote student awareness.* Describe the problem and its consequences. Ask students to talk about the problem in their own words and give specific examples. Ask them why they think the problem occurs and what they could do instead. Remember that promoting student awareness can increase knowledge but in isolation, is unlikely to change behavior.

 • *Teach self-monitoring:* Conduct interviews to determine whether they are aware of their behavior (Why it is a problem? Do they know why they do it? Do they wish to change? What are possible solutions?). Encourage journal keeping to record notes on social interactions, how their new interventions are working, and how others respond. See Appendix C.12 for a sample self-monitoring form.

• *Use contracts and post rules.* Identify skills and develop contracts that the student can sign. See Appendix C.12 for a sample contract.

• *Practice.* Having the student practice the targeted social skill and then giving feedback and reinforcement increases the likelihood of mastering the skill.

• *Use behavioral report cards.* When students utilize the social skills on their chart, they receive points that can be cashed in for a reward. See Appendices C.1, C.2, C.3, and C.4 for sample daily and weekly reports.

• *Use role playing to become aware of behavior.* The student is given scripts to role-play the targeted problem behavior. Afterwards, the student discusses his reactions to dealing with the targeted problem behavior in others.

• *Give praise and reinforcement.* Praise and encouragement must be part of any intervention.

• *Attend specialized summer camp programs.* Specialized summer camps are one way for students to practice social skills in other settings. (See Chapter 15.)

• *Utilize a "Social Skills Autopsy."*[19] Dr. Richard Lavoie created this process to examine and analyze "a social error to determine the cause of the error, the amount of damage that occurred and to learn about the causal factors in order to prevent reoccurrence in the future." The autopsy should teach new skills in a positive way; it is not intended to scold or punish. The child is a respected partner during the autopsy. Lavoie's autopsy utilizes five stages as explained in his book, *It's So Much Work to Be Your Friend.*

1) Ask the child to explain what happened. 2) Ask the child to identity the mistake he made. 3) Assist the child in determining the actual social error that he made. 4) The adult creates a brief story similar in nature to the social faux pas; then asks the child to explain the correct response. 5) Give social homework by asking the child to use the target skill in another setting and report back.

✓ **Institute a bullying prevention program.** Bullying prevention programs help students become more aware of their own behavior and how it impacts others. Students unknowingly give their unspoken support for bullying by silently acquiescing while another child is being taunted. These programs empower students to take a stand against bullying and give them the tools they need to cope with bullies. The Olweus Bullying Prevention Program has been endorsed by both SAMHSA (Substance Abuse and Mental Health Services Administration) and the OJJDP (Office of Juvenile Justice and Delinquency Prevention).

✓ **Implement a student-mediated conflict resolution program.** Schoolwide peer mediation programs teach students to resolve conflict in peaceful ways. Improved communication and specific strategies for settling disagreements and misunderstandings are taught. Involving students with AD/HD in a peer mediation program can help them reduce the aggressive, uncooperative behaviors that have resulted in their rejection. Mediation programs can be based inside the school or trained student mediators can be stationed on the playground during recess.

This chapter was adapted from an unpublished paper, "Social Skills for Teens with ADD and ADHD," by Chris A. Zeigler Dendy, M.S.

CHAPTER 13

Preparing for the Future

Chris A. Zeigler Dendy, M.S.

Adapted from *Teenagers with ADD and ADHD, 2nd edition*

Developing plans to help students with AD/HD transition into the adult work world is critical. It is so important that the federal education law, IDEA (Individuals with Disabilities Education Act), mandates that by age 16, career transition plans must be addressed in the IEP (Individual Education Plan) of students who receive special education.

Specifically, the law states that planning should help the student make the transition from high school to "post secondary education, vocational training, integrated employment (including supported employment), continuing and adult education, adult services, independent living or community participation."

The law also adds that the activities should be based upon "the individual student's needs taking into account the student's preferences and interests, and shall include instruction, community experiences, the development of employment and other post-school adult living objectives, and when appropriate, acquisition of daily living skills, and functional vocational evaluation."

Educational Needs After High School[1]

Additional education after high school is critical but can be deferred if students need a break from the stresses of school. With proper supports in place — accommodations and effective medication — many students with attention deficits can be successful in college. However, college is not the best choice for everyone. Students should know that good jobs are available that don't require a college degree. But they will need additional education to qualify for these highly skilled and technical jobs. Several activities can help prepare students for life after high school graduation:

✓ assessing vocational/career interests to increase self-awareness and identify potential career interest areas through interest surveys/inventories

✓ enrolling in vocational or technology classes that relate to the student's interest areas

✓ participating in job shadowing or mentoring programs

✓ practicing basic work skills, such as filling out job applications, writing a resume and role-playing job interviews. A program called *Job-related Social Skills* (JRSS) by Montague and Lund cam be helpful for students.[2]

Technical, Two- and Four-Year Colleges

Students who seek additional schooling can also benefit from assistance to ensure that accommodations are available for both entrance exams and post-secondary classes. For example, some students with AD/HD struggle with slow processing speed and require extended time on tests and some assignments. Typically students requesting accommodations, such as untimed tests, are currently receiving these accommodations in high school as part of services under IDEA or Section 504. Several steps must be completed to ensure that proper documentation is available for any student who wants accommodations on college entrance tests like the SAT or ACT:

1. Clearly *identify current classroom accommodations,* such as untimed tests, in the student's IEP or Section 504 plan.

2. Include a *statement in the IEP/504 plan* about the student's need for an untimed SAT or ACT and that the school will assist the student in making arrangements with the appropriate testing authority.

3. Typically, the guidance counselor helps the student *complete the application* for accommodations and then *submits any necessary supporting documentation.*

Increasingly, many colleges are now making SAT and ACT scores optional for admission to college. For students who don't test well, encourage them to check out the colleges with this optional requirement (http://www.fairtest.org).

Students and their parents should be advised that most of them will need additional supports once they enter college. Russell A. Barkley, Ph.D., reminds us that an 18-year-old entering college is more often like a 12- to 14-year-old, so supports appropriate for a 12- to 14-year-old will probably be needed. These supports should be planned with the full involvement of the teenager.

Helping the student select a technical program or college that is right for him or her is very important. Teachers and counselors can help with this decision by educating students and their families and advising them of helpful resources, such as those listed in Appendix A.

> "What's the point of rushing towards failure? It's okay to take more than four years to finish college."
>
> • Arthur Robin, Ph.D., psychologist

Obtaining Accommodations and Services

Although technical programs or college are not governed by IDEA requirements, Section 504 guidelines continue to apply in those settings if the institution receives federal funds. However, institutions with a religious affiliation are exempt from these requirements. Each school receiving federal funds has a Section 504 Coordinator, who is often an excellent resource to ensure a student's successful transition from high school.

Just as in high school, accommodations such as notetakers, extended time, tutors, early registration, or matching with teachers may be provided for eligible students. Some colleges offer a broader range of supportive services that can increase the student's chances of a successful transition to college. Some colleges specialize in serving students with special learning needs. For example, by paying extra tuition, the student is provided additional supervision, especially during the first year transition to college. As these students adjust to college life and gain confidence, they tend to require less supervision with each succeeding year.

Choosing a College

Accommodations and supportive services that are available for students with severe learning disabilities and/or AD/HD are described in several college directories, such as Peterson's, K & W's, and Lovejoy's,

which are available at most public libraries. These guides also provide general information about each school that may factor into the student's decision:

✓ If the student has decided upon a major, what are the degree requirements for graduation at different colleges? For example, one college may require foreign languages for a specific degree while another one does not for the same degree. If foreign languages are a nightmare for this particular student with AD/HD, avoid the degree program with the foreign language requirement.

✓ Consider the merits of a semester system versus a quarter system and whether it will make a difference in this student's performance. Some students with attention deficits say semester systems seem to last forever.

✓ Some colleges have cooperative education programs that offer degree-related work experience interspersed with course work.

Students can also learn more about various programs through personal recommendations. Based upon first-hand reports from other high school graduates, high school personnel are often able to advise students and parents about the desirability of certain colleges. Also, if a student has a clear idea of the career he wants to pursue, suggest he or she meet with an adult who works in the field to discuss colleges that offer the best program in this area.

Once students have narrowed down the number of colleges in which they are interested, they should consider visiting two or three of them:

✓ Suggest scheduling an appointment with the 504 coordinator during the campus visit to learn more about the accommodations and supportive services that are offered to eligible students

✓ Assist students in contacting universities or technical colleges early, perhaps during their junior year, since many require documentation of needs and updated evaluations to be eligible for accommodations.

CHAPTER 14

Educational Laws Regarding Students with AD/HD*

Mary Durheim, B.S.
Chris A. Zeigler Dendy, M.S.

Two federal laws, IDEA and Section 504, provide guidance for the education of all students with disabilities. Students with "ADD or ADHD" often qualify for services under one of these two laws because of the major academic and/or behavioral challenges they face. Approximately 30 to 50 percent of students with attention deficits qualify for services under *IDEA by the time they reach adolescence.*[1] However, these students don't necessarily require placement in a special education classroom, but rather can be successful in regular classroom settings with appropriate accommodations pursuant to either Section 504 or IDEA.

Generally speaking, these two key federal laws guarantee a free and appropriate public education, commonly known as FAPE, for all students with disabilities. More specifically, the laws differ slightly in their definitions of the components of FAPE.

1. **Section 504 of the Rehabilitation Act of 1973,** a civil rights law that prohibits discrimination and is often referred to as Section 504, addresses the educational needs of students in public as well as private, nonreligious schools receiving any federal funds.

2. **Individuals with Disabilities Education Act,** an education law known as IDEA, deals with students who are in public schools and have a disability that creates an adverse effect on learning, thus, creating an educational need.

According to a CHADD fact sheet for families, "Section 504 provides a faster, more flexible and less stigmatizing procedure for obtaining some accommodations and services for children with disabilities. By virtue of the looser eligibility criteria, some children may receive protection who are not eligible for services or protection under IDEA, and less information is needed to obtain eligibility. Thus, Section 504 can provide an efficient way to obtain limited assistance without the stigma and bureaucratic procedures attached to IDEA."[2]

With regard to eligibility, IDEA mandates that a child have a disability requiring special education services. Section 504 can be invoked when the child needs special education OR related services.[3] "Because of this distinction, children covered under Section 504 include those who typically either have less severe disabilities than those covered under IDEA or have

* This chapter is adapted from the resources listed in "References," Appendix B.
In most cases, AD/HD is used interchangeably throughout this Manual to describe both AD/HD predominately hyperactive-impulsive and AD/HD predominately inattentive. IDEA regulations refer to these two conditions as ADD and ADHD, respectively.

disabilities that do not neatly fit within the categories of eligibility under IDEA."[4]

In addition, a third law, the Americans with Disabilities Act (ADA), applies to all public and private schools, including post-secondary and the workplace.

Since roughly 90 percent of students with AD/HD will face serious struggles at school at some time during their academic career, it is reasonable to assume that the majority of students would benefit from some accommodations in the classroom, regardless of their eligibility for IDEA or Section 504. Brief summaries of provisions of these two laws are provided in this chapter.

Section 504

Section 504 is a federal *civil rights law* prohibiting discrimination against children with disabilities, ages 3 to 21. Additional qualifying guidelines, which vary from state to state, are provided for the 18 to 21 age group. This law applies to all public and private nonreligious schools, as well as colleges and technical schools that receive funds from the federal government. According to this federal law,

"No otherwise qualified individual with a disability in the United States…shall, solely by reason of her or his disability, be excluded from the participation in, be denied the benefits of, or be subjected to discrimination under any

program or activity receiving Federal financial assistance."

29 USC §794(a), 34 CFR §104.4(a)

Generally speaking, Section 504 has broader eligibility criteria and fewer regulations than IDEA and thus, more students may be eligible for services.

WHO IS AN INDIVIDUAL WITH A DISABILITY?

"An individual with a disability is a person who:
1. Has a physical or mental impairment that substantially limits one or more major life activity.
2. Has a record of such an impairment; or
3. Is regarded as having such impairment."

34 CFR §104.3(j)(1)

Students are eligible for services and an individual accommodation plan under Section 504 if they meet they meet the first criterion above. Students meeting the second and third criteria receive protections against discrimination but do not receive an accommodation plan until an evaluation determines that their disability meets the first eligibility criterion.

WHAT ARE "MAJOR LIFE ACTIVITIES"?

Major life activities include — but are not limited to — learning, concentrating, thinking, behavior, self-care, speaking, sitting, and interacting with others. Specific disorders that may impact major life activities include ADD, ADHD, dyslexia, Tourette Syndrome, depression, conduct disorder, oppositional defiant disorder, bipolar disorder, behavior disorders, and health challenges such as cancer, diabetes or asthma. The key phrase in determining eligibility is whether the condition "substantially limits" the student's ability to receive an "equal opportunity" to be successful in school.

WHAT DOES "SUBSTANTIALLY LIMITS" MEAN?

In a 2003 *Attention!* magazine article, Mary Durheim, CHADD President 2003–2005, educational consultant and Section 504 hearing officer, quotes an Office of Civil Rights (OCR) memo that clarifies the term "substantially limits."[5] According to the memo, a condition "substantially limits" when an individual is:

"significantly restricted as to the condition, manner or duration under which an individual can perform a particular major life activity when compared to the condition, manner or duration under which the average person in the general population can perform that same major life activity."

Ultimately, the definition of "substantial" is left for each 504 Committee to determine.

WHAT IS NECESSARY FOR A SECTION 504 EVALUATION?

Federal regulations state that "a variety of sources" must be used in the evaluation process. IQ tests or aptitude/achievement tests are NOT required, and an IQ score cannot be the only factor determining eligibility. Interpretation and implementation of Section 504 regulations varies by regions of the country. Check with your individual school system for a copy of their procedures for determining eligibility for services under Section 504.

WHAT SERVICES CAN ELIGIBLE STUDENTS RECEIVE?

The student must receive a free appropriate public education under both Section 504 and IDEA. FAPE consists of "regular or special education and related aids and services designed to meet the student's individual needs." However, the standards for the level of interventions are different under Section 504 and IDEA. Under Section 504, the student must have an "equal opportunity" to access and participate in the educational environment, when compared to nondisabled peers. With regard to extracurricular activities, however, if the student lacks the basic skills to participate in the activity, they don't have a "right" to participate simply because he or she has a disability. The FAPE provisions under IDEA require special education and related services designed to meet the individual educational needs of the student and must provide that student with *"educational benefit."*

Teachers frequently make simple academic or behavioral changes in the classroom that help children cope successfully with their attention deficits. These basic supports are often provided with or without Section 504 or IDEA eligibility by caring, dedicated teachers who want all students to be successful. (Examples of effective accommodations, including seating changes, shorter assignments, extended time, dictation to a scribe, and skills training, are provided in Chapters 4, 5, 8, and 10–12.)

IDEA

IDEA is a federal *education law* guaranteeing a free appropriate public education to all students with disabilities who have an educational need and meet eligibility criteria. This law applies to students served by public schools, from birth through high school, and in some cases through age 21. Schools receiving federal funds are required to provide necessary "special education and related services." Key provisions of IDEA include:

1. A free appropriate public education designed to meet a student's individual needs
2. Involvement of parents in educational decisions
3. Nondiscriminatory evaluations and assessments
4. An Individualized Education Program (IEP)
5. An education in the least restrictive environment (LRE)
6. A right to remedy or due process

Detailed written guidelines for IDEA and special education are available in each school district. State regulations must comply with federal regulations but can enact requirements that exceed federal minimums.

WHAT IS OTHER HEALTH IMPAIRMENT (OHI) AND WHY IS IT IMPORTANT?

In the 1999 IDEA regulations, "ADD and ADHD" were added to the list of eligible conditions under OHI. As a matter of best practice, most students with attention deficits should be considered for eligibility under the OHI category first instead of Specific

14

Learning Disability (SLD) or Emotional or Behavior Disorder (ED). According to current federal regulations, OHI

> "means having limited strength, vitality or alertness, including a heightened alertness to environmental stimuli, that results in limited alertness with respect to the educational environment, that…
>
> a. is due to chronic or acute health problems such as asthma, attention deficit disorder, or attention deficit hyperactivity disorders, diabetes, epilepsy, a heart condition, hemophilia, lead poisoning, leukemia, nephritis, rheumatic fever, and sickle cell anemia; and
>
> b. adversely affects a child's educational performance."

Please note that OHI criteria refer to educational performance, not academic performance. This means that factors other than test score discrepancies or a doctor's diagnosis should be considered in determining eligibility for services. For example, "relevant functional, developmental, and academic information" can include grades, homework completion, independent work habits, alertness, sleeping in class, class participation and attendance, ability to complete schoolwork and tests within specified time frames, relationships with peers, and compliance with rules.

WHAT SERVICES CAN ELIGIBLE STUDENTS RECEIVE?

Special education is defined under IDEA as "specially designed instruction, at no cost to parents, to meet the unique needs of a child with a disability." Special education strategies may be needed to address problem areas common to students with attention deficits, such as memorization, manipulation of information in working memory, written expression, and math computation. In addition, *accommodations* and *related services* may also be needed. Examples of related services are AD/HD education, counseling, parent training, and skills training in organization, time

management, anger management, or study strategies. The key is to identify skill deficits that create an "educational need" that is preventing school success and develop effective intervention strategies that will provide "educational benefit."

WHAT SHOULD BE INCLUDED IN AN IEP OR SECTION 504 PLAN?

The general purpose of both IEPs and 504 plans is similar: to provide eligible students an educational plan that addresses learning and/or behavior problems adversely affecting their learning educational performance. However, the requirements for these educational plans are different.

IEPs. A statement of the child's present level of educational performance is critically important in an IEP. All issues of concern should be listed in this section, including executive function deficits such as disorganization, working memory deficits, frequent morning tardiness, forgetting assignments, and difficulty completing long-term projects.

1. Present level of performance
   a. Present performance (academic, social, behavioral, developmental)
   b. Strengths
   c. Parental concerns
2. Goals: Measurable annual goals
3. Educational services to be provided
   a. Special education program
   b. Related services, such as counseling and assistive technology
   c. Accommodations, such as assistance with organizational skills and extended time
   d. Anticipated frequency, location of services, and person responsible for each task (for example, daily in regular class by Mrs. Smith)
   e. Modifications in statewide or district assessment (for example, extended time)
4. Method for assessing progress toward the annual goal
5. Individualized transition plans for those aged 16 years and older.

Section 504. Section 504 has significantly fewer formal mandates for educational plans than IDEA. For example, there are no formal requirements for a *written* educational plan. Typically, the 504 plan includes a list of accommodations that address the student's learning challenges. Specific learning issues of concern can also be identified in the minutes of the 504 meeting.

Frequently Asked Questions

1. ARE "ADD OR ADHD ELIGIBLE DISABILITIES?

Yes, in many situations. Federal policy states that eligible students with attention deficit disorder or attention deficit hyperactivity disorders may qualify under either Section 504 or IDEA. As stated earlier, "ADD and ADHD" are eligible conditions under the Other Health Impairment category.

In 1991, the U.S. Offices of Special Education, Civil Rights, and Elementary and Secondary Education issued a joint memo clearly stating that many students with "ADD or ADHD" have significant learning problems and may be eligible for services.[6] As is the case with other disabilities, "ADD and ADHD" exist on a continuum of severity from mild to severe. Consequently, those students with more complex cases of attention deficits and executive function deficits will be in need of special education and accommodations. The 1991 memo and subsequent policies have clarified that students with attention deficits should be considered for services under either Section 504 or IDEA.

If a multidisciplinary team determines that a student has "ADD or ADHD" and has an educational need that requires special education, the student may still be eligible for special education services even if he or she has no other disability. Many students with attention deficits (67 percent) have co-occurring disabilities, such as a learning disability or emotional disturbance, which are also qualifying disabilities under IDEA. In 2004, researchers reported that nearly two-thirds of youth served in classes for students with emotional problems also have an attention deficit.[7] It is not unusual to find a student in a special education class who also has undiagnosed attention deficits, so it is important for multidisciplinary teams to also screen for "ADD or ADHD"-related problems. If a student appears to have more than one of the disabilities defined by IDEA, he or she should be found eligible in each of the disability categories, and the IEP should address the unique needs of the student with respect to each of the disabilities.

Some states require diagnosis by a medical doctor for eligibility under the OHI category in addition to a variety of information from other sources; others do not. However, a medical diagnosis of AD/HD alone does not make a student eligible for services.

2. WHAT SHOULD A TEACHER DO IF "ADD OR ADHD" IS SUSPECTED?

A teacher may notice that a student who has not been diagnosed has behaviors characteristic of "ADD or ADHD." Often, experienced teachers say that they "know" a student has an attention deficit, even though he or she has not been evaluated or labeled. In this situation, teachers can recommend that a child be evaluated although they should never suggest a diagnosis. Teachers must walk the fine line between honoring their experience and avoiding premature conclusions and labels. Rather than ask, "Does this child have 'ADD or AD/HD?'" teachers should ask first, *"Is something interfering with the education of this child?"* If the answer is "yes," the next question should be, *"What is it?"* Typically, teachers take several steps to ensure that students are successful in school.

✓ **Schedule a parent conference.** If a teacher is concerned about a student who has symptoms of "ADD or ADHD," he or she should first *contact the parents* to explore possible causes and solutions. A few conditions and disorders share some common characteristics with attention deficits. For example, a hyperactive child or daydreaming teen may be adjusting to a new stepparent or sibling in the home or a family crisis, such as divorce or financial hardship, or have a health problem such as allergies, depression, or a sleep disorder. Typically, teachers describe the behaviors of concern and state facts to

14

illustrate them. For example, "Your son is not completing his school work and right now he has a 56 average in my Algebra class." Teachers are advised never to tell a parent that their child has an attention deficit because they can't officially diagnose the condition.

✓ **Offer simple interventions or accommodations.** Initially most teachers work with the student and parents to implement a few simple supports or accommodations to address learning problems. For example, parents can monitor Algebra homework completion and its return to school while the teacher can provide an extra Algebra book to keep at home and assign a peer to remind the student to write down assignments. These simple interventions, often called *prereferral strategies,* must be implemented prior to referring a child to a multidisciplinary team for evaluation.

✓ **Consult a multidisciplinary team for evaluation.** If the parent-teacher conference does not produce enough information or ideas, schools have a team of veteran educators that can be called in when teachers need more support for an individual child. This team discusses the behaviors of concern, generates possible solutions, and reconvenes to discuss the results of any interventions.

The teacher and other team members must first ask themselves whether they have reason to suspect that the student has a disability, as suspicion that a disability exists triggers legal obligations. If the student continues to struggle after implementation of simple supports in the classroom, the student should be scheduled for a more formal evaluation. The student is then screened for eligibility for services under either IDEA and Section 504. If students fail to meet IDEA criteria, then they should automatically be considered for eligibility under Section 504.

✓ **Develop, implement, and monitor an IEP or 504 plan.** Once eligibility is determined, an educational plan, known as a 504 plan or IEP, will be developed in conjunction with the IEP team, parents, and when appropriate, the students themselves. The IEP establishes goals that help students improve their academic performance or address other identified challenges. Several grade level-appropriate intervention strategies and accommodations to address specific deficits are available in Chapters 3–11.

3. WHAT ARE COMMON "ADD/ADHD BEHAVIORS" INDICATING THE NEED FOR AN IEP OR 504 PLAN?[8]

Several unique, yet less well-known, challenges face many students with attention deficits and should be addressed by the 504 plan or IEP. Many of their "ADD/ADHD behaviors" are also linked to deficits in executive function and their 30 percent developmental delay.

✓ **Deficits in working memory.** Students will have a limited capacity for holding information in mind, manipulating it, and then reorganizing it. This is a skill that is required for writing an essay, solving complex math problems, and reading comprehension. Students may lack the intuitive knowledge and study strategies required to memorize basic facts, such as multiplication tables, or study for tests.

✓ **Difficulty activating and maintaining effort.** Students will have difficulty getting started on tasks and persisting until the work is finished.

✓ **An impaired sense of time.** Students cannot accurately judge the passage of time. Consequently, they are often late and have difficulty estimating how long a task will take to complete. In addition, they will have difficulty planning ahead and managing the time and work required to complete long-term projects.

✓ **Poor regulation of emotions.** These students will be more emotionally reactive and have major problems with self-control so they are less likely to stop and think before they act or speak. Thus, they may talk excessively, impulsively blurt out in class, talk back to teachers, or get into fights at school.

✓ **Difficulty using "self-talk" to control behavior.** Internalized speech will be delayed, which means these students are less likely to use self-talk to direct their behavior to complete future tasks or to control their own behavior. They may have trouble following rules, don't learn as easily from past mistakes, and may repeat misbehavior.

✓ **Difficulty analyzing, reconstituting, and problem-solving.** Students will have problems with the complex problem-solving skills required for critical tasks at school and in life. For example, this deficit impacts their verbal fluency and speed of verbal processing, ability to communicate clearly and concisely with others, complete complex math problems, write essays, sequence information, and organize ideas. The student may have wonderful ideas for an essay topic that he is unable to capture, organize, and write down on paper. In addition, they may not fully comprehend directions from the teacher regarding expectations for assignments or behavior in the classroom.

✓ **Slow processing speed and slow retrieval of information.** Taking an abnormally long time to complete work is another manifestation of executive function deficits. This deficit may impact both written work and verbal expression. Students with "ADD" are more likely to have difficulty completing work as quickly as their peers and may avoid answering questions in class.

✓ **Disorganization.** Many of these deficits contribute to a sense of chronic disorganization among these students. Lockers are often a "black hole" where homework papers are lost forever. Homework is completed but not turned in. These students require extensive supervision from parents or teachers to help them organize work materials and time. When disorganization is debilitating, teachers must provide *developmentally appropriate supervision,* which means more supervision and more often than for other students.

✓ **Forgetfulness.** Students are extremely forgetful. Forgetfulness is not simply a matter of choice or laziness; it is one of the diagnostic criteria for attention deficits. Although they forget tasks they want to avoid, they also forget enjoyable events and activities in which they *want* to participate. Home-

work assignments are often forgotten or postponed, resulting in failure to submit homework in a timely manner. Thus, students often receive more zero grades on homework and long-term projects than their classmates. They may forget to stay after school for detention or to take home their books needed for homework.

✓ **Undiagnosed coexisting conditions.** Teachers should be watchful for other coexisting conditions, such as learning disabilities, depression, anxiety, or bipolar disorder. Sleep disturbances are also present in over half of these children, resulting in extreme difficulty falling asleep, waking up, and getting restful sleep. As a result, students may be late to school or appear tired and sleep in class. If other conditions are suspected, discuss the issue with your multidisciplinary team and decide whether to encourage parents to talk with their doctor.

4. CAN STUDENTS WITH ADD OR ADHD ALSO HAVE LEARNING DISABILITIES?

Yes, 25 to 50 percent of students with AD/HD qualify as having a specific learning disability under federal laws. Russell Barkley, Ph.D., has reported significant learning disabilities in several areas: reading (8 to 39 percent), math (12 to 30 percent), and spelling (12 to 27 percent).[9] In addition, two researchers, Susan Mayes, Ph.D., and Susan Calhoun, M.S., found that 65% of these students had deficits in written expression.

5. DOES A STUDENT HAVE TO BE FAILING ANY CLASSES TO BE ELIGIBLE FOR SERVICES?

No, federal law makes it clear that a student does not have to be failing to be eligible for services. According to an April 5, 1995 policy statement from the U.S. Department of Education Office of Special Education Programs (Letter to Lillie, 23 IDELR 714, OSEP):[11]

The evaluation should "consider information about outside or extra learning support provided to the child when determining whether a child who received satisfactory grades is nevertheless not achieving at age level. The child's current educational achievement may reflect the service augmentation not what the child's achievement would be without such help. Such information may also have bearing on the evaluation team's conclusions, required by (law), on whether the child has a severe discrepancy between achievement and ability that is not correctable without special education and related services." The 1999 regulations also indicated that the student "could be passing from grade to grade…"

In other words, educators should also take into consideration that students with attention deficits may be passing their classes primarily because of medication or the Herculean efforts of students, parents, or tutors. If these supports are withdrawn, the student's academic performance may decline significantly. Very bright students may learn enough information to pass tests simply by attending class, but regardless of how bright, if students are failing, extra supports will be needed.

According to Dixie Jordan, an educational consultant of the PACER Center, the student's ability to meet "age/grade-appropriate standards of personal independence and social responsibility" should also be taken into consideration during an evaluation. The importance of these skills is often overlooked. Unfortunately, because of their significant developmental delay and executive function deficits,[12] students with attention deficits often seem immature and unmotivated. In reality, they simply lack the necessary skills for independence.

6. WHAT ABOUT CHILDREN WHO ARE ON GRADE LEVEL BUT ARE BRIGHT AND NOT ACHIEVING UP TO THEIR ABILITY LEVELS?

These children may be eligible for services in certain situations. The 1995 OSEP memo also noted that

"…a student may be eligible for services if the team determines that the child does not achieve commensurate with his or her age and ability levels…"

One simple way of interpreting this statement is that "age level" refers to being on grade level and "ability level" refers to children who are intellectually capable of functioning at a higher level of academic achievement.

7. ARE CHILDREN WITH A HIGH IQ ELIGIBLE FOR SERVICES?

Yes, the 1995 OSEP memo states that "there is no categorical exclusion for children with high IQs…therefore, if a student with a high IQ is not achieving at this expected performance standard," and also meets eligibility criteria, the student can be eligible for services. The student could have dual classification as Gifted-OHI or Gifted-LD. "Each child who is evaluated for a suspected learning disability must be measured against his own expected performance, and not against some arbitrary general standard."

This means that a gifted child who is achieving on grade level could still be eligible for services. Furthermore, some students with attention deficits can score high on some achievement test categories but have really low scores on math computation or written expression sufficient to meet eligibility criteria.

8. WHAT SHOULD BE DONE IF A STUDENT HAS AN IEP BUT CONTINUES TO STRUGGLE?

According to Ms. Jordan of the PACER Center:

"We should never have a child with an IEP who is failing. That is a clear signal that something is terribly wrong with the IEP. Perhaps, expectations were too high, interventions were not intensive enough, or the duration of the intervention was not long enough. School failure is a signal for scheduling an IEP meeting immediately and revising the goals or adding needed services."

Ms. Jordan adds that "a 504 plan or IEP may be ineffective for a variety of reasons, for example:
✓ All learning problems not have been identified.
✓ Executive function deficits have not been addressed.

✓ Effective accommodations or modifications have not been put in place or are not being implemented consistently.

✓ Appropriate accommodations are not yet being provided.

✓ Some teachers may not be following the requirements of the IEP or 504 plan.

Regardless of the reasons for the ineffective IEP or 504 plan, the bottom line is this: if the student has an educational plan and is still struggling or perhaps even failing, something is terribly wrong! *Changes must be made to the IEP or 504 plan so that the student is more likely to be successful in school.* An IEP meeting may be requested at *any* time to revise the plan. A Functional Behavior Assessment (FBA) can be conducted to aid in the development of a Behavior Intervention Plan (BIP) or Behavior Management Plan."

9. IF A STUDENT HAS AN IEP THAT REQUIRES ACCOMMODATIONS, IS A CLASSROOM TEACHER REQUIRED TO PROVIDE THEM?

Yes, teachers are obligated to comply with IEPs developed by the local IEP team. In 1993, a West Virginia teacher refused to read tests orally to a student as required by the IEP. Even after urging by the principal and superintendent, the teacher refused to comply with the IEP. The student failed history and was barred from extracurricular activities. Subsequently, the parents sued and won a $15,000 judgment from the teacher alone.[13] Because the school system, principal, and superintendent fully supported provision of the accommodation, they did not have to pay any legal fines.

10. WHAT ARE POSITIVE BEHAVIOR SUPPORTS?

Changes to IDEA in the late 1990s require more frequent use of positive behavior supports with students to prevent future problems. George Sugai, Ph.D., of the University of Oregon, director of OSEP's official website on Positive Behavioral Interventions and Supports (PBIS), is recognized as one of the leading authorities on this topic. Dr. Sugai pioneered *school-wide positive behavioral intervention and support programs,*

which are extremely effective not only in reducing behavior problems and special education referrals but also in improving academic performance. Visit **http://www.pbis.org** for more detailed information on PBIS, FBA, and BIP. Additional information on PBIS is available in Chapter 5.

11. WHAT ARE FUNCTIONAL BEHAVIOR ASSESSMENTS AND BEHAVIOR INTERVENTION PLANS?[14]

When students have shown a pattern of several disruptive incidents at school especially if they place the student at risk of school suspension, the multidisciplinary teams should meet to discuss strategies to prevent future reoccurrence of the problem behavior.

A good FBA will address several key issues: behavior, context, antecedent or trigger behavior, contributing factors, function of behavior, teachers' response and student reaction, continuation of behavior, potential rewards, and previous effective interventions. This analysis of problem behaviors will help in the development of an effective behavioral intervention plan (BIP)."[14]

12. IF A STUDENT WITH "ADD OR ADHD" IS SUSPENDED FOR BEHAVIOR PROBLEMS, WHAT INTERVENTIONS SHOULD THE SCHOOL PROVIDE PURSUANT TO THE IEP OR 504 PLAN?

When characteristics of "ADD or ADHD," such as impulsivity and forgetfulness, are contributing to behavior problems, the school must develop a positive behavioral intervention plan to address the behavior. A Functional Behavior Assessment should be conducted and a positive Behavior Intervention Plan developed to address the behavior. The school should also reconsider any existing IEP or 504 plans. The plan may have to be revised with more appropriate interventions or accommodations or is not being implemented correctly. Punishment alone is not sufficient. The teachers may also need training for coping with AD/HD behaviors.

If a student who has an IEP or 504 plan has been suspended more than 10 days, the school must conduct

14

a "manifestation determination hearing" to see if the misbehavior subject to disciplinary action is linked to the disability. Alternative disciplinary procedures to existing school policies can be written into the IEP or 504 plan.

13. WHY IS IT IMPORTANT TO ESTABLISH DISABILITY ELIGIBILITY NO LATER THAN HIGH SCHOOL?

Some students with mild "ADHD or ADD" and have extremely supportive school environments, complete with accommodations and parents who are actively involved, may not need services under IDEA or Section 504 even in high school. However, these students may be "just getting by" and if these supports are withdrawn when the student reaches college or technical school, they may flounder and fail. Consequently, establishing Section 504 or IDEA eligibility no later than the secondary school years is important for obtaining services in college or vocational school environments. Post-secondary institutions provide students the same accommodations that they received in high school but require documentation of the student's learning problems and the subsequent provision of specific accommodations. Section 504 and IDEA provide important documentation of the need for accommodations in college or vocational school.

Since 1995, meeting eligibility criteria for accommodations on the SAT and ACT has become increasingly difficult. Both the SAT and ACT have endorsed a policy statement, developed by a group known as the ADHD Consortium, that states that an IEP or Section 504 plan are important, but in isolation are not sufficient documentation for accommodations. The new policy requires a lengthy comprehensive evaluation that is not older than three years and is conducted by a licensed professional.[15]

Conclusion

Unaddressed academic and behavioral needs of students with attention deficits take a toll on their educational performance as evidenced by higher dropout rates, lower graduation rates, lower grade averages, higher rates of suspensions and expulsions, and lower college attendance. Unfortunately, academic problems among these students also take a tremendous emotional toll on the whole family since the student is aware that he is smart enough to "do better" and yet is at a loss to explain why he or she can't do the work. The tragedy here is that many special education class placements could have been avoided if the AD/HD had been treated and effective intervention strategies offered during earlier school years.

The information given in this chapter is stated in general terms and is not intended as legal advice. Local school districts frequently have their own individual policies and procedures. Furthermore, each of the fifty states and many local jurisdictions have their own set of laws. Should a legal issue arise, please consult your local school administration or an attorney.

Model Programs

Chapter 15: Promising Practices in Education

Ten model programs are featured in this chapter.

PRESCHOOL AND ELEMENTARY
✓ The Regional Intervention Program
✓ First Step to Success

ELEMENTARY
✓ The Irvine Paraprofessional Program (IPP)
✓ Summer Treatment Program (STP)

MIDDLE SCHOOL
✓ Challenging Horizons Program (CHP)

HIGH SCHOOL
✓ The Lehigh University — Consulting Center for Adolescents with Attention Deficit Disorders (LU–CCAADD)

ALL GRADE LEVELS
✓ CLASS Act
✓ Kenosha WI School District Continuum of Care

COLLEGE
✓ The SALT Center

PARENTS
✓ CHADD Parent-to-Parent Training Program (P2P)

Promising Practices in Education

Mark Katz, Ph.D.

C HADD believes schools benefit from an awareness of exceptional programs that serve students with AD/HD. Model programs are often featured at CHADD's annual conferences as well as in articles in *Attention!* Magazine. Some programs have proven remarkably effective in reversing the developmental trajectories of young children prone to aggressive and poorly controlled behavior. Others have facilitated cooperative working relationships between parents and local schools to ensure that students with AD/HD are successful in school. Perhaps you may find one of these programs worthy of replication in your own school district.

Preschool and Elementary

The first two programs for preschool and early elementary age children have been recognized nationally for their effectiveness. They have also received CHADD's Innovative Program of the Year Award.

1. THE REGIONAL INTERVENTION PROGRAM[1]

The Regional Intervention Program specializes in providing parents with the tools they need to effectively teach their preschool and kindergarten age children to better manage and control their behavior. The program, which draws upon a variety of evidence-based practices, is specifically designed around the needs of parents of children prone toward aggression or other forms of acting out behavior or who struggle in their ability to listen, follow directions,

and get along with others. The program requires that at least one parent or guardian attend training sessions with their child twice a week. During sessions, parents are coached on how to attend to behaviors that need to increase and how to ignore behaviors that need to decrease. Importantly, they practice the skills in situations that look a lot like those where tantrums and out-of-control behavior are common – when the child hears the word "no," for example, when a parent is talking on the phone, or when company comes to visit. Parents practice these skills until they're mastered. All children also participate in a classroom-based social skills training program. Here, children learn skills necessary for making friends and getting along with others. All children also participate in a preschool classroom module where they learn and practice specific skills they need to adjust successfully to school, both in the short-term and years down the road.

Program Information
http://www.ripnetwork.org

Contact Information
Kate Driskill Kanies
Regional Intervention Program
3411 Belmont Boulevard
Nashville, TN 37215
615-963-1177
kate.kanies@state.tn.us

Research Information
Matthew Timm, Ph.D.
Tennessee Voices for Children
1315 8th Avenue South
Nashville, TN 37203
mtimm@tnvoices.org

Phillip Strain, Ph.D.
University of Colorado
1380 Lawrence Street, Suite 650
Denver, CO 80204
phil_strain@ceo.cudenver.edu

2.   FIRST STEP TO SUCCESS[2]

Developed by researchers at the University of Oregon's Institute on Violence and Destructive Behavior (IVDB) under the direction of Hill Walker, Ph.D., *First Step to Success* includes three modules: 1) a universal screening procedure for all kindergarten age school children; 2) a school intervention component that includes the active participation of the teacher, the at-risk child, and the child's classmates; and 3) a parent/caregiver component that involves a home-based parent training program, along with strategies designed to foster home-school collaborative practices. Initially, the trainer teaches a lesson for 20 to 30 minutes; later on, the teacher teaches the lesson with supervision from the trainer. Finally, during the maintenance phase, lessons are integrated into the school day's routine, and as the students master skills, behavioral rewards are scaled back.

The home component consists of a weekly series of lessons, games, and activities that target six areas related to school performance: 1) communication and sharing in school; 2) cooperation; 3) limit setting, 4) problem solving, 5) friendship making, and 6) development of confidence.

Program Information
First Step to Success
Sopris West Publishing
800-547-6747

Contact Information
Hill Walker, Ph.D., Co-Director
Institute on Violence and Destructive Behavior
University of Oregon
1265 University of Oregon
Eugene, OR 97403
541-346-3592
hwalker@oregon.uoregon.edu

Elementary School

These nationally recognized innovative models have both been recognized as CHADD Innovative Programs of the Year. The IPP trains paraprofessional behavioral specialists to assist teachers in the regular classroom. The summer camp program (STP) provides intensive academic and behavioral interventions and follow-up interventions at home and at school.

3.   THE IRVINE PARAPROFESSIONAL PROGRAM (IPP)[3]

An outgrowth of the University of California, Irvine Child Development Center (UCI-CDC) treatment model — a highly successful and nationally recognized comprehensive multimodal treatment model developed by James Swanson, Ph.D., for children with severe AD/HD — IPP trains undergraduate university students to function as paraprofessional behavioral specialists in regular elementary school classrooms. Teachers within surrounding school districts who are struggling to manage one or more children in their regular education classrooms can call upon these trained behavioral specialists to assist them. At the teacher's request, and under the supervision of the school's psychologist, the behavioral specialist designs and implements a specific 10 to 12 week behavioral program that addresses the needs of one or more struggling students. And perhaps just as important, this person also assists the teacher in providing extra help and enrichment to all of the other children in class.

A hallmark of all individualized behavioral plans is how frequently and immediately children with AD/HD are caught doing the "right thing" in class. At the outset, this occurs every 15 minutes over a several hour period of time. As the child's behavior and time on task improves, time intervals are expanded, eventually to 45 minutes. Once the child is able to maintain gains up to 45 minutes, behavioral specialists begin transferring the behavioral plan to the teacher.

Initial outcome studies showed a 50 percent reduction in disruptive behaviors for children receiving IPP services over the course of an academic year. Children in the control group, on the other hand, showed a 15 percent increase in disruptive behaviors over the same time period. The program, under the direction of Ron Kotkin, Ph.D., has been so effective that it has been replicated in over 200 schools across the country and was part of the landmark Multimodal Treatment Study on AD/HD sponsored by the National Institute of Mental Health and the U.S. Department of Education.

Contact Information
Ron Kotkin, Ph.D., Director
Day Treatment and Community-Based Programs
UCI Child Development Center
UCI Medical Center
101 The City Drive South
Orange, CA 92868
949-824-2343
rakotkin@uci.edu

4. SUMMER TREATMENT PROGRAM (STP)

Intensive summer camps established by William Pelham, Jr., Ph.D., are a nationally recognized model program. Five different forms of intervention are utilized in this six to eight week program that runs for six to nine hours on weekdays. Both academic and peer problems are addressed. Most of the day is spent participating in recreational activities, such as baseball and soccer, where skills, strategy, and rules are taught. Additionally, campers are provided intensive practice in social and problem-solving skills, good teamwork, decreasing negative behaviors, and developing close friendships.

Two hours are reserved for academics, including related skills such as organization. During the school year, follow-up services are available via direct contacts and phone consultations with teachers. Parent training and intensive follow-up in the home are also provided.

Detailed guidelines for establishing a school-home daily report card are also provided. This program has been replicated at several sites around the country as shown on its website.

Program Information
http://wings.buffalo.edu/adhd

Contact Information
William Pelham, Jr., Ph.D., Director
Professor of Psychology, Pediatrics & Psychiatry
Center for Children and Families
The State University of New York at Buffalo
318 Diefendorf Hall
3435 Main Street
Buffalo, NY 14214
716-829-2244

Middle School

These innovative programs are designed to help middle schoolers with AD/HD.

5. THE CHALLENGING HORIZONS PROGRAM (CHP)

Working in collaboration with a local middle school in Harrisonburg, VA, researchers at James Madison University, under the direction of Steven W. Evans, Ph.D., have developed an innovative and cost-effective multimodal treatment model that addresses common AD/HD middle school trouble spots at school (incomplete assignments, notetaking problems, difficulties with transitions), at home (completing homework), and within the context of social and recreational settings (recognizing nonverbal cues, knowing how to join in a game or activity). The treatment model weaves together four school-based service components:

1) **Debriefing with a mentor after school.** In 30-minute individual counseling sessions after school, the "mentor," a university-trained student or graduate student, talks with the student as they debrief about events of the school day.

15

2) **Participating in social skills training and practice.** Students attend an interpersonal skills group where they review and practice different social skills, especially those relating to actual social situations encountered at school or in the afterschool program. Roleplaying and videotaping different social situations are integral parts of the program.

3) **Participating in recreational activities.** Students are coached not only on rules underlying different games and sports activities, but also on the subtleties — the unwritten rules, in other words — like how to join in a pick-up game of basketball.

4) **Practicing academic skills.** Program staff simulate an actual classroom situation and have students practice critical classroom skills like notetaking, organizing materials for class, or successfully transitioning from one subject or class to another. Students also begin working on their homework.

Before leaving, students meet again with their individual counselor to be sure they're ready to handle the evening's homework assignments and to troubleshoot other potential upcoming problem areas. Program staff follow up with teachers to get feedback and ensure that program goals are addressing areas that teachers feel are most important. Parents also receive training and meet with staff on an ongoing basis to assess progress and help troubleshoot any problems at home.

Program Information
http://chp.cisat.jmu.edu

Contact Information
Steven W. Evans, Ph.D.
Challenging Horizons Program
Alvin V. Baird Attention and Learning
   Disabilities Center
James Madison University
Blue Ridge Hall, MSC 9013
Harrisonburg, VA 22807
chp@jmu.edu
540-568-6484

Bob Scott, Principal
Montevideo Middle School
7648 McGaheysville Road
Penn Laird, VA 22846
540-289-3401

6. THE LEHIGH UNIVERSITY— CONSULTING CENTER FOR ADOLESCENTS WITH ATTENTION DEFICIT DISORDERS (LU-CCAADD).

The LU-CCAADD project, funded by the U.S. Department of Education, was developed by George DuPaul, Ph.D., and Edward Shapiro, Ph.D. This important school-based program provides three basic levels of services:

✓ In-service training for educational staff in assessment, school-based interventions, parent training, collaboration with the community, and peer-relationship interventions

✓ Behavioral consultation for identifying students with AD/HD, designing treatment plans, communicating with physicians, and assisting in implementation of parent, social skills, self-management, and program evaluation services

✓ Advance knowledge, dissemination, and consultation to educational staff

Results

Outcome studies from the LU-CCAADD projects are promising. Teachers…

✓ increased their knowledge about AD/HD.

✓ were satisfied with the services provided by the program.

✓ were still using the strategies they learned in the program.

✓ adapted strategies for new students who were not in the program.

✓ wanted more information on AD/HD.

Program Information

Although this program is no longer operational, their final report to the DOE is available through ERIC (document number ED419328) at http://www.eric.ed.gov.

All Grade Levels

Several model programs have been established in local communities that exemplify the ideal working relationship between school systems and local CHADD leaders. Two programs have set a high standard for developing effective educational programs for students with AD/HD who would otherwise struggle terribly in school. Several CHADD members have been involved in the development of these programs: Kathy Hubbard Weeks, M.S.W., Anne Teeter Ellison, Ed.D., Joan Helbing, B.A., and Paula Stewart, R.N., in Wisconsin and Linda Smith, B.A., in Utah. These programs could be implemented in other communities without significant additional funding.

7. CLASS ACT, DAVIS COUNTY SCHOOLS, UTAH

A unique school-parent partnership, Collaborative Learning Accommodation Services for Students, better known as CLASS Act, was created to serve students with attention deficits or other learning problems. Through this innovative program, an individualized educational plan is developed for *all* students who are struggling. Students who do not qualify for special education yet appear to have a disability are automatically referred to the school Section 504 coordinator for consideration

Davis District has managed to develop this model program systemwide in all 77 schools, despite Utah having one of the lowest per capita spending rates and the highest number of students per classroom. The program was so effective in the 2002-2003 school year that Davis County did not expel any students or refer any to an institution. The key elements of the CLASS Act/504 program include these impressive components:

✓ District level Director
✓ Secondary and elementary 504 coordinators

✓ Section 504 coordinator in each school (not just at the county level)
  – 10 hours of training each year
  – Reference manual for each 504 Coordinator and school administrator
✓ Trainer of Trainers Model for CLASS Act Teachers
  – Seven Master CLASS Act Teacher trainers
  – Designated CLASS Act Teacher at each school
  – 10 to 12 hours of training for each CLASS Act Teacher
✓ Parent training
  – 14 hours of training for parents, "AD/HD 101," offered three times a year
  – Training is cotaught by parents and school personnel
  – Training from nationally known experts
✓ Students
  – Provided individual supports as needed
  – Study skills classes at middle and high school levels

Results

Improved grades and citizenship for 91 percent of students served.

Program Information

http://www.davis.k12.ut.us/district/classact/504/index.html

Contact Information

Ellen Stantus, Director
Davis District
CLASS Act/504 Department
70 East 100 North
Farmington, UT 84025
801-402-5143

8. KENOSHA WI SCHOOL DISTRICT CONTINUUM OF CARE.

Another innovative program for students who are struggling, especially those with attention deficit disorder, was initiated in the Kenosha Wisconsin

15

Unified Public School District in 1990 under the leadership of Kathy Hubbard Weeks, M.S.W. After the successes achieved by the Kenosha Project, as it was known, AD/HD consultants were established statewide for several school systems. Here are highlights of their program components:

✓ AD/HD Consultant to help teachers
✓ Intensive training on AD/HD for teachers (16 hours)
  – A year-long 30-hour advanced study group
  – In-service credits
✓ Counseling groups for students with attention deficits
✓ Attention deficit education plans
✓ Parent education and an annual conference plus regular training
✓ Reading Recovery, which helps students achieve grade level
✓ Bridges Programs, which provides intensive instruction to students who are behind
✓ Graduation make-up credits via a self-paced computer program
✓ Partnership with local businesses to offer a range of high tech career training

Program Information
http://www.kusd.edu/departments/ssps/add/addhome.htm

Contact Information
Melissa Werner
262-653-6332
mwerner@kusd.edu

College
Finally, this innovative program was designed to help college students cope with AD/HD.

9. THE SALT CENTER
The University of Arizona's SALT Center (Strategic Alternative Learning Techniques) provides students with AD/HD and learning disabilities a wide array of services that go well beyond simple accommodations and, in the process, significantly increases their likelihood of academic success. Over 75 percent of SALT students graduate within five years, exceeding the campuswide average graduation rate of 55 percent.

For each eligible incoming freshman, the SALT Center learning specialists play a pivotal role in helping them transition into university life, and eventually into their chosen major and career path. Together, they develop an individualized learning plan that, among other things, spells out those academic, organizational and time management strategies, tutoring services, campus resources, and additional supports that match up best with the student's learning strengths and challenges. Learning plans are also reviewed on an ongoing basis, and the learning specialist remains available to the student, as needed, until graduation. Program components include:

✓ 10 trained learning specialists
✓ 100+ content tutors
✓ Access to a writer's lab and writing tutors
✓ Computer software and educational technologies
✓ State-of-the-art assistive technologies
✓ Workshops on key skills and important career-related topics
  – Strategies for testtaking, study, organizational and time management, memorization, notetaking, and editing
  – Introduction to assistive technologies, including voice-activated and read-and-write software
  – Guidance on choosing a major and an eventual career path

Through the SALT LEAP Program (Learning to Excel Academically with Pride), seventh and eighth graders with learning disabilities or AD/HD, along with their parents and teachers, are invited to campus to meet successful college students who themselves struggled with learning and attention problems. These students are coached on preparing for college early and are provided with a checklist of activities that will help them anticipate and overcome the typical college barriers. The program's mission is to encourage these students to stay in school and not lose hope of someday being able to attend college and achieve their career goals.

Program Information
http://www.salt.arizona.edu

Contact Information
Jeff Orgera, Director
SALT Center
University of Arizona
P.O. Box 210136
Tucson, AZ 85721
520-621-1427
jorgera@u.arizona.edu

Parents
Educators may also be interested in referring parents to participate in the "Parent to Parent (P2P)" training module that CHADD has developed. Teachers may also be interested in attending the CHADD training and becoming certified P2P teachers.

10. PARENT TO PARENT: FAMILY TRAINING ON AD/HD.

"Parent to Parent" (P2P) provides a series of workshops containing educational information and support for individuals and families who are dealing with AD/HD. The sessions offer strategies for navigating the challenges of AD/HD across the lifespan. P2P is an intensive, 7-week, 14-hour course. The curriculum was developed by Beth Kaplanek, R.N., Linda Smith, B.A., and Mary Durheim, B.S. who, in addition to having professional expertise on AD/HD, have also lived the experience of parenting a child with this challenging condition. In addition, these parents received input from the best researchers and practitioners in the country. The course includes over 350 transparencies, extensive teacher notes, articles, reference materials, handouts, and home-work assignments. Here is an overview of the content:

✓ Overview of AD/HD
✓ Assessment and Multimodal Treatment
✓ The Impact of AD/HD on the Family
✓ Creating Developmentally Appropriate and Positive Behavioral Interventions
✓ Developing Parenting Strategies and Interventions to Strengthen Family Relationships
✓ What Do I Do When My Child is Having Difficulty at School?: Understanding the Federal Education Laws
✓ Working with Schools: Building an Education Team that Works
✓ AD/HD Across the Life Span: Teens and Adults with AD/HD

Program Information
http://www.chadd.org

Contact Information
Parent to Parent Administrative Assistant
CHADD
8181 Professional Place, Suite 150
Landover, MD 20785
301-306-7070, ext. 133

Summary
In summary, a small sampling of innovative programs and practices benefiting those impacted by AD/HD have been presented in this chapter. Those interested in learning about other programs are encouraged to attend CHADD's annual national conference, where an entire session is devoted exclusively to highlighting promising practices from around the country. New innovative programs are also regularly featured in CHADD's *Attention!* Magazine.

15

APPENDIX A

Resources By Chapter

Chapter 1 — Introduction and Overview

AD/HD and Coexisting Disorders (What We Know Sheet #5).
http://www.help4adhd.org, CHADD, 2003.
AD/HD Predominantly Inattentive Type (What We Know Sheet #8).
http://www.help4adhd.org, CHADD, 2004.
Attention Deficit Disorder. T.E. Brown. Yale University Press, 2005.
Attention Deficit Disorders and Comorbidities in Children, Adolescents and Adults. T.E. Brown (Ed.). American Psychiatric Press, 2000.
Attention-Deficit Hyperactivity Disorder (3rd ed.). R.A. Barkley. Guilford Press, 2006.
Attention Deficit Hyperactivity Disorder: State of the Science — Best Practices. P.S. Jensen, J.R. Cooper. Civic Research Institute, 2002.
Interventions for ADHD. P.A. Teeter. Guilford Press, 2000.
Kids in the Syndrome Mix of ADHD, LD, Asperger's, Tourette's, Bipolar, and More! M. Kutscher. Jessica Kingsley Publishers, 2005.
Managing Medication for Children and Adolescents with AD/HD (What We Know Sheet #3). http://www.help4adhd.org, CHADD, 2004.
The ADHD Handbook for Schools. H.C. Parker. Specialty Warehouse, 2005.
The Disorder Named AD/HD (What We Know Sheet #1). http://help4adhd.org, CHADD, 2004.
Understanding and Managing Children's Classroom Behavior. S. Goldstein. John Wiley & Sons, Inc., 1994.

Chapter 2 — Diagnosis

ADHD in Adolescents. A.L. Robin. Guilford Press, 1998.
Attention-Deficit Hyperactivity Disorder (3rd ed.). R.A. Barkley. Guilford Press, 2006.
Critical Issues in Assessing AD/HD. NASP Communiqué, Vol. 28, No. 6, 2000.
Mental Health: Culture, Race, and Ethnicity, A Supplement to Mental Health: A Report of the Surgeon General. Office of the U.S. Surgeon General, 2001.
School Neuropsychology of Attention-Deficit/Hyperactivity Disorder. P.A. Teeter Ellison. In R. D'Amato, E. Fletcher-Jansen, C. Reynolds (Eds.), The Handbook of School Neuropsychology (pp. 460–486). John Wiley & Sons, Inc., 2005.

Chapters 3–5 — Key Academic Issues

IMPACT OF ADHD ON SCHOOL PERFORMANCE
ADHD. R.A. Lougy, D.K. Rosenthal. Hope Press, 2002.
ADHD & LD (Video). S.F. Rief. http://www.sandrarief.com, Educational Resource Specialists, 2004.
ADHD in the Schools, 2nd ed. G.J. DuPaul, G.J. Stoner. Guilford Press, 2004.
How to Reach and Teach All Children in the Inclusive Classroom, 2nd Ed. S.F. Rief, J. Heimburge. Jossey-Bass, 2006.
How to Reach and Teach Children with ADD/ADHD, 2nd ed. S.F. Rief. Jossey-Bass, 2005.
Interventions for ADHD. P.A. Teeter. Guilford Press, 2000.
Practical Suggestions for ADHD. C.B. Jones, LinguiSystems, 2003.
Problem Solver Guide for Students with ADHD. H.C. Parker, Specialty Press, 2002.
Strategies for Teaching Students with Learning and Behavior Problems. C. Bos, S. Vaughn. Allyn & Bacon, 1994.

Teaching Teens with ADD and ADHD. C.A.Z. Dendy. Woodbine House, 2000.
Teenagers with ADD and ADHD, 2nd ed. C.A.Z. Dendy. Woodbine House, 2006.
The ADD/ADHD Checklist. S.F. Rief. Jossey-Bass, 2003.
The ADHD Book of Lists. S.F. Rief. Jossey-Bass, 1998.

PREVENTING AND REDUCING BEHAVIORAL PROBLEMS
1-2-3 Magic, 3rd ed. T.W. Phelan. ParentMagic, Inc., 2003.
ADD/ADHD Behavior-Change Resource Kit. G.L. Flick. Jossey-Bass, 1998.
ADHD. R.A. Lougy, D.K. Rosenthal. Hope Press, 2002.
ADHD in the Schools, 2nd ed. G.J. DuPaul, Gary J. Stoner. Guilford Press, 2004.
All About ADHD. L.J. Pfiffner. Scholastic, 1996.
Fred Jones Tools for Teaching. F.H. Jones, B. Jones. Fredric H. Jes & Associates, Inc., 2000.
From Chaos to Calm. J.E. Heininger, S.K. Weiss. Perigee Books, 2001.
From Defiance to Cooperation. J.F. Taylor, Prima Publishing, 2001.
How to Reach and Teach Children with ADD/ADHD, 2nd ed. S.F. Rief. Jossey-Bass, 2005.
How to Reach and Teach All Children in the Inclusive Classroom, 2nd Ed. S.F. Rief, J. Heimburge. Jossey-Bass, 2006.
Interventions for ADHD. P.A. Teeter. Guilford Press, 2000.
Managing Unmanageable Students. E.K. McEwan, M. Damer, Corwin Press, 1999.
Positive Parenting Practices for Attention Deficit Disorder. T. Illes. Jordan School District, Utah, 2002.
Practical Suggestions for ADHD. C.B. Jones, LinguiSystems, 2003.
Raising Resilient Children. R. Brooks, S. Goldstein, Contemporary Books, 2001.
Taking Charge of ADHD (Rev. Ed.). R.A. Barkley. Guilford Press, 2000.
Teaching Teens with ADD and ADHD. C.A.Z. Dendy. Woodbine House, 2000.
The Acting-Out Child. H.M. Walker. Sopris West, 1995.
The ADD/ADHD Checklist. S.F. Rief. Jossey-Bass, 2003.
The ADHD Book of Lists. S.F. Rief. Jossey-Bass, 1998.
The ADHD Handbook for Schools. H.C. Parker. Specialty Warehouse, 2005.
The Teacher's Encyclopedia of Behavior Management. R.S. Sprick, L.M. Howard. Pacific Northwest Publishing, 1998.
The Tough Kid Book. G. Rhode, W.R. Jenson, H.K. Reavis. Sopris West, 1996.
The Tough Tool Box. W.R. Jenson, G. Rhode, H.K. Reavis. Sopris West, 1995.
Understanding and Managing Children's Classroom Behavior. S. Goldstein. John Wiley & Sons, Inc., 1994.
Violence Prevention and Reduction in Schools. W.N. Bender, G. Clinton, R.L. Bender (Eds.). Pro-Ed, Inc., 1999.

POSITIVE BEHAVIOR INTERVENTION STRATEGIES (PBIS)
Behaviorally Effective School Environments. G. Sugai, R. Horner, F. Gresham. In M. Shinn, H. Walker, G. Stoner (Eds.), Interventions for Academic and Behavior Problems II (pp. 315-350). NASP, 2002.
Effective Behavior Support. T.J. Lewis, G. Sugai. Focus on Exceptional Children, Vol. 31, No. 6, pp. 1-24, 1999.
Integrated Approaches to Preventing Antisocial Behavior Patterns Among School-age children and Youth. H.M. Walker, R.H. Horner, G. Sugai, M. Bullis, J.R. Sprague, D. Bricker, M.J. Kaufman. Journal of Emotional and Behavioral Disorders, Vol. 4, No. 4, pp. 194-209, 1996.

School-wide Positive Behavior Support. R.H. Horner, G. Sugai. In L. Bambara, L. Kern (Eds.), Positive Behavior Support (pp.359-390). Guilford Press, 2005.

The Evolution of Discipline Practices. G. Sugai, R.H. Horner. Child and Family Behavior Therapy, Vol. 24, Nos. 1-2, pp. 23-50. 2002.

Chapter 6 — Preschool

ACADEMIC AND LEARNING ISSUES

Interventions for ADHD. P.A. Teeter. Guilford Press, 2000.

Sourcebook for Children with Attention-Deficit disorder (Rev. ed.). C.B. Jones. Psychological Corporation, 1998.

DISCIPLINE/DIFFICULT BEHAVIOR

1-2-3 Magic for Teachers. T.W. Phelan, S.J. Schonour, D. Farrell. ParentMagic, Inc., 2004.

First Step to Success. Institute on Violence and Destructive Behavior, College of Education, University of Oregon, Eugene, OR.

Psychosocial Treatment for Children and Adolescents with AD/HD (What We Know Sheet #7). http://www.help4adhd.org, CHADD, 2004.

The Explosive Child. R.W. Greene. Harper Collins, 2005.

SOCIAL ISSUES

Raise Your Child's Social IQ. C. Cohen. Advantage Books, 2000.

Skillstreaming in Early Childhood. E. McGinnis, A.P. Goldstein. Research Press, 2003.

PARENTING ISSUES

CHADD Parent to Parent Training. http://www.chadd.org, 800-233-4050.

1-2-3 Magic. T.W. Phelan. Child Management Press, 1990.

Parenting a Child with AD/HD (What We Know Sheet #2). http://www.help4adhd.org, CHADD, 2004.

The ADHD Workbook for Parents. H.C. Parker. Specialty Press, 2005.

Triple P — Positive Parenting Program. http://www.triplep-america.com, 803-787-9944.

Chapter 7 — Elementary School

ACADEMIC AND LEARNING ISSUES

A Teacher's Guide: Attention Deficit Hyperactivity Disorders in Children. S. Goldstein, M. Goldstein. Neurology, Learning & Behavior Center, 2000.

ADHD in the Schools, 2nd ed. G.J. DuPaul, G.J. Stoner. Guilford Press, 2004.

Attention Deficit Disorder. C.B. Jones. Psychological Corp, 1998.

CHADD Parent to Parent Training. http://www.chadd.org, 800-233-4050

Helping Children Learn. J.A. Naglieri, E. Pickering. Paul H. Brookes Publishing, 2003.

How to Reach and Teach Children with ADD/ADHD, 2nd ed. S.F. Rief. Jossey-Bass, 2005.

Interventions for ADHD. P.A. Teeter. Guilford Press, 2000.

MyADHD.com. An on-line fee for service system to help parents and professionals minitor a student's academic performance.

Practical Suggestions for ADHD. C.B. Jones, LinguiSystems, 2003.

Problem Solver Guide for Students with ADHD. H.C. Parker, Specialty Press, 2002.

Seven Steps to Homework Success. S.S. Zentall, S. Goldstein. Specialty Press, 2000.

Study Strategies Made Easy. L. Davis, S. Sirotowitz, H.C. Parker. Specialty Warehouse, 1996.

The ADD Hyperactivity Workbook for Parents, Teachers, and Kids (3rd Ed.). H.C. Parker. Specialty Press, 1999.

The ADHD Book of Lists. S.F. Rief. Jossey-Bass, 1998.

The ADHD Handbook for Schools. H.C. Parker. Specialty Warehouse, 2005.

Understanding and Managing Children's Classroom Behavior. S. Goldstein. John Wiley & Sons, Inc., 1994.

DISCIPLINE AND DIFFICULT BEHAVIOR

1-2-3 Magic for Teachers. T.W. Phelan, S.J. Schonour, D. Farrell, ParentMagic, Inc., 2004.

Angry Children, Worried Parents. S. Goldstein, R. Brooks, S.K. Weiss. Specialty Press, 2004.

Elementary Teacher's Discipline Problem Solver. K. Shore. Jossey-Bass, 2003.

First Step to Success. Institute on Violence and Destructive Behavior, College of Education, University of Oregon, Eugene, OR 97403.

How to Handle a Hard-To-Handle Kid. C.D. Edwards. Free Spirit Publishing, 1999.

Psychosocial Treatment for Children and Adolescents with AD/HD (What We Know Sheet #7). http://www.help4adhd.org, CHADD, 2004.

Responding to Problem Behavior in Schools. D.A. Crone, R. Horner, L.S. Hawken. Guilford Press, 2003.

Why Johnny Doesn't Behave. B.D. Bateman, A. Golly. Attainment Publication, 2003.

Your Defiant Child. R.A. Barkley, C.M. Benton. Guilford Press, 1998.

SOCIAL SKILLS

Seven Steps to Improve Your Child's Social Skills. K. Hagar, S. Goldstein, R. Brooks. Specialty Press, 2006.

Skillstreaming in Early Childhood. E. McGinnis, A.P. Goldstein. Research Press, 2003.

Teaching Social Skills to Youth, 2nd Ed. T. Dowd, J. Tierney. Boys Town Press, 2005.

PARENTING ISSUES

1-2-3 Magic. T.W. Phelan. Child Management Press, 1990.

Attention, Please!. E.D. Copeland, V.L. Love. Specialty Press, 1995.

CHADD Parent to Parent Training. http://www.chadd.org, 800-233-4050

Dr. Larry Silver's Advice to Parents on ADHD (2nd Ed.). L. Silver. Three Rivers Press, 1999.

From Chaos to Calm. J.E. Heininger, S.K. Weiss. Perigee Books, 2001.

Understanding Girls with AD/HD. K.G. Nadeau, E.B. Littman, P.O. Quinn. Advantage Books, 2000.

Making the System Work for Your Child with ADHD. P.S. Jensen. Guilford Press, 2004.

Parenting a Child with AD/HD (What We Know Sheet #2). http://help4adhd.org, CHADD, 2004.

Preventive Parenting with Love, Encouragement, and Limits. T.J. Dishion, S.G. Patterson. Castalia Publishing Co., 1996.

Straight Talk about Psychiatric Medications for Kids, Rev. Ed. T.E. Wilens. Guilford Press, 2004.

The ADHD Workbook for Parents. H.C. Parker. Specialty Press, 2005.

Triple P — Positive Parenting Program. http://www.triplep-america.com, 803-787-9944.

Why Is My Child's ADHD Not Better Yet? D. Gottlieb, T. Shoaf, R. Graff. McGraw-Hill, 2005.

MATERIALS FOR CHILDREN

A Walk in the Rain with a Brain. E.M. Hallowell. Regan Books, 2004.

Learning to Slow Down and Pay Attention (3rd Ed.). K.G. Nadeau, E.B. Dixon. Magination Press, 2004.

Putting on the Brakes, Rev. Ed. P.O. Quinn, J.M. Stern. Magination Press, 2001.

Shelly, The Hyperactive Turtle, 2nd Ed. D.H. Moss. Woodbine House, 2006.

The Social Skills Picture Book. J.E. Baker. Future Horizons, 2003.

Chapter 8 — Advanced Behavioral Strategies

Angry Children, Worried Parents. S. Goldstein, R. Brooks, S.K. Weiss. Specialty Press, 2004.

Defiant Teens. R.A. Barkley, G.H. Edwards, A.L. Robin. Guilford Press, 1998.

First Steps to Success: Institute on Violence and Destructive Behavior, College of Education, University of Oregon, Eugene, OR 97403

From Chaos to Calm. J.E. Heininger, S.K. Weiss. Perigee Books, 2001.

It's Nobody's Fault. H. Koplewicz. Random House, 1997.

Responding to Problem Behavior in Schools. D.A. Crone, R. Horner, L.S. Hawken. Guilford Press, 2003.

The Explosive Child. R.W. Greene. Harper Collins, 2005.

Your Defiant Child. R.A. Barkley, C.M. Benton. Guilford Press, 1998.

ASSISTIVE TECHNOLOGY

Beeper Tape: Listen, Look and Think Program. H.C. Parker. http://addware-house.com, ADD WareHouse.

MyADHD.com. An on-line fee for service system to help parents and professionals minitor a student's academic performance.

Time Timer©. http://www.timetimer.com.

Chapters 9–11 — Middle and High School

ACADEMIC AND LEARNING ISSUES

Academic Success Strategies for Adolescents with Learning Disabilities and ADHD. E. Minskoff, D. Allsopp. Paul H. Brookes Publishing, 2003.

ADHD in the Schools, 2nd ed. G.J. DuPaul, G.J. Stoner. Guilford Press, 2004.

Educational Care, 2nd Ed. M. Levine. Educators Publishing Service, 2002.

Executive Skills in Children and Adolescents. P. Dawson, R. Guare. Guilford Press, 2004.

Helping the Student with ADHD in the Classroom. http://www.naspcenter.org (Special Populations). NASP, 2002.

Interventions for ADHD. P.A. Teeter. Guilford Press, 2000.

Multisensory Algebra. B. Witzel, www.msalgebra.com

The ADHD Workbook for Parents. H.C. Parker. Specialty Press, 2005.

Problem Solver Guide for Students with ADHD. H.C. Parker, Specialty Press, 2002.

Teaching Adolescents with Learning Disabilities, 2nd Ed. D.D. Deshler, E.S. Ellis, B.K. Lenz. Love Publishing, 1996.

Teaching Strategies for Twice-Exceptional Students. S. Winebrenner. Intervention in School and Clinic, Vol. 38, No. 3, pp. 131-137, 2003.

Teaching Teens with ADD and ADHD. C.A.Z. Dendy. Woodbine House, 2000.

Teaching the Tiger. M.P. Dornbush, S.K. Pruitt. Hope Press, 2007.

The ADHD Book of Lists. S.F. Rief. Jossey-Bass, 1998.

The ADHD Handbook for Schools. H.C. Parker. Specialty Warehouse, 2005.

GIFTED STUDENTS

Teaching Gifted Kids in the Regular Classroom (Rev. and Updated Ed.). S. Winebrenner. Free Spirit Publishing, 2000.

ASSISTIVE TECHNOLOGY

Electronic Tools

Alphasmart: www.alphasmart.com; 800-656-6740

Calculator

Computer

MyADHD.com: An on-line fee for service system to help parents and professionals monitor a student's academic performance.

PDA: Palm Pilot, IPAQ, Wizard, Zire

Software

Dragon Naturally Speaking (child can dictate information to be converted to text); www.dragontalk.com

Inspiration (older child can organize ideas and information more easily); www.inspiration.com; 800-877-4292

Kidspiration (younger child can organize ideas and information more easily)

Type to Learn: Sunburst Communication: 800-786-3155

Mavis Bacon Teaches Typing for Kids: www.learningcompany.com; 800-395-0277

STUDY SKILLS

Learning to Learn. G. Frender. Incentive Publications, 2004.

Middle School Study Skills. J. Ernst. Teacher Created Materials, Inc., 1999.

Study Strategies Made Easy. L. Davis, S. Sirotowitz, H.C. Parker. Specialty Warehouse, 1996.

Thinking Smarter. C. Crutsinger. Brainworks, 1992.

GRAPHIC ORGANIZERS

50 Graphic Organizers for Reading, Writing & More: Grades 4-8. K. Bromley, L. Irwin-DeVitis, M. Modlo. Scholastic Professional Books, 1999.

Teaching Teens with ADD and ADHD. C.A.Z. Dendy. Woodbine House, 2000.

Thinking Smarter. C. Crutsinger. Brainworks, 1992.

Using Graphic Organizers for Learning and Assessment in Middle Level Classrooms. L. Irwin-DeVitis, D. Pease. Middle School Journal, Vol. 26, No. 5, pp. 57-64, 2005.

Using Graphic Organizers to Make Sense of the Curriculum. E. Ellis. Masterminds, 1999.

TIME MANAGEMENT

Schwab Learning. http:// www.schwablearning.org

Talking Timer (TelTime). http://www.maxiaids.com (gives auditory prompts as time counts down)

Time Management: Learning to Use a Day Planner (What We Know Sheet #11). http://www.help4adhd.org, CHADD, 2003.

TIMERS

Time Timer. http://www.timetimer.com (gives visual representation of elapsed time)

WatchMinder. http://www.watchminder.com (a programmable vibrating watch that also gives messages)

PROSOCIAL SKILLS

Creative Coaching. (for elementary and middle school). N. McDougall, J. Roper. Youthlight, Inc., 2001.

It's So Much Work to Be Your Friend. R. Lavoie. Touchstone, 2005.

Psychosocial Treatment for Children and Adolescents with AD/HD (What We Know Sheet #7). http://www.help4adhd.org, CHADD, 2004.

Ready-to-use Social Skills Lessons & Activities for Grades 7-12. R. Weltmann Begun. Jossey-Bass, 1996.

Skillstreaming the Adolescent. A.P. Goldstein, E. McGinnis. Research Press, 1997.

Seven Steps to Improve Your Child's Social Skills. K. Hagar, S. Goldstein, R. Brooks. Specialty Press, 2006.

Social Skills in Adults (What We Know Sheet #15). http://www.help4adhd.org, CHADD, 2003.

Teaching Social Skills to Children and Youth. G. Cartledge, J. Fellows Milburn. Allyn & Baco, 1995.

Teaching Social Skills to Youth, 2nd Ed. T. Dowd, J. Tierney. Boys Town Press, 1996.

The Use of Classroom-Based Social Skills Training to Improve Student Behavior: A Project ACHIEVE Training Manual. G.M. Batsche, H.M. Knoff. University of South Florida, 1995.

What Does Everybody Else Know That I Don't. M. Novotni. Specialty Press, 1999.

Why Don't They Like Me? S. Sheridan. Sopris West, 1998.

DISCIPLINE AND DIFFICULT BEHAVIOR

Defiant Teens. R.A. Barkley, G.H. Edwards, A.L. Robin. Guilford Press, 1998.

It's Nobody's Fault. H. Koplewicz. Random House, 1997.

Responding to Problem Behavior in Schools. D.A. Crone, R. Horner, L.S. Hawken. Guilford Press, 2003.

The Explosive Child. R.W. Greene. Harper Collins, 2005.

Your Defiant Child. R.A. Barkley, C.M. Benton. Guilford Press, 1998.

Youth Suicide Prevention: School-Based Guide — Overview (FMHI Series Publication #218-0). K. Lazear, S. Roggenbaum, K. Blase. http://cfs.fmhi.usf.edu, Department of Child and Family Studies, Division of State and Local Support, Louis de la Parte Florida Mental Health Institute, University of South Florida, 2003.

PARENTING ISSUES

AD/HD & Driving. M. Snyder. Whitefish Consultants, 2001.

CHADD Parent to Parent Training. http://www.chadd.org, 800-233-4050

Making the System Work for Your Child with ADHD. P.S. Jensen. Guilford Press, 2004.

Maybe You Know My Teen. M. Fowler. Broadway Books, 2001.

Parents and Adolescents Living Together: The Basics. G.R. Patterson, M.S. Forgatch. Research Press, 2005.

Parents and Adolescents Living Together: Family Problem Solving. M.S. Forgatch, G.R. Patterson. Research Press, 2005.

Put Yourself in Their Shoes. H.C. Parker. Specialty Press, 1998.

Straight Talk about Psychiatric Medications for Kids, Rev. Ed. T.E. Wilens. Guilford Press, 2004.

Surviving Your Adolescents (2nd ed.). T.W. Phelan. ParentMagic, Inc., 1998.

Teenagers with ADD and ADHD, 2nd ed. C.A.Z. Dendy. Woodbine House, 2006.

Understanding Girls with AD/HD. K.G. Nadeau, E.B. Littman, P.O. Quinn. Advantage Books, 2000.

MATERIALS FOR TEENS

A Bird's-eye View of Life with ADD and ADHD. C.A.Z. Dendy, A. Zeigler. Cherish the Children, 2003.

ADHD: A Teenager's Guide. J.J. Crist. Childsword/Childsplay, 1997.

Bringing Up Parents. A.J. Packer. Free Spirit Publishing, 1992.

Help4ADD@High School. K. Nadeau. Advantage Books, 1998.

Positively ADD. C.A. Corman, E.M. Hallowell. Walker Books for Young Readers, 2006.

Putting on the Brakes, Rev. Ed. P.O. Quinn, J.M. Stern. Magination Press, 2001.

Teen to Teen (Video; available in English and Spanish). C.A.Z. Dendy. Cherish the Children, 2003.

Teens with ADHD. CHADD's Annual International Conference 2004 in Nashville, TN. Available from National Conference Recording Service, https://www.ncrsusa.com, 303-807-1404.

The Girls' Guide to AD/HD. B. Walker. Woodbine House, 2004.

What About Medicines for ADHD? Questions From Teens Who Have ADHD. AAP, 2005. Available from http://www.help4adhd.org.

What Is ADHD Anyway? Questions From Teens? AAP, 2005. Available from http://www.help4adhd.org.

Chapter 12 — Social Skills for Children and Adolescents

GENERAL INFORMATION

ADHD in Children, Adolescents, and Adults. R.A. Barkley. New England Educational Summer Institutes, 2004.

It's So Much Work to Be Your Friend. R. Lavoie. Touchstone, 2005.

Jarvis Clutch: Social Spy. M. Levine. Educators Publishing, 2001.

Psychosocial Treatment for Children and Adolescents with AD/HD (What We Know Sheet #7). http://www.help4adhd.org, CHADD, 2004.

Seven Steps to Improve Your Child's Social Skills. K. Hagar, S. Goldstein, R. Brooks. Specialty Press, 2006.

Social Skills and Children with Attention Deficit Hyperactivity Disorder and/or Learning Disabilities Realities and Direction for Treatment. A.H. Fine, R.A. Kotkin. In A.H. Fine, R.A. Kotkin (Eds.), Therapist's Guide to Learning and Attention Disorders (pp. 295-334). Academic Press, 2003.

Teaching Adolescents with Learning Disabilities, 2nd Ed. D.D. Deshler, E.S. Ellis, B.K. Lenz. Love Publishing, 1996.

Teaching Social Skills to Children and Youth. G. Cartledge, J.F. Milburn. Allyn & Baco, 1995.

Teenagers with ADD and ADHD, 2nd ed. C.A.Z. Dendy. Woodbine House, 2006.

The ADHD Handbook for Schools. H.C. Parker. Specialty Warehouse, 2005.

What Does Everybody Else Know That I Don't? M. Novotni. Specialty Press, 1999.

SOCIAL SKILL ASSESSMENT

Social Skills Rating System (SSRS). F.M. Gresham, S.N. Elliott. American Guidance Service, 1991.

Walker-McConnell Scale of Social Competence and School Adjustment. H.M. Walker, S.R. McConnell. Pro-Ed, Inc., 1998.

SOCIAL SKILLS CURRICULA

Creative Coaching (for elementary and middle school). N. McDougall, J. Roper. Youthlight, Inc., 2001

SCORE Skills: Social Skills for Cooperative Groups. J. Schumaker, S. Vernon, D. Deshler. Edge Enterprises (Box 1304, Lawrence, KS 66044; 913-749-1473), 1996.

Skillstreaming in Early Childhood. E. McGinnis, A.P. Goldstein. Research Press, 2003.

Skillstreaming the Adolescent. A.P. Goldstein, E. McGinnis. Research Press, 1997.

Teaching Social Skills to Youth, 2nd Ed. T. Dowd, J. Tierney. Boys Town Press, 2005.

The Walker Social Skills Curriculum: ACCEPTS Program Curriculum Guide (K-6). H.M. Walker. Pro-Ed, Inc., 1983.

BULLYING PREVENTION

Olweus Bullying Prevention Program, Clemson University, http://www.clemson.edu/olweus. Marlene Snyder, nobully@clemson.edu.

Chapter 13 — Preparing for the Future

ADD and the College Student. P.O. Quinn. Magination Press, 2001.

Finding a Career That Works for You. W. Fellman. Specialty Press, 2000.

Succeeding in College (What We Know Sheet #13). http://www.help4adhd.org, CHADD, 2003.

Teenagers with ADD and ADHD, 2nd ed. C.A.Z. Dendy. Woodbine House, 2006.

Chapter 14 — Educational Laws

GENERAL

Educational Rights for Children with AD/HD (What We Know Sheet #4). http://www.help4adhd.org, CHADD, 2003.

HELPFUL WEBSITES

AD/HD

CHADD — http://www.chadd.org

National Resource Center — http://www.help4adhd.org

Academics

ACT — http://www.act.org

All Kinds of Minds — http://www.allkindsofminds.org

Books on tape: Recording for the Blind and Dyslexic — http://www.rfbd.org

College Board (SAT) — http://www.collegeboard.com

Coordinated Campaign for Learning Disabilities — http://www.focusonlearning.org

Critical Issues in Assessing AD/HD. NASP Communiqué, Vol. 28, No. 6, 2000.

Diagnosis and Treatment of Attention Disorders: Roles for School Personnel. http://www.naspcenter.org/factsheets/add_fs.html, NASP, 2005.

Intervention Central — http://www.interventioncentral.org

Learning Disabilities Association of America — http://www.ldaamerica.org

LRP Special Ed Connection — http://www.specialedconnection.com

MyADHD.com: www.myadhd.com.

NASP Fact Sheets on Special Populations — http://www.naspcenter.org/special_populations/index.html

National Association for the Education of African American Children with Learning Disabilities — http://www.aacld.org

National Council on Learning Disabilities — http://www.ncld.org

National Dropout Prevention Centers (OSEP) — http://www.dropoutprevention.org

OSEP Ideas that Work — http://www.osepideasthatwork.org/toolkit

Position Statement on Students with Attention Problems. http://www.nasponline.org/information/pospaper_add.html, NASP, 2003.

Schwab Learning — http://www.schwablearning.org

TeachingLD (CEC) — http://www.teachingld.org

Teaching Children with Attention Deficit Hyperactivity Disorder — http://www.ed.gov/about/reports/annual/osep/index.html

The Council for Educators of Students with Disabilities, Inc. — http://www.504idea.org

The University of Kansas Center for Research on Learning: summer institutes: teaching strategies for reading, writing, studying, and test taking — http://www.ku-crl.org

Gifted Students

ERIC Information Center on Disabilities and Gifted Education (Under Gifted Education/Dual Exceptionalities) — http://www.ericec.org.

IDEA/IEP

CHADD — http://www.chadd.org, http://www.help4adhd.org

Doing It Right: IEP goals and objectives to address behavior — http://www.dpi.wi.gov/sped/doc/iepbehavor.doc

Family and Advocates Partnership for Education (PACER) — http://www.fape.org

IDEA Practices (CEC) — http://www.ideapractices.org

National Dissemination Center for Children with Disabilities — http://www.nichcy.org

✓ Tips for IEP development for student and parents

✓ State-by-state listings: resources for children with challenges, congressional representatives, and university evaluation centers

Parent Advocacy Coalition for Educational Rights (PACER) — http://www.pacer.org

Special Education Law

Harbor House Law Press, The Beacon — http://www.harborhouselaw.com/newsletter.html

National Disability Rights Network (formerly known as the National Association of Protection and Advocacy Systems) — http://napas.org

Reed Martin, Special Education Law and Strategies — http://www.reedmartin.com

Wright's Law — http://www.wrightslaw.com

APPENDIX B

References By Chapter

Chapter 1

1. Centers for Disease Control and Prevention. (2005). Mental health in the United States: Prevalence of diagnosis and medication treatment for attention–deficit/hyperactivity disorder — United States, 2003. *Morbidity and Mortality Weekly Report, 54,* 842–847.
2. Goldman, L.S., Genel, M., Bezman, R., & Sianetz, P.J. (1998). Diagnosis and treatment of attention–deficit/hyperactivity disorder in children and adolescents. *Journal of the American Medical Association, 279,* 1100–1107.
3. Durston, S., Tottenham, N.T., Thomas, K.M., Davidson, M.C., Eigsti, I.M., Yang, Y., et al. Differential patterns of striatal activation in young children with and without ADHD. *Biological Psychiatry, 53,* 871–878.
4. Schultz, K.P., Fan, J., Tang, C.Y., Newcorn, J., Buchsbaum, M.S., Cheung, A.A., et al. (2004). Response inhibition in adolescents diagnosed with attention deficit hyperactivity disorder during childhood: An event-related fMRI study. *American Journal of Psychiatry, 161,* 1650–1657.
5. Castellanos, F.X. (1999). Psychobiology of ADHD. In H.C. Quay & A.E. Hogan (Eds.), *Handbook of disruptive behavior disorders* (pp. 179–198). New York: Kluwer Academic/Plenum Publishers.
6. Faraone, S., Perlis, R.H., Doyle, A.E., Smoller, J.W., Goralnick, J.J., Holmgren, M.A., et al. (2005). Molecular genetics of attention-deficit/hyperactivity. *Biological Psychiatry, 57,* 1324–1335.
7. Wilcutt, E.G., Doyle, A., Nigg, J.T., Faraone, S., & Pennington, B.P. (2005). Validity of the executive function theory of attention-deficit hyperactivity disorder: A meta-analytic review. *Biological Psychiatry, 57,* 1336–1346.
8. Pliszka, S.R. (2003). *Neuroscience for the mental health clinician.* New York: Guilford Press.
9. Brown, T.E. (2005). *Attention deficit disorder.* New Haven, CT: Yale University Press.
10. Barkley, R.A. (1997). *ADHD and the nature of self-control.* New York: Guilford Press.
11. Castellanos, 1999.
12. Brown, 2005.
13. Schuck, S.E.B., & Crinella, F.M. (2005). Why children with ADHD do not have low IQs. *Journal of Learning Disabilities, 38,* 262–280.
14. Brown, 2005.
15. Barkley, R.A. (2000, June 17). *Dr. Russell Barkley on AD/HD.* Presentation at Schwab Foundation for Learning. Transcript retrieved August 10, 2002, from http://www.schwablearning.org/pdfs/2200_7-barktran.pdf
16. Brown, 2005.
17. Brown, 2005.
18. MTA Cooperative Group. (1999). A 14-month randomized clinical trial of treatment strategies for attention-deficit/hyperactivity disorder. *Archives of General Psychiatry, 56,* 1073–1086.
19. Tannock, R., & Brown, T.E. (2000). Attention deficit disorders with learning disorders in children and adolescents In T.E. Brown (Ed.), *Attention deficit disorders and comorbidities in children, adolescents and adults* (pp. 231–295). Washington, DC: American Psychiatric Press.
20. Tannock, R. (2000). Attention-deficit/hyperactivity disorder with anxiety disorders, in Attention Deficit Disorders and Comorbidities in Children, Adolescents and Adults. In T.E. Brown (Ed.), *Attention deficit disorders and comorbidities in children, adolescents and adults* (pp. 125–170). Washington, DC: American Psychiatric Press.
21. Brown, T.E. (Ed.). (2000). *Attention deficit disorders and comorbidities in children, adolescents and adults.* Washington, DC: American Psychiatric Press.
22. Pliszka, 2003.
23. Barkley, R.A. (2006). *Attention-deficit hyperactivity disorder, third edition.* New York: Guilford Press.
24. Brooks, R., & Goldstein, S. (2001). *Raising resilient children.* Chicago: Contemporary Books.
25. American Academy of Pediatrics. (2001). Clinical practice guideline: Treatment of the school-aged child with attention-deficit/hyperactivity disorder. *Pediatrics, 108,* 1033–1044.
26. American Academy of Child and Adolescent Psychiatry. (2002). Practice parameter for the use of stimulant medications in the treatment of children, adolescents and adults. Journal of American Academy of Child and Adolescent *Psychiatry, 41*(Suppl. 2), 26–49.
27. Wolraich, M.L., Wibbelsman, C.J., Brown, T.E., Evans, S.W., Gotlieb, E.M., Knight, et al. (2005). Attention-deficit/hyperactivity disorder among adolescents: A review of the diagnosis, treatment and clinical implications. *Pediatrics, 115,* 1734–1746.
28. MTA Cooperative Group. (1999). A 14-month randomized clinical trial of treatment strategies for attention-deficit/hyperactivity disorder. *Archives of General Psychiatry, 56,* 1073–1086.
29. MTA, 1999.
30. Barkley, 2006.
31. Connor, D.F. (2006) Stimulants. In R.A. Barkley (Ed.), *Attention-deficit Hyperactivity Disorder,* third edition (pp. 608-647). New York: Guilford Press.
32. Spencer, T.J. (2006) Antidepressant and specific norepinephrine reuptake inhibitor treatments. In R.A. Barkley (Ed.), *Attention-deficit Hyperactivity Disorder,* third edition (pp. 648-657). New York: Guilford Press.
33. Brown, 2005.
34. MTA, 1999.
35. Dendy, C.A.Z. (2000). *Teaching teens with ADD and ADHD (2nd ed.).* Bethesda, MD: Woodbine House.
36. DuPaul, G.J., & Stoner, G. (2003). *ADHD in the schools.* New York: Guilford Press.
37. Rief, S.F. (2005). *How to reach and teach children with ADD/ADHD, second edition.* San Francisco, CA: Jossey-Bass.
38. Teeter, P.A. (1998). *Interventions for ADHD.* New York: Guilford Press.
39. Evans, S.W., Pelham, W.E., Gnagy, E. M., Smith, B. H., Bukstein, O., Greiner, A.R., et al. (2001). Dose-response effects of methylphenidate on ecologically valid measures of academic performance and classroom behavior in adolescents with ADHD. *Experimental and Clinical Psychopharmacology, 9,* 163–175.
40. Wilens, T.E. (2004) *Straight talk about psychiatric medications for kids,* Rev.Ed. New York: Guilford Press

Chapter 2

REFERENCES FOR CHAPTER TEXT

1. Teeter Ellison, P.A. (2005). School neuropsychology of attention-deficit/hyperactivity disorder. In R. D'Amato, E. Fletcher-Jansen, & C. Reynolds (Eds.), *The handbook of school neuropsychology* (pp. 460–486). New York: John Wiley & Sons, Inc.
2. Jensen, P.S., Kettle, L., Roper, M.T., Sloan, M.T., Dulcan, M.K., Hoven, C., et al. (1999). Are stimulants overprescribed? Treatment of ADHD in four U.S. communities. *Journal of the American Academy of Child and Adolescent Psychiatry, 38,* 797–804.
3. Office of the U.S. Surgeon General. (1999). *Mental Health: A Report of the Surgeon General.* Washington, DC: Author.

B

4. Office of the U.S. Surgeon General. (2001). *Mental Health: Culture, Race, and Ethnicity, A Supplement to Mental Health: A Report of the Surgeon General*. Washington, DC: Author.

5. Dendy, C.A.Z. (2000). *Teaching teens with ADD and ADHD* (2nd ed.). Bethesda, MD: Woodbine House.

6. Teeter, P.A. (1998). *Interventions for ADHD*. New York: Guilford Press.

7. Weiss, G., & Hecht, L. (1993). *Hyperactive children grown up* (2nd ed.). New York: Guilford Press.

REFERENCES FOR GIRLS

a. Gaub, M., & Carlson, C.L. (1997). Gender differences in ADHD: A meta-analysis and critical review. *Journal of the Academy of Child and Adolescent Psychiatry, 36,* 1036–1045.

b. Sharp, W.S., Walter, J.M., Marsh, W.L., Ritchie, G.F., Hamburger, S.D., & Castellanos, F.X. (1999). ADHD in girls: Clinical comparability of a research study. *Journal of the American Academy of Child and Adolescent Psychiatry, 38,* 40–47.

c. Biederman, J., Faraone, S., Mick, E., Williamson, S., Wilens, T., Spencer, T., et al. (1999). Clinical correlates of ADHD in females: Findings from a large group of girls ascertained from pediatric and psychiatric referral sources. *Journal of the American Academy of Child and Adolescent Psychiatry, 38,* 966–975.

REFERENCES FOR MINORITIES

a. Jensen, P.S., Kettle, L., Roper, M.T., Sloan, M.T., Dulcan, M.K., Hoven, C., et al. (1999). Are stimulants overprescribed? Treatment of ADHD in four U.S. communities. *Journal of the American Academy of Child and Adolescent Psychiatry, 38,* 797–804.

b. Rowland, A.S., Umbach, D.M., Stallone, L., Naftel, A.J., Bohlig, E.M., & Sandler, D.P. (2002). Prevalence of medication treatment for attention deficit-hyperactivity disorder among elementary school in children in Johnston County, North Carolina. *American Journal of Public Health, 92,* 231–234.

c. Dosreis, S., Zito, J.M., Safer, D.J., Soeken, K.L., Mitchell, J.W., & Ellwood, L.C. (2003). Parental perceptions and satisfaction with stimulant medication for attention-deficit hyperactivity disorder. *Journal of Developmental & Behavioral Pediatrics, 24,* 155–161.

d. Rowland, et al., 2002.

e. Bussing, R., Zima, B.T., Perwien, A.R., Belin, T., & Widawski, M. (1998). Children in special education programs: Attention deficit hyperactivity disorder, use of services and unmet needs. *American Journal of Public Health, 88,* 880–886.

f. Mattox, G. (March, 2001). Presentation at the 30th annual conference of the Black Psychiatrists of America, Atlanta, GA.

g. Harris Interactive. (April 29, 2003). Barriers to the diagnosis and treatment of attention deficit hyperactivity disorder (ADHD) among African American and Hispanic children. *Health Care News, 3*(7), 1–4.

h. Bauermeister, J.J. (2005). Medication treatment of ADHD in Latino/Hispanic children. Child and Adolescent Psychopharmacology News, 10(5), 7–11.

i. Office of the U.S. Surgeon General. (2001). *Mental Health: Culture, Race, and Ethnicity, A Supplement to Mental Health: A Report of the Surgeon General*. Washington, DC: Author.

REFERENCES FOR ASSESSMENT

a. DuPaul, G.J., & Stoner, G. (2003). *ADHD in the schools*. New York: Guilford Press.

b. Teeter Ellison, P.A. (2005). School neuropsychology of attention-deficit/hyperactivity disorder. In R. D'Amato, E. Fletcher-Jansen, & C. Reynolds (Eds.), *The handbook of school neuropsychology* (pp. 460–486). New York: John Wiley & Sons, Inc.

Chapter 3

1. Barkley, R.A. (2000, June 17). *Dr. Russell Barkley on AD/HD*. Presentation at Schwab Foundation for Learning. Transcript retrieved August 10, 2002, from http://www.schwablearning.org/pdfs/2200_7-barktran.pdf

2. Rief, S.F. (2005). *How to reach and teach children with ADD/ADHD, second edition*. San Francisco, CA: Jossey-Bass.

3. Rief, S.F. (2003). *The ADHD book of lists*. San Francisco: Jossey-Bass.

4. Dendy, C.A.Z. (2000). *Teaching teens with ADD and ADHD (2nd ed.)*. Bethesda, MD: Woodbine House.

Chapter 4

1. Rief, S.F. (2005). *How to reach and teach children with ADD/ADHD, second edition*. San Francisco, CA: Jossey-Bass.

2. Rief, S.F. (2003). *The ADHD book of lists*. San Francisco: Jossey-Bass.

3. Rief, S.F. (1998). *The ADD/ADHD checklist*. San Francisco: Jossey-Bass.

4. Rief, S.F., & Heimburge, J. (2006). *How to reach and teach all children in the inclusive classroom, second edition*. San Francisco: Jossey-Bass.

Chapter 5

1. Rief, S.F., & Heimburge, J. (2006). *How to reach and teach all children in the inclusive classroom, second edition*. San Francisco: Jossey-Bass.

2. Rief, S.F. (2005). *How to reach and teach children with ADD/ADHD*. San Francisco, CA: Jossey-Bass.

3. Rief, S.F. (2003). *The ADHD book of lists*. San Francisco: Jossey-Bass.

4. Pelham, W.E. (2002). *ADHD. Buffalo,* NY: Center for Children and Families. http://wings.buffalo.edu/adhd

Chapter 6

1. Barkley, R.A. (2006). *Attention-deficit hyperactivity disorder*. New York: Guilford Press.

2. Teeter, P.A. (1998). *Interventions for ADHD*. New York: Guilford Press.

3. Jensen, P. (2002). Longer term effects of stimulant treatments for attention-deficit/hyperactivity disorder. *Journal of Attention Disorders, 6*(Suppl. 1), S31–S43.

4. Barkley, 2006.

5. Jones, C.B. (1998). *Sourcebook for children with attention deficit disorder* (Rev. ed.). San Antonio: Psychological Corporation.

6. Teeter, 1998.

7. Tirosh, E., & Cohen, A. (1998). Language deficit with attention deficit disorder: A prevalent comorbidity. *Journal of Child Neurology, 13,* 493–497.

8. Teeter, 1998.

9. Farran, D.C. (1990). Effects of intervention with disadvantaged and disabled children. In S.J. Meisels & J.P. Shonkoff (Eds.), *Handbook of early intervention*. New York: Cambridge University Press.

10. Walker, H.M., Colvin, G., & Ramsey, E. (2000). *Antisocial behavior in schools*. Belmont, CA: Brooks/Cole.

11. Walker, H.M. & Sylwester, R. (1991) "Where is school along the pathway to prison?" *Educational Leadership.* September 1991.

12. CHADD. (draft). *Toddlers and preschoolers with AD/HD (What We Know)*. Landover, MD: Author.

13. Barkley, 2006.

14. Dawson, P., & Guare, R. (2004). *Executive skills in childhood and adolescents*. New York: Guilford Press.

15. Levine, M. (2002). *Educational care* (2nd ed.). Cambridge, MA: Educators Publishing Service.

16. Heininger, J.E., & Weiss, S. (2001). *From chaos to calm*. New York, NY: Perigee Books.

17. Barkley, 2006.

18. Barkley, 2006.

19. Abramowitz, A.J., O'Leary, S.G., & Rosen, L.A. (1987). Reducing off-task behavior in the classroom: A comparision of encouragement and reprimands. *Journal of Abnormal Child Psychology, 15,* 153–163.

20. Heininger & Weiss, 2001.

21. Phelan, T. (2003). *1-2-3 Magic: Training your child to do what you want!* (3rd ed.). Glen Ellyn, IL: ParentMagic, Inc.

22. McCain, A.P., & Kelly, M.L. (1993). Managing the classroom behavior of an ADHD peschooler: The efficacy of a school-home note intervention. *Child and Family Behavior Therapy, 15,* 22–44.

23. Cohen, C. (2000). *How to raise your child's social IQ*. Washington, DC: Advantage Books.

24. Barkley, 2006.

25. MTA Cooperative Group. (1999). A 14-month randomized clinical trial of treatment strategies for attention-deficit/hyperactivity disorder. *Archives of General Psychiatry, 56,* 1073–1086.

26. Teach, J. (personal correspondence, 2005)

27. CHADD Parent to Parent Training: http://www.chadd.org, 800-233-4050

28. Bor, W., Sanders, M., & Markie-Dodds, C. (2002). The effects of Triple P-Positive Parenting Program on preschool children with co-occurring disruptive behavior and attentional/hyperactive difficulties. *Journal of Abnormal Child Psychology, 30,* 571–587.

29. Barkley, 2006.

30. MTA, 1999.
31. Barkley, 2006.
32. Connor, D.F. (2002). Preschool attention deficit hyperactivity disorder: A review of prevalence, diagnosis, neurobiology, and stimulant treatment. *Journal of Developmental Behavior Pediatrics, 23*(Suppl. 1), S1–S9.
33. Teeter, 1998.
34. Greenhill, L.L., Jensen, P.S., Abikoff, H., Blumer, J.L., Deveaugh-Geiss, J., Fisher, C., et al. (2003). Developing strategies for psychopharmacological studies in preschool children. *Journal of the American Academy of Child and Adolescent Psychiatry, 42*, 406–414.
35. McGoey, K., DuPaul, G., Eckert, T., Volpe, R., & VanBrackle, M. (2005). Outcomes of a multi-component intervention for preschool children at-risk for attention-deficit/hyperactivity disorder. *Child and Family Therapy, 27*, 34–56.
36. Good news about bad things that happen to your kids [Special issue]. *USA Weekend.* (2004, January 4).
37. Teeter, 1998.
38. DuPaul, G.J., & Stoner, G. (1994). *ADHD in schools.* New York: Guilford Press.

Chapter 7

REFERENCES FOR CHAPTER TEXT

1. Jones, C.B. (1998). *Sourcebook for children with attention deficit disorder* (Rev. ed.). San Antonio: Psychological Corporation.
2. Barkley, R.A., & Mash, E.J. (1996). *Child psychopathology.* New York: Guilford Press
3. Zentall, S. S. (1993). Research on the educational implications of attention deficit hyperactivity disorder. *Exceptional Children, 60*, 143–153.
4. Barkley, R.A. (2006). *Attention-deficit hyperactivity disorder, third edition.* New York: Guilford Press.
5. Milich, R. (1994). The response of children with ADHD to failure: If at first you don't succeed, do try, try, again? *School Psychology Review, 23*, 11–28
6. August, G.J., & Garfinkel, G.D. (1998). Behavioral and cognitive subtypes of ADHD. *Journal of the American Academy of Child and Adolescent Psychiatry, 28*, 739–748.
7. Barkley, 2006.
8. Jones, C.B. (2003). *Practical suggestions for AD/HD.* East Moline, IL: Lingui-Systems.
9. Pennington, B.F., & Bennetto, L. (1993). Main effects or transactions in the neuropsychology of conduct disorder? Commentary on the "The neuropsychology of conduct disorder." *Development and Psychopathology, 5*, 151–164.
10. Milich, R., & Landau, S. (1989). The role of social status variables in differentiating subgroups of hyperactive children. In L.M. Bloomingdale & J. Swanson (Eds.), *Attention-deficit disorder* (pp. 1–16). New York: Pergamon Press.
11. Whalen, C.K. & Henker, B. (1985). The social worlds of hyperactive children. *Clinical Psychology Review, 5*, 1–32.
12. Barkley, R.A. (2000, June 17). *Dr. Russell Barkley on AD/HD.* Presentation at Schwab Foundation for Learning. Transcript retrieved August 10, 2002, from http://www.schwablearning.org/pdfs/2200_7-barktran.pdf
13. Goldstein, S., & Jones, C. (1998). Managing and educating children with ADHD. In S. Goldstein & M. Goldstein (Eds.), *Managing attention deficit hyperactivity disorder in children* (pp. 545–591). New York: John Wiley & Sons, Inc.
14. Zentall, S.S. (1995). Modifying classroom tasks and environments. In S. Goldstein (Ed.), *Understanding and managing children's classroom behavior* (pp. 356–374). New York: John Wiley & Sons, Inc.
15. Goldstein & Jones, 1998.
16. Jones, V.F., & Jones, L.S. (1986). *Comprehensive classroom management.* Boston: Allyn & Bacon.
17. Jones, C.B. (1998). *Attention deficit disorder.* San Antonio, TX: Communication Skill Builders.
18. Jones, 2003.
19. Kelly, M.L. (1990). *School-home notes.* New York: Guilford Press.
20. Imber, S.C., Imber, R.D., & Rothstein, C. (1979). Modifying independent work habits: An effective teacher-parent communication program. *Exceptional Children, 45*, 218–221.
21. Witt, J.C., Hannafin, M.J., & Martens, B.K. (1983). Homebased reinforcement: Behavioral covariation between academic performance and inappropriate behavior. *Journal of School Psychology, 21*, 337–348.
22. Zentall, S.S., & Krucsek, T. (1988). The attraction of colors for active attention problem children. *Exceptional Children, 54*, 357–362.
23. Zentall, S.S. (1989). Attention cuing and spelling tasks for hyperactive and comparison regular classroom children. *Journal of Special Education, 23*, 83–93.
24. Zentall, 1993.

REFERENCES FOR CHALLENGIING BEHAVIORS

a. Barkley, 2006.
b. Barkley, 2006.
c. Barkley, 2006.

Chapter 8

REFERENCES FOR CHAPTER TEXT

1. Heininger, J.E., & Weiss, S. (2001). *From chaos to calm.* New York, NY: Perigee Books.
2. MTA Cooperative Group. (1999). A 14-month randomized clinical trial of treatment strategies for attention-deficit/hyperactivity disorder. *Archives of General Psychiatry, 56*, 1073–1086.
3. Parker, H.C. (2005). *The ADHD Handbook for Schools.* Plantation, FL: Specialty Press.
4. Barkley, R.A. (2006). *Attention-deficit hyperactivity disorder, third edition.* New York: Guilford Press.

REFERENCES FOR ONE CHILD'S STORY

a. Barkley, 2006.
b. Barkley, 2006.

Chapter 9

REFERENCES FOR CHAPTER TEXT

1. MTA Cooperative Group. (1999). A 14-month randomized clinical trial of treatment strategies for attention-deficit/hyperactivity disorder. *Archives of General Psychiatry, 56*, 1073–1086.
2. Wolraich M.L., Wibbelsman, C.J., Brown, T.E., Evans, S.W., Gotlieb, E.M., Knight, J.R., et al. (2005). Attention-deficit/hyperactivity disorder among adolescents: A review of the diagnosis, treatment and clinical implications. *Pediatrics, 115*, 1734–1746.
3. Wolraich, et al., 2005.
4. Dendy, C.A.Z., & Zeigler, A. (2003). *A bird's-eye view of life with ADD and ADHD.* Cedar Bluff, AL: Cherish the Children.
5. Barkley, R.A. (2006). *Attention-deficit hyperactivity disorder, third edition.* New York: Guilford Press.
6. Brown, T.E. (Ed.) (2000). *Attention deficit disorders and comorbidities in children, adolescents and adults.* Washington, DC: American Psychiatric Press.
7. Wolraich, et al., 2005.
8. Barkley, R.A. (2000, June 17). *Dr. Russell Barkley on AD/HD.* Presentation at Schwab Foundation for Learning. Transcript retrieved August 10, 2002, from http://www.schwablearning.org/pdfs/2200_7-barktran.pdf
9. Barkley, 2006.
10. Levine, M. (2002). *Educational care* (2nd ed.). Cambridge, MA: Educators Publishing Service.
11. Deshler, D., Ellis, E.S., & Lenz, B.K. (1991). *Teaching adolescents with learning disabilities.* Denver, CO: Love Publishing.
12. Barkley, 2006.
13. Mayes, S.D., & Calhoun, S. (2000). Prevalence and degree of attention and learning problems in ADHD and LD. *The ADHD Report, 8*(2), 14–16.
14. Teeter, P.A. (1998). *Interventions for ADHD.* New York: Guilford Press.
15. Quinn, P.O., & Nadeau, K.G. (Eds.). (2002). *Gender issues and AD/HD.* Silver Spring, MD: Advantage Books.
16. Gaub, M., & Carlson, C.L. (1997). Gender differences in ADHD: A metaanalysis and critical review. *Journal of the Academy of Child and Adolescent Psychiatry, 36*, 1036–1045.
17. Biederman, J. (2006). Comorbidity in girls with ADHD. In R.A. Barkley (Ed.), *Attention-deficit hyperactivity disorder, third edition.* New York: Guilford Press.
18. Rucklidge, J.J., & Kaplan, B.J. (1997). Psychological functioning of women identified in adulthood with attention-deficit/hyperactivity disorder. *Journal of Attention Disorders, 2*, 167–176.

REFERENCE FOR CHALLENGIING BEHAVIORS

a. Walker, R. (personal interview, 2006)

Chapter 10

1. DuPaul, G., & Hennington, P. (1993). Peer tutoring effects on the classroom performance of children with attention deficit hyperactivity disorder. *School Psychology Review, 22*, 134–143.
2. Kellam, S., Mayer, L., Rebok, G., & Hawkins, W. (1998). Effects of improving achievement on aggressive behavior and of improving aggressive behavior on achievement through two preventive interventions: An investigation of causal paths. In B. Dohrenwend (Ed.), *Adversity, stress, and psychopathology* (pp. 486–505). New York: Oxford University Press.

B

3. Atkins, M. (personal communication, March 1, 2006)
4. Robin, A. (1998). *Adolescents with ADHD.* New York: Guilford Press.
5. Deshler, D., Ellis, E.S., & Lenz, B.K. (1991). *Teaching adolescents with learning disabilities.* Denver, CO: Love Publishing.
6. Dendy, C.A.Z. (2000). *Teaching teens with ADD and ADHD* (2nd ed.). Bethesda, MD: Woodbine House.
7. Crutsinger, C. (1992). *Thinking smarter.* Carrollton, TX: Brainworks.
8. Welch, A. (1999). Increasing academic engagement of students with ADHD. *The ADHD Report, 7*(3), 1–5.
9. Ellis, E. (1998). *Using graphic organizers to make sense of the curriculum and strategic graphic organizer instruction.* Lillian, AL: Masterminds.
10. Welch, 1999.
11. Zentall, S.S., & Dywer, A.M. (1989). Color effects on the impulsivity and activity of hyperactive children. *Journal of School Psychology, 27,* 165–173.
12. Deshler, et al., 1991.
13. Covey, S.R. (1989). The 7 habits of highly effective people. New York: Simon and Schuster.
14. Zentall, S., & Goldstein, S. (1999). *Seven steps to homework success.* Plantation, FL: Specialty Press.
15. NEA & PTA. *Policy paper on homework.* http://www.nea.org.
16. Barkley, R.A. (2006). *Attention-deficit hyperactivity disorder, third edition.* New York: Guilford Press.
17. Ellis, 1998.
18. Barkley, 2006.
19. Reid, R. (1999). Attention deficit hyperactivity disorder: Effective methods for the classroom. *Focus on Exceptional Children, 32*(4), 1–20.
20. Jones, C.B. (1998). *Strategies for school success: Middle school through high school.* Presentation at the 1998 CHADD National Conference.
21. Pfiffner, L.J., & Barkley, R.A. (1990). Educational placement and classroom management. In R.A. Barkley (Ed.), *Attention-deficit hyperactivity disorder, third edition.* New York: Guilford Press.

Chapter 11

1. Barkley, R.A. (2006). *Attention-deficit hyperactivity disorder, third edition.* New York: Guilford Press.
2. Welch, A. (1999). Increasing academic engagement of students with ADHD. *The ADHD Report, 7*(3), 1–5.
3. Abramowitz, A.J., O'Leary, S.G., & Rosen, L.A. (1987). Reducing off-task behavior in the classroom: A comparision of encouragement and reprimands. *Journal of Abnormal Child Psychology, 15,* 153–163.
4. Dendy, C.A.Z. (2000). *Teaching teens with ADD and ADHD* (2nd ed.). Bethesda, MD: Woodbine House.
5. Dendy, 2000.
6. Dendy, 2000.
7. Covey, S.R. (1989). *The 7 habits of highly effective people.* New York: Simon and Schuster.
8. NICHCY (National Dissemination Center for Children with Disabilities). (2002, January). *A student's guide to the IEP.* Retrieved June 1, 2006 from http://www.nichcy.org/pubs/stuguide/st1book.htm
9. *National Technical Assistance Center on Positive Behavioral Interventions and Supports* (PBIS), http://www.pbis.org

Chapter 12

1. Gresham, F., & Elliott, S. (1993). *Social intervention guide.* Binghamton, NY: The Haworth Press, Inc.
2. CHADD. (2003). *Social skills in adults with AD/HD (What We Know Sheet #15).* Retrieved June 1, 2006 from http://www.help4adhd.org/en/living/relandsoc/WWK15
3. Barkley, R.A. (2006). *Attention-deficit hyperactivity disorder, third edition.* New York: Guilford Press.
4. Anderson, N.H. (1968). Likeableness rating of 555 personality trait words. *Journal of Social Psychology, 9,* 272–279.
5. Unnever, J.D., & Cornell, D.G. (2003). Bullying, self-control, and ADHD. *Journal of Interpersonal Violence, 81*(2), 129–147.
6. Levine, M. (2002). *Educational care* (2nd ed.). Cambridge, MA: Educators Publishing Service.

7. Barkley, R.A. (1997). *ADHD and the nature of self-control.* New York: Guilford Press.
8. Deshler, D., Ellis, E.S., & Lenz, B.K. (1991). *Teaching adolescents with learning disabilities.* Denver, CO: Love Publishing.
9. CHADD, 2003.
10. Barkley, 2006.
11. Anderson, 1968.
12. CHADD. (2004). *Psychosocial treatment for children and adolescents with AD/HD (What We Know Sheet #7).* Retrieved June 1, 2006 from http://www.help4adhd.org/en/treatment/behavioral/WWK7
13. Lavoie, R. (2005). *It's so much work to be your friend.* New York: Simon and Schuster.
14. Barkley, 2006.
15. Barkley, 2006.
16. CHADD, 2004.
17. CHADD, 2004.
18. Barkley, 2006.
19. Lavoie, 2005.

Chapter 13

1. Dendy, C.A.Z. (2006). *Teenagers with ADD and ADHD, 2nd edition.* Bethesda, MD: Woodbine House.
2. Montague, M., & Lund, K. (1991). *Job related social skills.* Reston, VA: Exceptional Innovations.

Chapter 14

1. Reid, R. (1999). Attention deficit hyperactivity disorder: Effective methods for the classroom. *Focus on Exceptional Children, 32*(4), 1–20.
2. Durheim, M. (2003). parent's guide to Section 504. *ATTENTION! Magazine, 10*(1), 36–41.
3. Davila, R.R., Williams, M.L., & MacDonald, J.T. (1991). Clarification of policy to address the needs of children with attention deficit disorders within general and/or special education. Washington, DC: U.S. Department of Education, Office of Special Education and Rehabilitation Services.
4. CHADD. (2003). Educational rights for children with AD/HD (What We Know Sheet #4). Retrieved June 1, 2006 from http://www.help4adhd.org/documents/WWK4.pdf
5. Davila, et al., 1991.
6. Wagner, M., & Sumi, W.C. (2006, February). A national look at the mental health and support services provided to children with emotional disturbances. Presentation at the RTCCMH (Research and Training Center for Children's Mental Health) Conference.
7. Dendy, C.A.Z. (2000). Teaching teens with ADD and ADHD (2nd ed.). Bethesda, MD: Woodbine House.
8. Dendy, 2000.
9. Barkley, R.A. (2006). *Attention-deficit hyperactivity disorder, third edition.* New York: Guilford Press.
10. Mayes, S.D., & Calhoun, S. (2000). Prevalence and degree of attention and learning problems in ADHD and LD. *The ADHD Report, 8*(2), 14–16.
11. Letter to Lillie, 23 IDELR 714 (OSEP 1995).
12. Barkley, 2006.
13. Doe v. Withers, 20 IDELR 422 (W.Va. Cir. Ct. 1993)
14. *National Technical Assistance Center on Positive Behavioral Interventions and Supports* (PBIS), http://www.pbis.org
15. Dendy, 2000.

Chapter 15

1. Strain, P.S., & Timm, M.A. (2001). Remediation and prevention of aggression. An evaluation of the Regional Intervention Program over a quarter century. *Behavioral Disorders, 26,* 297–313.
2. Walker, H.M., Kavanaugh, K., Stiller, B., Golly, A., Severson, H.H., & Feil, E.G. (1998). First Step to Success: An early intervention approach for preventing school antisocial behavior. *Journal of Emotional and Behavioral Disorders, 6,* 66–80.
3. Kotkin, R. (1998). The Irvine Paraprofessional Program: Promising practice for serving students with ADHD. *Journal of Learning Disabilities, 31,* 556–564.

APPENDIX C

Sample Charts and Forms

Several forms are available to assist teachers with behavioral programs. These forms can be downloaded from the CHADD website at the following link: www.chadd.org/forms. These forms are made available thanks to several contributing authors: Chris Dendy, Joan Helbing, Terry Illes, Harvey Parker, Sandra Rief, and Alex Zeigler. Appendices include:

C.1–C.3 Daily or weekly report forms for various age students

C.4 Classroom behavior rubric

C.5 Behavior contract

C.6 Homework contract

C.7 Response cost chart

C.8 Functional Behavior Assessment (FBA)

C.9 Hand raising form

C.10 I beat the clock

C.11 Was I paying attention?

C.12 Getting along

C.1   **C.2**   **C.3**

C.4   **C.5**   **C.6**   **C.7**

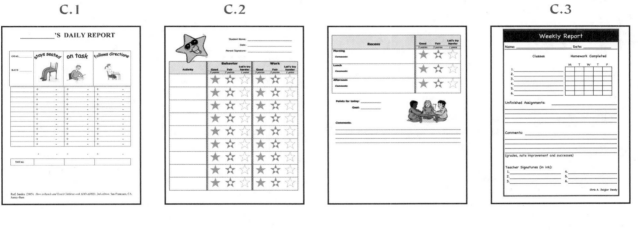

C.8

C.9

C.10

C.11

C.12

Index

ORDER THE
EDUCATOR'S MANUAL
on Attention Deficit Disorder

A tool for educators, treatment professionals, advocates and family members

This comprehensive manual provides an overview of the latest information regarding common learning challenges often associated with AD/HD. Specific academic and behavioral interventions are suggested for students at the preschool, elementary, middle and high school levels. An easy-to-use summary of the most common academic and behavioral challenges is included for each age level.

This invaluable tool offers critical information regarding diagnosis and treatment of AD/HD, social skills, transition planning, relevant educational laws and promising educational practices.

A team of veteran educators and nationally recognized experts on AD/HD collaborated to produce this state-of-the-art tool for key professionals and family members.

USE THIS FORM TO PLACE YOUR ORDER!

CHADD Improves the Lives of Children and Adults with AD/HD

AD/HD is a lifespan disorder and CHADD Membership provides families, adults and professionals with:

✓ Support — There are more than 200 CHADD affiliates nationwide. If a local support group exists in your area, you will receive support, resources and the latest information from professionals, as well as critical information on local laws and policies affecting your family.

✓ *Attention!,*® CHADD's bimonthly magazine offering advice and information about AD/HD from the field's leading experts.

✓ Access to the members-only portion of CHADD's redesigned Web site and monthly chats with guest experts at **www.chadd.org**

✓ A free copy of *The CHADD Information and Resource Guide to AD/HD*, a 170+ page guide to life with AD/HD (a $34.95 value).

✓ Discounts on many CHADD educational products for families, adults with AD/HD, educators, medical professionals and others, including videotapes, audiotapes and books.

✓ Reduced registration fee to CHADD's Annual Conference and other events.

✓ Advocacy — CHADD promotes the rights and concerns of individuals with AD/HD

CHADD®
CHILDREN AND ADULTS WITH
ATTENTION-DEFICIT/HYPERACTIVITY DISORDER

JOIN CHADD TODAY!

CHADD SUCCESS SIGN-UP

Name _____ Occupation _____

Address _____ City _____ State _____ Zip _____

Telephone (Day) _____ (Evening) _____ Fax Number _____

E-Mail: _____ Organization (if organizational member) _____

REGULAR MEMBERSHIP
❑ New Member ❑ Renewal Membership
❑ $45 individual/family ❑ **$45 educator** ❑ $35 student ❑ $75 international student ❑ $100 international individual/family ❑ $100 international educator
❑ I would like to donate a $45 membership for someone less fortunate

PROFESSIONAL MEMBERSHIP
❑ $100 professional member ❑ $175 professional plus member* ❑ $190 international professional member ❑ $265 international professional plus member*

ORGANIZATIONAL MEMBERSHIP
❑ $275 organizational member ❑ $350 organizational plus member* ❑ $425 international organizational member (outside U.S. and Canada)
❑ $500 international organizational plus member*
* Membership includes a listing in *CHADD's online Directory of Professionals, Products & Services*

PAYMENT
❑ Check ❑ MasterCard ❑ Visa ❑ American Express ❑ Discover

Name on Card _____ Card Number _____ Exp. Date _____

Signature _____ Chapter Affiliation _____

Total Payment $_____

MAIL OR FAX TO: CHADD, 8181 Professional Place, Suite 150, Landover, MD 20785 • Fax: 301-306-7090

OR ENROLL ONLINE: WWW.CHADD.ORG

QUESTIONS OR FURTHER INFORMATION? Call CHADD at 800-233-4050 or visit our Web site at **www.chadd.org**

All funds submitted must be in U.S. dollars, drawn on U.S. banks.

The **NEW** CHADD Information and Resource Guide to AD/HD

CHADD®

CHILDREN AND ADULTS WITH
ATTENTION-DEFICIT/
HYPERACTIVITY DISORDER

The New CHADD Information and Resource Guide to AD/HD

What We know – and What Works

Attention-Deficit/Hyperactivity Disorder is a lifespan condition with scholastic, social, emotional and professional impact. *The New CHADD Information and Resource Guide to AD/HD*, published by Children and Adults with Attention-Deficit and Hyperactivity Disorder (CHADD) brings together a wealth of information about how to manage – and succeed – with AD/HD.

From family issues to tips on managing medication, the Guide helps patients and families cope with the disorder. A sampling of the topics covered:

- Understanding AD/HD
- Tips for parents, guidelines for pediatricians
- Parenting a child with AD/HD
- Homework strategies
- Transitioning to middle school
- Teen drivers with AD/HD
- Strategies for college students
- Dealing with the impact of AD/HD on marriage
- Coaching
- Medication and complementary treatments
- Legal rights: higher education and the workplace
- Life Stories: Living with AD/HD

The Information and Resource Guide is just one benefit of membership in CHADD; a $35 value, the Guide is provided free to new and renewing members.

For more information on membership, go to *www.chadd.org*, the CHADD website.

For more information on AD/HD, go to *www.help4adhd.org,* the website of The National Resource Center on AD/HD: a program of CHADD, funded by the Centers for Disease Control and Prevention.

Contents

8181 Professional Place, Suite 150
Landover, MD 20785

(800) 233-4050 or (301) 306-7070